A Practice-based Model of STEM Teach

D1086437

A Practice-based Model of STEM Teaching

STEM Students on the Stage (SOS)™

Edited by

Alpaslan Sahin
Harmony Public Schools, Houston, USA

SENSE PUBLISHERS
ROTTERDAM/BOSTON/TAIPEI

A C.I.P. record for this book is available from the Library of Congress.

ISBN: 978-94-6300-017-8 (paperback)
ISBN: 978-94-6300-018-5 (hardback)
ISBN: 978-94-6300-019-2 (e-book)

Published by: Sense Publishers,
P.O. Box 21858,
3001 AW Rotterdam,
The Netherlands
https://www.sensepublishers.com/

Printed on acid-free paper

TABLE OF CONTENTS

MARGARET J. MOHR-SCHROEDER

FOREWORD

It's easy to come up with new ideas; the hard part is letting go of what worked for you two years ago, but will soon be out of date.

— Roger von Oech

Teachers today are being asked to think "outside of the box" in order to prepare their students for a career and a life that is largely unknown due to the warp speed changing needs and desires of society today. While many teachers today happily accept the challenge and are driven by curiosity and motivation to succeed, it can become a very daunting and overwhelming task. The STEM SOS™ (Students on Stage) model, and this book in particular, helps to bridge that gap between daunting and overwhelming to doable and successful. While much literature exists regarding project-based instruction, no book or article has provided such a comprehensive look and guide to successful (and what success looks like!) implementation of interdisciplinary STEM project-based instruction, through the STEM SOS™ model, as Dr. Alpaslan Sahin has done here with this book.

While I was trained as a mathematician and mathematics educator, I also had a deep passion for the life sciences. I dreamed of becoming a neonatologist when I was growing up, but I also had a deep passion for teaching and helping people understand mathematics and science. In the end, that passion for learning and teaching won out and I eventually ended up in my current position as a teacher educator at a major research university. As a budding STEM enthusiast, my research and work over the years led to the creation of the first ever major in STEM Education in the United States. It was through this work that I reconnected with Alpaslan and his grass roots interdisciplinary STEM school efforts.

I first met Dr. Sahin while doing my doctoral work at Texas A&M University. As a fellow doctoral student, Alpaslan and I were deeply entrenched in a multi-million dollar research project that involved lots and lots of video coding and analysis. You always knew when we had a deadline coming up – one would walk into our office room and we all would be sitting in our cubicles, headphones on, huddled over our monitors, furiously tallying away. It was in these moments that Dr. Sahin and I's conversations about connections and interdisciplinarity began. Dr. Sahin has always had a deep curiosity for mathematics content and how it was taught and presented in the United States. I remember during our video coding sessions, he would always wonder and discuss why United States teachers were always so focused on teaching a particular concept, instead of focusing on the application and interconnectedness of a concept, skill or generalization. He would share stories about how he had seen and experienced mathematics as a student. As someone who had been discouraged from majoring in mathematics and biology in college because they were so "dissimilar", I was fascinated with Dr. Sahin's knowledge and passion about applications and connections.

While I took a more traditional "professorial" route after graduation, Dr. Sahin continued pursuing his passion of helping people understand the importance of applications and connections, especially through the lens of interdisciplinary, project-based instruction. Through his work as a research scientist at the Aggie STEM Center at Texas A&M University in College Station, Dr. Sahin was an integral part in building and nurturing the foundation for innovative STEM schools in the area. This work springboarded him into the Harmony Public Schools where he has carefully studied and helped teachers and administrators implement and embrace the STEM SOS™ (Students on the Stage) model. Over the past several years, he has studied, designed and trained STEM teachers of STEM academies, with his work appearing in a variety of books and journals.

The STEM SOS™ model has been shown to improve student knowledge and conceptual understanding, and STEM interest, and other important 21st century skills including self-confidence, communication and collaboration, ultimately improving students' college and career readiness. In this book, Dr. Sahin's work shines through in codifying and telling the story of the STEM SOS™ model. While there have been books and articles published affirming the positive effects of project-based instruction, none have presented it in a ready-made curriculum, making this an essential go-to book to have in your library. Not only does it set a foundational stage for integrating project-based instruction into classrooms, it also contains examples of what the STEM SOS™ model looks like at the classroom level and at the school level; its connections to standards; and even contains appendices of full lesson plans, teacher resources, authentic assessment samples, etc.

This book tells the story of that implementation and how you - whether a teacher, an administrator, a teacher educator, a scientist, an engineer, or even a STEM enthusiast – can regularly, actively engage students in STEM, through shared work in collaborative and social settings, in order to help them see STEM as a socially desirable and attractive profession for them to consider in their futures.

Margaret J. Mohr-Schroeder
Associate Professor of Middle/Secondary Mathematics Education
STEM Enthusiast
Department of STEM Education
University of Kentucky

PREFACE

The purpose of this book is to describe the Harmony STEM approach called the *STEM SOS Model* and its components, from creation to assessments to teacher training. This book describes an easy-to-use project-based learning (PBL) model and classroom-ready materials that help make implementation as simple and seamless as possible. At its heart, however, this book provides useful information about STEM education, including its history, current PBL models and their similarities and differences, and most importantly, detailed information about the STEM SOS model and implementation strategies.

The STEM SOS model was developed by Harmony Public Schools with the goal of teaching rigorous content in an engaging, fun and effective way. In the book, you will find that the STEM SOS model is not only helping students learn STEM content and develop 21st-century skills, but also helping teachers improve their classroom climate through increased student-teacher communication and a reduction in classroom management issues.

This is an innovative book in at least two ways: First, you will find student videos and websites associated with QR codes. Readers can use their QR readers to watch student videos related to the content in the chapter and see student e-portfolio samples at their Google sites. This provides readers with the opportunity to see that what is discussed in the book actually happened, either within a classroom or in outside activities. Second, the book is not about a theory; it is an actual implemented model that has evolved through the years and has been used in more than 25 schools since 2012. Every year, the model continues to be improved to increase its rigor and ease of implementation for both teachers and students. In addition to using the book as a classroom teacher resource and/or guide, it can also be used as a textbook in Master's level mathematics, science and/or STEM education programs. Curriculum and instruction and/or educational leadership programs may also benefit from the explanations, research and discussion around the implementation, development, and sustainability of a STEM teaching model from scratch. Therefore, STEM educators, leaders, pre-service and in-service teachers, and graduate students may all benefit from reading this book.

Appendices will be one of the favorite aspects of this book for teachers who are constantly looking for ready-to-use student and teacher handouts and activities. Full handouts, including formative and summative assessments materials and grading rubrics, will provide an opportunity for teachers and curriculum directors to understand the ideas and secrets behind the STEM SOS model. Lastly, STEM directors will find one of the best STEM teaching model examples on the market due to their ability to either adopt or revise the model to make it their own.

The Editor

ACKNOWLEDGEMENTS

Many individuals contributed to this book through their encouragement, ideas and examples and it is not possible to thank all of them due to space constraints. However, there are some specific individuals who have given their time, support and wisdom to whom I wish to express my gratitude and appreciation.

I would like to thank the following authors who contributed chapters for the book: Margaret J. Mohr-Schroeder, Maureen Cavalcanti, Kayla Blyman, S. Enrico, P. Indiogine, Niyazi Erdogan, Todd Dane Bozeman, Namik Top, Ozgur Ozer, Ismail Ayyildiz, Nickola Esch, Pam Srinivasan, Freda Husic, Cynthia Sargent, Robert Thornton, Kerri Bell, Burak Yilmaz, Eugene Kennedy, Tevfik Eski, Ulvi Celepcikay, Soner Tarim, Bulent Dogan, Bernard Robin, Farjana Yasmin, Kadir Almus, Steven Busch, and Angus J. Macneil.

Dr. Ozcan E. Akgun, Assistant Professor in the Department of Computer and Instructional Technology, Sakarya University, was with me when I was working on this model. His inspirational ideas and support helped me develop the name of the model, "STEM Students on the Stage."

Levent Sakar, HPS Physics Curriculum Director and STEM Activity Coordinator and one of the developers and advocates of the STEM SOS model, contributed valuable insights and provided sample STEM SOS lessons, assessment materials and rubrics for the book. He also answered all my questions without showing any signs of weariness while I was working on codifications of the model. Likewise, Ishmael Ayyildiz, Director of Curriculum-Secondary and ISWEEEP Program Director also provided valuable insights during the project. Dr. Ozgur Ozer, Chief Academic Officer and Associate Superintendent of Harmony Public Schools, supported the idea of writing and codifying the model as well as helping me determine the content of the book.

I would also like to thank Margaret J. Mohr-Schroeder, Associate Professor of Middle and Secondary Mathematics Education in the College of Education, University of Kentucky, who agreed to write the foreword for this book even though she has been swamped with her own projects and responsibilities.

Meredith Takahashi, Editorial Assistant, reviewed the book multiple times for grammar and format. This book is better as a result of her meticulous efforts.

And, finally, it is without reservation that I acknowledge my debt to Dr. Soner Tarim, Professor Robert M. Capraro, Mr. Zekeriya Yuksel, Dr. Kadir Almus and Professor Gerald Kulm for their exceptional leadership and support during this endeavor. Thank you!

Alpaslan Sahin, Ph.D.
Houston, TX
October 2014

SECTION 1

LITERATURE ABOUT STEM EDUCATION

How did STEM education start? What made STEM education important? Do we really have problems educating students in STEM fields? Are there any differences between ethnic groups in mathematics and science achievement? Section I helps you assess your preparedness for STEM education and increase your readiness to appreciate the variety of STEM learning models.

MARGARET J. MOHR-SCHROEDER, MAUREEN CAVALCANTI,
AND KAYLA BLYMAN

1. STEM EDUCATION: UNDERSTANDING THE CHANGING LANDSCAPE

This chapter provides a brief history of Science, Technology, Engineering and Mathematics (STEM) education in the United States, including key movements that have helped shape it and have kept it sustainable. This chapter is foundational to understanding the context of STEM education and its interdisciplinary nature.

INTRODUCTION

It is well-known that the today's youth are tomorrow's innovators and leaders. They are our *Generation Z* or *Post-Millennials* (Horovitz, 2012). They are our most diverse population cohort yet and are considered to be digital natives. Yet they are amidst a STEM "crisis." Research, legislation, media and even infographics (see Figure 1 for an example) everywhere point to the dire need for educational reform in STEM (Kelly et al., 2013); for creating a *STEM literate* workforce (National Research Council, 2009, 2014a; National Academy of Engineering, 2008; Varmus et al., 2003); for more women and people of color in STEM fields (National Science Foundation, 2013); and for more individuals in general to be interested in STEM careers (Carnevale, Smith, & Melton, 2011; Langdon, McKittrick, Beede, Khan, & Doms, 2011; National Science Board, 2014). Additionally, employers today believe that *all* people, especially young people, need some form of technological and STEM literacy in order to become productive citizens, even if they never intend to enter a STEM-related career (National Academy of Engineering and National Research Council, 2014).

There have been multitudes of reports published in the last 30 years that call for major changes, expansions, opportunities and improvements in STEM education (e.g., AAAS, 1990, 1993; Council on Competitiveness, 2005; NGA, 2007; NRC, 1996, 2007a, 2012a; NSB, 2007; PCAST 2012). Major changes and initiatives have emerged from these calls to action, including, but not limited to:

- The Common Core State Standards for Mathematics and Literacy in the Sciences (CCSSO, 2010);
- A Framework for K-12 Science Education (NRC, 2011) and the subsequent Next Generation Science Standards (NGSS Lead States, 2013);

A. Sahin (Ed.), A Practice-based Model of STEM Teaching, 3–14.

- Assessment consortia aiming to create assessments aligned with the new standards (e.g., PARCC, Smarter Balanced Assessment Curriculum);
- STEM-focused schools; and
- STEM partnership networks (e.g., STEMx, Ohio STEM Learning Network, iSTEM, Washington STEM).

These initiatives have led to a renewed focus on the exact definition of STEM education, what constitutes effective teaching in STEM and a general overall

Figure 1. Example STEM need infographic (Washington STEM, washingtonstem.org).

knowledge of STEM and the development of a STEM literate population. This chapter will provide a brief history of STEM education and its influences and present a framework and definition of STEM education that will set the stage for the model presented in this book. Here, we aim to present a model that will help teachers operationalize STEM education through interdisciplinary instructional practices. Doing so will provide support for teachers transitioning to STEM teaching and learning and make content accessible and meaningful to students, both within and across disciplines (Basham, 2010). The need to develop curricula that operationalizes STEM education has been studied (Wang, Moore, Roehrig, & Park, 2011), but the models themselves are still being developed. This book aims to fill this gap in a way that connects research, perception and practice.

A BRIEF HISTORY OF STEM EDUCATION

Almost 60 years ago, on October 5, 1957, the launch of the Russian satellite *Sputnik* caused a deep stir in the United States, one that was fueled by fear (of falling behind) and the United States' competitive nature. In President Eisenhower's famous speech after the launch of *Sputnik*, he challenged Americans and called for action:

> The Soviet Union now has – in the combined category of scientists and engineers – a greater number than the United States. And it is producing graduates in these fields at a much faster rate . . . We need scientists in the ten years ahead. They (the President's advisors) say we need them by thousands more than we are now presently planning to have. The Federal government can deal with only part of this difficulty, but it must and will do its part. The task is a cooperative one. Federal, state, and local governments, and our entire citizenry must all do their share.

Very quickly thereafter, the National Aeronautics and Space Administration (NASA) was formed in 1958. Through the rapid growth and success of the space program, the United States soon emerged as the world leader in the number of students attaining engineering degrees, graduating about 80,000 per year in the mid-1980s, according to the Engineering Workforce Commission.

As an incentive to continue the reform efforts, including those focused on developing more critical thinking and problem-solving skills rather than rote memorization and facts, the Reagan Administration's National Commission on Excellence in Education published *A Nation at Risk* (1983). Shortly after, in 1985 - the year Halley's Comet passed near earth – the American Association for the Advancement of Science (AAAS) created *Project 2061* – the year we will see the return of Halley's Comet (for a more complete history, see http://www.aaas.org/program/project2061/about). Project 2061 set out to identify factors that would create a science literate population, which led to the 1989 publication of *Science for All Americans* and the subsequent *Benchmarks for Science Literacy* that are still widely cited and utilized today.

5

Although the call to action in STEM heightened after the 1957 Sputnik launch, the United States has had an extensive history of recognizing the importance of scientific issues, phenomena, and research, dating as far back as the First Congress (1787, www.TeachingAmericanHistory.org) and President George Washington's First Annual Message to Congress on the State of the Union on January 8, 1790, at which time he called upon Congress to promote scientific knowledge:

> Nor am I less persuaded that you will agree with me in opinion that there is nothing which can better deserve your patronage than the promotion of science and literature. Knowledge is in every country the surest basis of public happiness. In one in which the measures of government receive their impressions so immediately from the sense of the community as in ours it is proportionably [sic] essential.

The drive to be competitive and outpace our international partners continues today. Fifty-two years after Sputnik and 219 years after President Washington's State of the Union speech, Congress and the American people are still being called upon to be innovative and achievers in science and mathematics. President Obama called on Americans to renew that charge of almost 60 years ago in his 2009 State of the Union Address:

> We will not just meet, but we will exceed the level achieved at the height of the Space Race, through policies that invest in basic and applied research, create new incentives for private innovation, promote breakthroughs in energy and medicine, and improve education in math and science. ... Through this commitment, American students will move... from the middle to the top of the pack in science and math over the next decade – for we know that the nation that out-educates us today will out-compete us tomorrow.

Policy

While one can see that policy has played a pivotal role in the history of STEM, its role over the past 10 years has significantly impacted how we view and what we call STEM today. During his tenure as president, Barack Obama and his administration has passed two specific initiatives to improve STEM teaching and learning. They first launched *Educate to Innovate* in 2009, followed by *Change the Equation* in 2010. Change the Equation was a specific call to action for the business community to become more involved in STEM education, which was also one of the goals of Educate to Innovate (http://changetheequation.org/). Additional goals of Educate to Innovate include increasing diversity within STEM fields and careers, improving STEM teacher quality and having the government invest more in STEM at the federal level. One way President Obama has worked towards a more effective and diverse STEM workforce for the future of the United States has been to invest in improving undergraduate STEM learning in order to positively impact future generations (http://www.whitehouse.gov/issues/education/k-12/educate-innovate).

Before President Obama, President George W. Bush passed the *American Competitiveness Initiative* (2006), which had similar goals to those of President Obama.'s initiatives. The American Competitiveness Initiative had a goal to improve mathematics and science performance in the United States in the interest of making the United States a world leader in the STEM fields. This call to action specifically addressed training more highly-qualified mathematics and science teachers, increasing the number of people involved in innovation and providing additional grant money to schools to encourage them to more readily adopt and implement research-based mathematics curricula and interventions (http://georgewbushwhitehouse.archives.gov/stateoftheunion/2006/aci/index.html#section2).

Curricula

While presidential initiatives come and go with changes in administration and tend to be nothing more than "calls to action," actionable change happens at the local level through the use of innovative curricular methods such as the one described in this book. While continuous, collaborative and interdisciplinary STEM education remains a dream and goal of many teachers, the realities of current classrooms and the cultural climate of accountability testing can bring an innovative project to a halt before the idea even gets off the ground. However, the passion and drive that teachers and educators bring to the STEM content areas have helped overcome these barriers through grassroots efforts. While there are many that have helped shape STEM as we know it today, two engineering education projects have become nationwide projects and these two programs highlight the interdisciplinary nature and project-based instruction framework we propose in this book.

Figure 2. A student demonstrating his Level II project. (Please use your QR reader to scan the QR code to watch the video).

Project Lead The Way.   The steps towards the birth of this widely successful program began in 1986 when a high school teacher named Richard Blais began teaching basic engineering to his students. In 1997, the project was funded to expand beyond Blais' school by the Charitable Leadership Foundation. Over the years, Project Lead The Way has continued to grow with partnerships, grants and endorsements from many notable government programs and Fortune 500 companies. Because of the support the project has received, it has managed to expand beyond the initial goal of educating K-12 students about engineering while encouraging them to consider a career in and/or majoring in an engineering-related major in college. Today, Project Lead The Way's curricula are more wholly inclusive of STEM, while working toward a broader mission of "[preparing] students to be the next generation of problem solvers, critical thinkers, and innovators for the global economy" (https://www.pltw.org/).

Engineering is Elementary.   Another such project is Engineering is Elementary. This project was founded by the National Center for Technological Literacy (http://legacy.mos.org/nctl/), which was launched by the Museum of Science, Boston, in 2004. While it is not as widely known as Project Lead The Way, Engineering is Elementary has a more narrow focus for its audience. Specifically, Engineering is Elementary targets elementary school students and teachers with a mission to "[support] educators and children with curricula and professional development that develop engineering literacy" (http://www.eie.org/). While the project has expanded to include middle grades materials through the Engineering Everywhere curricula and to high school with the Engineering the Future course, its expansion to other STEM fields remains limited; however, they have expanded geographically and now have their curricula used in all 50 states. (http://www.eie.org/).

The Pivotal Role of the National Science Foundation

Throughout the history of STEM education, several Presidents and their administrations and hundreds of various organizations have impacted STEM as we know it today and as it is being formed for future generations. However, it can be argued that none have had more of a pivotal impact than that of the National Science Foundation. While World War I, the subsequent Great Depression and World War II took many resources from the American people, those events became test beds and discovery zones that focused on scientific advances related to wartime needs. For example, cyanoacrylates, aka, superglue, were discovered in 1942 while searching for materials for clear plastic gun sights for World War II (MIT, 2010). Duck tape (or duct tape) was developed during World War II for use in sealing ammunition cases (Gurowitz for Johnson & Johnson, www.kilmerhouse.com). Wanting to continue with the scientific advances even though the war was over, President Franklin D. Roosevelt called upon Vannevar Bush for help. Bush's solution, presented to the President in 1945, was a "National Research Foundation." The "National Science Foundation" – a name suggested by Senator Harley Kilgore of West Virginia

– was introduced as a series of bills in 1945 and passed by Congress in 1947. However, President Truman vetoed the bill because he was not allowed to name the director of the agency. Finally, in 1950, the bill passed, creating the *National Science Foundation* (NSF), with Alan T. Waterman as the first director and an initial appropriation of $225,000 (equivalent of about $1,875,000 in today's dollar). (For a more complete history of the NSF, please see http://www.nsf.gov/about/history/overview-50.jsp#1940s.) Although the NSF began funding educational innovations as early as 1954, it did not see significant amounts of funding until after the launch of Sputnik, when Congress more than tripled its education funding in 1958.

While there were several calls for a renewed focus on science education throughout NSF's history (e.g., 1971, 1972, 1980), it wasn't until 1989 that we saw the beginnings of the calls for multidisciplinary research through the Small Grants for Exploratory Research program. This call for multidisciplinary, innovative research was originally coined *SMET* – Science, Mathematics, Engineering and Technology. Although the history of the acronym SMET is largely unknown, it did appear as early as 1993 in NSF 93-143 Guide to Programs documents:

> One major NSF goal is to improve the quality of the Nation's science, mathematics, engineering, and technology (SMET) education.

Additionally, congressional hearings in 1997 in the Committee of Science show the use of the SMET terminology as well. However, in 2001, Judith Ramaley, then a director at NSF, decided that the words needed reordering to show a more interdisciplinary emphasis:

> I did so because science and math support the other two disciplines and because STEM sounds nicer than SMET. The older term subtly implies that science and math came first or were better. The newer term suggests a meaningful connection among them. (Chute, Feb. 10, 2009)

The term is wildly popular today, long surpassing analysts and critics who thought it was just a trend or fetish. Despite its growing popularity, the definition of STEM and, more specifically, the definition of STEM education, remains very broad and open to various interpretations amongst its stakeholders (Breiner, Harkness, Johnson, & Koehler, 2012).

DEFINING STEM EDUCATION: AN INTERDISCIPLINARY APPROACH

In defining STEM education, the current state and focus of that education must be considered. There is an increased focus on college and career readiness with the recent release of the Common Core State Standards and the Next Generation Science Standards, including a new focus on integrating engineering into science classrooms. Add into the mixture literacy across the disciplines, STEM literacy and 21st century skills, it has become a very broad field with a great deal of overlap. Across the literature, although STEM education consistently focuses on a more holistic approach where sense-making is essential, the starting point for doing so varies (Labov, Reid, & Yamamoto, 2010). For example, the NRC (2003) advocates for effective STEM instruction to foster "inquisitiveness, cognitive skills of evidence-based reasoning, and an understanding and appreciation of the process of scientific investigation" (p. 25). However, one of the first integrative STEM education programs in the US suggests starting with engineering so as to focus on the application of the field (Sanders, 2009). Regardless of the starting point, the most important thing to consider is that the context in which we conceptualize STEM education impacts our definition. For example, Breiner et al. (2012) surveyed faculty members at a public Research I institution concerning their conceptions of STEM. While 72% possessed a relevant conception of STEM, they did not share a common conceptualization. This disjoint in conceptualization is likely due to their various academic disciplines and/or the impacts of STEM on their daily lives.

Therefore, for the purposes of this book, we sought to define STEM education that (a) took into consideration a common context for our conceptualization of STEM education (namely, project-based instruction); (b) considered the application of STEM to real-world settings within the project-based instruction environment; (c) rooted itself in an interdisciplinary approach (described later); and (d) led to the STEM literate society. Tsupros, Kohler, and Hallinen's (2009) definition of STEM education most closely met our criteria:

> STEM education is an interdisciplinary approach to learning where rigorous academic concepts are coupled with real-world lessons as students apply science, technology, engineering, and mathematics in contexts that make connections between school, community, work, and the global enterprise enabling the development of STEM literacy and with it the ability to compete in the new economy.

Interdisciplinary and *integrated* are two terms commonly used to describe theoretical and instructional approaches to STEM education. Perceptions of these terms have the potential to carry different meanings and may, in fact, lead to misapplications of prior experiences by novices as they try to apply theory to practice (NRC, 2014; Rivet & Krajcik, 2008). Our focus on supporting the practice of STEM education will be best accomplished in this book by further defining *interdisciplinary* as it is applied to incorporating STEM teaching and learning in educational contexts. Specifically, there should be a focus on depth of content knowledge within a specific [STEM] discipline while engaging in learning across two or more [STEM] disciplines. As depicted in Figure 3, we can visualize the interdisciplinary nature of STEM education in which goals, outcomes, integration and implementation are clearly defined within the disciplinary expertise, and practice within and across STEM are essential (Mohr-Schroeder, Jackson, Schroeder, & Wilhelm, in press). Note that we are not advocating for a single model of cross-sector collaboration, but rather a variety of different models that are relevant to the communities they serve and reflect cultures, environments and stakeholders.

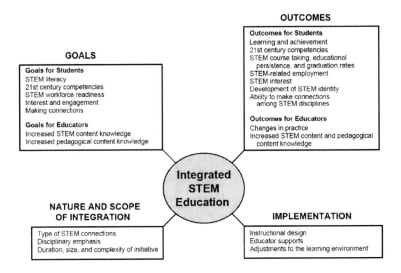

Figure 3. Interdisciplinary STEM education framework (National Academy of Engineering and National Research Council, 2014).

For example, let's explore what it means to be *STEM literate* using our idea of interdisciplinary STEM education. We can consider literacy as defined in terms of STEM compared to literacy as it is defined for individual disciplines. Literacy has become increasingly more specialized (Shanahan & Shanahan, 2008). The misconception of literacy as a concern limited to the English Language Arts is being corrected as the concept of disciplinary literacy gains traction and the experts are increasingly those within a given discipline. We can apply a common definition of disciplinary literacy to the four STEM disciplines, both individually and then more holistically. A frequently cited definition of *disciplinary literacy* addresses the context of a discipline, the unique practices used by those within a discipline and how the knowledge and abilities possessed by those in a discipline are used to create, communicate and use knowledge to engage in the work of that discipline (Shanahan & Shanahan, 2008, 2012). Applied to the STEM fields, experts in individual STEM disciplines could identify those unique tools related to engaging in that discipline. The commonalities across the disciplines, as previously described in defining a transdisciplinary approach, create yet another unique tool set and ability to create and use knowledge that we classify as STEM literacy. Novices can become experts as they learn how to create, communicate and use knowledge within and across STEM fields.

FULL STEM AHEAD

The perspectives held by teachers and students help shape the implementation of STEM education. In this chapter, we sought to present a brief history and a framework that will help teachers operationalize STEM education through transdisciplinary instructional practices such as the STEM SOS model on which this book focuses. Professional development and supplemental materials such as this book that are geared toward STEM education practices are necessary to effectively meld perception and practice in the classroom. While teachers today know and understand the value of inquiry-based instruction, such as that of project-based instruction, without proper training and support, they tend to revert to traditional instruction that is rooted in the work of the Harvard Committee of Ten (NEA, 1894) that placed an individual focus on subject areas. While discrete subjects are important, that focus challenges today's call for 21st century skills, critical thinking and application, and making cross-disciplinary connections that industries desire (NRC, 2014).

Imagine an education that includes solving hundreds of such challenges over the course of the 13 years of schooling that lead to high school graduation – challenges that increase in difficulty as the children age . . . Children who are prepared for life in this way would be great problem solvers in the workplace, with the abilities and the can-do attitude that are needed to be competitive in the global economy. Even more important, they will be more rational human beings - people who are able to make wise judgments for their family, their community and their nation. (Alberts, as quoted in NRC, 2014, p. 10-11)

REFERENCES

American Association for the Advancement of Science. (1990). *Science for all Americans*. New York, NY: Oxford University Press.

American Association for the Advancement of Science. (1993). *Benchmarks for science literacy*. New York, NY: Oxford University Press.

Basham, J. D., Israel, M., & Maynard, K. (2010). An ecological model of STEM education: Operationalizing STEM for all. *Journal of Science Education and Technology, 25*(3), 9–19.

Breiner, J. M., Harkness, S. S., Johnson, C. C., & Koehler, C. M. (2012). What is STEM? A discussion about conceptions of STEM in education and partnerships. *School Science and Mathematics, 112*(1), 3–11.

Carnevale, A. P., Smith, N., & Melton, M. (2011). *STEM*. Washington, DC: Georgetown University Center on Education and the Workforce.

Chute, E. (2009, February 10). STEM education is branching out. *Pittsburgh Post-Gazette*. Retrieved from http://www.post-gazette.com/news/education/2009/02/10/STEM-education-is-branching-out/stories/200902100165

Council of Chief State School Officers [CCSSO]. (2010). *Common core state standards for mathematics*. Retrieved from www.corestandards.org

Council on Competitiveness. (2005). *Innovate America*. Retrieved from www.compete.org/images/uploads/File/PDF%20Files/NII_Innovate_America.pdf

Gurowitz, M. (2009). Duct tape: Invented here! *Johnson & Johnson*. Retrieved from http://www.kilmerhouse.com/2009/08/duct-tape-invented-here/

Horovitz, B. (Mary 5, 2012). After Gen X, Millennials, what should the next generation be? *USA Today*. Retrieved from http://usatoday30.usatoday.com/money/advertising/story/2012-05-03/naming-the-next-generation/54737518/1

Kelly, D., Xie, H., Nord, C. W., Jenkins, F., Chan, J. Y., & Kastberg, D. (2013). *Performance of U.S. 15-year-old students in mathematics, science, and reading literacy in an international context: First look at PISA 2012*. Washington, DC: National Center for Education Statistics.

Labov, J. B., Reid, A. H., & Yamamoto, K. R. (2010). Integrated biology and undergraduate science education: a new biology education for the twenty-first century? *CBE-Life Sciences Education, 9*(1), 10–16.

Langdon, D., McKittrick, G., Beede, D., Khan, B., & Doms, M. (2011). *STEM: Good jobs now and for the future.* ESA Issue Brief #03-11. Washington, DC: U.S. Department of Commerce.

MIT. (2004). *Inventor of the week archive.* Lemelson-MIT Program. Retrieved from http://lemelson.mit. edu/

Mohr-Schroeder, M. J, Jackson, C., Schroeder, D. C., & Wilhelm, J. (in press). Developing a STEM education teacher preparation program to help increase STEM Literacy amongst preservice teachers. In P. Jenlink (Ed.), *STEM teaching and Common Core Standards: An interdisciplinary approach.* Lanham, Maryland: Rowman & Littlefield.

National Academy of Engineering. (2008). *Grand challenges for engineering.* Retrieved from http:// www.engineeringchallenges.org

National Academy of Engineering and National Research Council. (2014). *STEM integration in K-12 education: Status, prospects, and an agenda for research.* Washington, DC: The National Academies Press.

National Governors Association. (2007). *Innovation America: A final report.* Retrieved from www.nga. org/files/live/sites/NGA/files/pdf/0707INNOVATIONFINAL.PDF

NGSS Lead States. (2013). *Next generation science standards: For states, by states.* Washington, DC: The National Academies Press.

National Research Council. (1996). *National Science Education Standards.* Washington, DC: The National Academies Press. Retrieved from www.nap.edu/catalog.php?record_id=4962

National Research Council. (2003). *Improving undergraduate instruction in science, technology, engineering, and mathematics: Report of a workshop.* Washington, DC: The National Academies Press.

National Research Council. (2007). *Rising above the gathering storm: Energizing and employing America for a brighter economic future.* Available at www.nap.edu/catalog.php?record_id=114639

National Research Council [NRC]. (2009). *Learning science in informal environments: People, places, and pursuits.* Committee on Learning Science in Informal Environments, P. Bell, B. Lewenstein, A. W. Shouse, and M. A. Feder (Eds.). Board on Science Education, Center for Education, Division of Behavioral and Social Sciences and Education. Washington, DC: The National Academies Press.

National Research Council. (2012). *A framework for K–12 science education: Practices, crosscutting concepts, and core ideas.* Washington, DC: The National Academies Press.

National Research Council. (2014a). *Convergence: Facilitating transdisciplinary integration of life sciences, physical sciences, engineering, and beyond.* Committee on Key Challenge Areas for Convergence and Health. Board on Life Sciences, Division on Earth and Life Studies. Washington, DC: The National Academies Press.

National Research Council. (2014b). *STEM learning is everywhere: Summary of a convocation on building learning systems.* S. Olson and J. Labov, Rapporteurs. Planning Committee on STEM Learning Is Everywhere: Engaging Schools and Empowering Teachers to Integrate Formal, Informal, and Afterschool Education to Enhance Teaching and Learning in Grades K-8, Teacher Advisory Council, Division of Behavioral and Social Sciences and Education. Washington, DC: The National Academies Press.

National Research Council. (2014c). *STEM integration in K-12 education: Status, prospects, and an agenda for research.* Washington, DC: The National Academies Press.

National Science Board. (2007). *National action plan for addressing the critical needs of the U.S. science, technology, engineering and mathematics education system.* Retrieved fromwww.nsf.gov/ nsb/documents/2007/stem_action.pdf

National Science Board. (2014). *Science and engineering indicators 2014.* Arlington, VA: National Science Foundation.

National Science Foundation. (2013). *Women, minorities, and persons with disabilities in science and engineering: 2013.* Arlington, VA: Author.

Nicolescu, B. 2002. *Manifesto of transdisciplinarity.* Albany, NY: State University of New York Press.

PCAST (President's Council of Advisors on Science and Technology). 2012. Report to the President. *Engage to excel: Producing one million additional college graduates with degrees in science, technology, engineering and mathematics.* Retrieved from www.whitehouse.gov/sites/default/files/microsites/ostp/pcast-engage-to-excel-final_feb.pdf

Rivet, A. E., & Krajcik, J. S. (2008). Contextualizing instruction: Leveraging students' prior knowledge and experiences to foster understanding of middle school science. *Journal of Research in Science Teaching, 45*(1), 79–100.

Sanders, M. (2009). STEM, STEM education, STEMmania. *The Technology Teacher, 68*(4), 20–26.

Shanahan, T., & Shanahan, C. (2008). Teaching disciplinary literacy to adolescents: Rethinking content-area literacy. *Harvard Educational Review, 78*(1), 40–59.

Shanahan, T., & Shanahan, C. (2012). What is disciplinary literacy and why does it matter?. *Topics in Language Disorders, 32*(1), 7–18.

Thompson Klein, J., Grossenbacher-Mansuy, W., Häberli, R., Bill, A., Scholz, R. W., & Welti, M. (Eds.). 2001. *Transdisciplinarity: Joint problem solving among science, technology, and society: An effective way for managing complexity.* Basel, Switzerland: Birkhäuser Basel.

Tsupros, N., Kohler, R., & Hallinen, J. (2009). *STEM education: A project to identify the missing components.* Pennsylvania: Intermediate Unit 1: Center for STEM Education and Leonard Gelfand Center for Service Learning and Outreach, Carnegie Mellon University.

Varmus, H., Klausner, R., Zerhouni, E., Acharya, T., Daar, A. S., & Singer, P. A. (2003). Grand challenges in global health. *Science, 302*(5644), 398–399.

Wang, H. H., Moore, T. J., Roehrig, G. H., & Park, M. S. (2011). STEM integration: Teacher perceptions and practice. *Journal of Pre-College Engineering Education Research, 1*(2), 1–13.

Margaret J. Mohr-Schroeder
Associate Professor of Middle/Secondary Mathematics Education
Secondary Mathematics Program Chair
STEM Enthusiast
University of Kentucky

Maureen Cavalcanti
Graduate Research Assistant
University of Kentucky

Kayla Blyman
Graduate Research Assistant
University of Kentucky

2. THE ACHIEVEMENT GAPS IN MATHEMATICS AND SCIENCE

INTRODUCTION

The purpose of this chapter is to discuss and outline the findings from studies on the achievement gaps (AGs) in science and mathematics. I also review the interventions that have been implemented to mitigate or overcome those gaps.

I begin this analysis by (1) looking at the background of AGs by investigating the meaning and origin of AGs and discussing the several types of AGs. Then (2) I examine the relevance of AGs to the lives and prospects of the students and our nation, asking "What is the economic and strategic impact of the AGs?" (3) I then present the results of research on the causes of AGs, and (4) examine the outcomes of interventions to address AGs that have been implemented by the schools and school districts.

BACKGROUND

In a contemporary society where universal education has become a reality, the focus of attention has shifted from the availability of public education to its quality. There is a widespread perception in the United States that K-12 public education is not at the level it should be. This issue is thought to have a number of negative effects, ranging from the narrowing of career opportunities for students all the way to reducing national competitiveness in an increasingly competitive global economy. Many attempts have been made to quantify the quality of education in our public schools. Looking at the several available metrics, including graduation rate, funding per student, time in school and educational levels of teachers, it comes as no surprise that the preferred metrics are test scores, preferably from standardized tests. This can be seen in the following quote by Maloney and Mayer (2010, p. 333).

> The phrase "achievement gap" in education and political circles signifies the long-term and steady score gap between white, black, and Hispanic/Latino youth on standardized tests. Using the National Assessment of Educational Progress (NAEP) and SAT scores, researchers have shown that this gap, first recognized in the 1960s, fell by 20% to 40% (depending on the estimate) in the 1970s and 1980s, but then began widening in the late 1990s. (Lee 2002; English 2002; Haycock 2001)

A. Sahin (Ed.), A Practice-based Model of STEM Teaching, 15–28.

The NAEP scores are computed at the national level and disaggregated by ethnic and racial group by the National Center for Education Statistics, an agency of the U.S. Department of Education. The SAT is administered by the Educational Testing Service on behalf of the College Board.

In other words, at the national level, there are persistent and significant differences between ethnic/racial groups in which students of Asian and European descent have significantly higher scores than Native American students and students of African or Hispanic descent. Concurrent with these differences in achievement scores based on race/ethnicity are the differences in wealth. The effect of disparity in income on educational outcomes is at least as incisive as the previous differences. This phenomenon has been called the "racial, ethnic, income, or national achievement gap" (NAG).

The national achievement gap is not a phenomenon that is restricted to the public school system in the U.S. It also exists in private schools, although less is known about the NAG in private schools. However, it seems that the NAG is narrower in private schools (Coulson, 2005; Neal, 1997). Similarly, little is known about the NAG in home-schooling but there again, it seems that the gap is narrower if not eliminated (Home School Legal Defense Association, 2001, pp. 4-5).

Test scores have also been aggregated according to nation by the International Association for the Evaluation of Educational Achievement, administrator of the Programme for International Student Assessment (PISA), and the Organization for Economic Cooperation and Development, which offers the Trends in International Mathematics and Science Study (TIMSS). In these international rankings, the U.S. usually places at the middle to bottom among developed countries. This phenomenon is often called the "international achievement gap" (IAG).

The IAG is defined and understood in slightly different ways by various authors. The general concept is that there is a disparity between the proficiency of students in U.S. and other countries that are considered its "peers." A recent author on the subject, Wagner (2008), defined this gap as the disparity between the "new skills" needed in "today's highly competitive global knowledge economy" and what students are taught in class) (p. xxi).

A more prosaic understanding of the IAG is simply about the ranking of the U.S. in international studies. However, this is a very crude way of understanding the issue. Ranking is often misleading because the differences in score points are not statistically significant. For example, the document that in a certain sense started it all, *A Nation at Risk* (National Commission on Excellence in Education, 1983), was later reanalysed and much less threatening results were found in the data. According to Carson, Heulskamp, and Woodall (1993), Simpson's paradox made several trends appear to go in the opposite of their actual direction. This type of paradox occurs when the statistical data of distinct groups are pooled, i.e., each group may exhibit a positive trend, but when combined, the overall trend becomes negative. However, according to Stedman (1994) there were still reasons for concern even though the situation was not as dire as generally portrayed. The standardized tests themselves

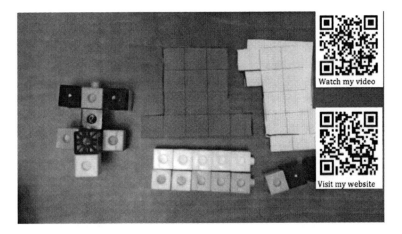

Figure 1. A student demonstrating her Level II project. (Please use your QR reader to scan the QR codes to watch her video and/or see her e-portfolio website.)

have been subjected to extensive criticism. For example, a simple renorming would make any idea of trends meaningless. Others such as Downey, Steffy, Poston, and English (2009) have a more nuanced view:

> The first important step to take in confronting the achievement gap problem is to abandon the idea that one single thing, or even a few things in combination, will crack this apparently baffling educational conundrum. And the first factor to confront is that there is no single "achievement gap" but many kinds of gaps. (p.1)

Using a national educational longitudinal data set, Carpenter, Ramirez, and Severn (2006) found "not one, but multiple achievement gaps, within and between groups" (p. 120) and that "gaps between races may not be the most serious of them" (p. 123). The gender AG has received less attention because the gender imbalance in public schools has swung in favour of female students and has only remained relevant in advanced placement (AP) courses in the STEM fields where female students are typically underrepresented (e.g., Robinson & Lubienski, 2011).

RELEVANCE

Although schools teach a wide variety of subjects, the focus of attention has primarily been on English language and mathematics and, more recently, science. These fields of knowledge are considered vital for national security and prosperity. Of these subjects, the preeminent one has been English, which is the "unofficial official" language of the nation. The latest wave of immigration into the U.S. distinguishes itself from the previous ones by its members being less eager to relinquish their native languages in favour of English. However, more recent harsh economic realities have shifted the spotlight to the teaching and learning of mathematics and science. These academic subjects are considered to be critical for the formation of a workforce capable of participating and succeeding in a competitive and technologically advanced economic system that now spans the entire planet.

The achievement gap is now an indelible part of the public discourse on education at all levels. There are two major markers of this phenomenon. The first was the publication in 1983 of the previously mentioned report, *A Nation at Risk* (National Commission on Excellence in Education, 1983), and the second was the passing of the "No Child Left Behind" Act of 2001 (NCLB). The topic is closely intertwined with burning issues of the U.S. social life such as de-industrialization, globalization and the disappearance of "well-paying jobs" for those having a high school degree or less.

A recent example of the popularity of this subject is an article that appeared in *The New York Times*, written by Garfunkel and Mumford and dated August 24, 2011.

There is widespread alarm in the United States about the state of our math education. The anxiety can be traced to the poor performance of American students on various international tests, and it is now embodied in George W. Bush's No Child Left Behind law, which requires public school students to pass standardized math tests by the year 2014 and punishes their schools or their teachers if they do not.

DESCRIPTION AND CAUSES

The majority of the research on AGs has been conducted without specific reference to math or science. Most of these studies focused on identifying the causes of the underachievement of African American students. Among these studies are Chambers (2009) who detected a "differential treatment by school personnel as early as elementary school" (p. 1). The study by Rowley and Wright (2011), based on the Educational Longitudinal Study of 2002, confirmed the Black/White gap, but also made the statement that among its causes is "discrimination based on race" (p. 1). However, the paper itself did not offer any substantiation of racial discrimination, but rather pointed to the inequity of the U.S. public school system. This is an almost uniquely U.S. phenomenon based on the preponderance of local funding of schools in the United States.

A relatively recent trend in AG studies is the focus on Hispanic students. The term Latino/a is also used. Among those studies are those of Reardon and Galindo (2009), Heilig, Williams, and Jez (2010), and Madrid (2011).

Gill (2011) conducted a study in which both ethnic groups, Black and Hispanic, were taken into consideration. The author did not find any statistically significant differences in the Virginia "Standards of Learning" scores between those two groups, but both had scores that were statistically different from the group of White students.

An additional item on the topic of study is the socioeconomic status of the families (SES). However, Condron (2009) studied both and, surprisingly, found that schools widen the Black/White disparities, but narrow the social class gaps. He concluded that school factors affect the racial AG and non-school factors drive the income AG. Later, Burchinal et al. (2011) obtained the same type of result in a longitudinal study of elementary school students.

Among the studies about the causes of AGs, a topic of research is school and class size (McMillen, 2004). There is a policy aspect to the size of schools and classes because it is determined by policy and funding. McMillen stated that:

> The number of public schools serving the secondary grades in the U.S. has largely held steady between 23,000 and 26,000 since 1930. During that same time, however, the number of public high school students in the U.S. nearly tripled, from approximately 4.4 million to over 13 million. As consolidation trends have created larger schools, the issue of school size has become of great interest to educators and policymakers alike. (p.)

Cultural aspects of AGs were discussed by Cholewa and West-Olatunji (2008) and Demerath, Lynch, Milner, Peters, and Davidson (2010). These researchers discussed the AGs in light of the "wave theory." The first wave was the primordial hunter-gatherer culture; the second wave consisted of the agrarian civilization; the third wave was the industrial society; and the fourth is the post-industrial society. The author noticed how in a fourth wave society, such as the U.S. of today, "[a]dvanced literacy and numeracy skills are absolutely essential for competing within the 4th wave workforce" (p. 15). Adams (2005) showed how differences in habits between racial/ethnic groups impact academic success, such as hours spent watching television, time dedicated to homework and parental expectations.

The gap between the culture of the teachers, the majority of whom are of European descent, and those of who do not share this culture creates what Cholewa and West-Olatunji (2008) called "cultural discontinuity" (p. 1). The authors considered this phenomenon to be a major cause of the AGs. A different approach was taken by Demerath et al. (2010), who pointed out that "we need to decode success, rather than continue the autopsy of failure" (citing Hilliard, 2002, p. 2937). The authors analysed how children from middle and upper-class backgrounds are able to extract from schools the best they have to offer to better compete in society.

A more focused analysis of the various immigrant groups was performed by Han (2006), who took into consideration the number of generations after immigration as well as the ethnic origin of students and concluded that "[c]hild and family characteristics were the most important factors to these [immigrant family] young children's academic achievements" (pp. 313-314). Basically, some ethnic groups scored higher (e.g., East Asian) than the U.S. average, while others (e.g., Mexican) scored lower. Schwartz and Stiefel (2006) similarly found that countries of origin were important. For example, Russian children scored above average and children from the Dominican Republic scored lower. However, on average, immigrant students

19

did better than native students in New York. Konstantopoulos (2009) performed a rigorous correlational statistical analysis of the achievement of Asian American students and confirmed what is considered common knowledge. The Asian-White AG is clearly in favour of Asian American students, even though it is smaller in reading than in mathematics. However, Pang, Han and Pang (2011) showed in their study of this group of students in California that we should not consider all Asian American students as a homogeneous group, but rather need to disaggregate between subgroups. Briefly, Asian Americans can be divided into a group of above-average achievers, corresponding to North East Asians (Chinese, Koreans, and Japanese) and South East Asians (Filipinos, Cambodians, Pacific Islanders, etc.), who achieve below average. Some studies on the achievement of immigrant students are even more granular. Simms (2012) studied the effect of educational selectivity of parents. This term denotes how the education level of parents compares with the average in the country of origin. The author found that educational selectivity had more explanatory power than SES. Related to immigration is the issue of how language has an effect on achievement (Han, 2012). The author described how mixed bilingual students were able to close the AGs, but non-English dominant bilinguals and non-English monolinguals did not. Halle, Hair, Wandner, McNamara and Chien (2012) studied the effects of the grade at which English proficiency was attained and the AGs. Their study found that the sooner that proficiency was attained, the sooner the gap was narrowed or closed.

A minor, but still important, area of research is the comparison between public and private schools. Usually, the private schools are Catholic because they are (1) a large system, and (2) unlike many private schools, not for the nation's elite, but for all groups of students. Hallinan and Kubitschek (2010) provided an example of this kind of study. The authors compared Catholic schools to public schools in Chicago with regards to the influence of poverty on student achievement. This study showed, not surprisingly, that poverty hampers achievement, but that this effect was mitigated in Catholic schools.

Some studies are fairly technical and critique the statistical measurement of the AGs themselves. For example, Verdugo (2011) studied the effect of dropouts on the AGs. Because the academically weakest students are those who typically are the most likely to leave the school systems, the achievement scores looked better than they actually were.

Considerable research has been done on the causes of the mathematics AG. The typical study of this type involves a detailed statistical analysis in which several factors are considered: race/ethnic group, SES, parental involvement, teacher, class and school size, and knowledge of English. See, for example, Berends and Penaloza, (2010), Braun, Chapman, and Vezzu (2010), Georges and Pallas (2010), Abedi and Herman (2010), and Riegle-Crumb and Grodsky (2010).

Among the most interesting types of statistical analysis is the longitudinal study. The efficacy of NCLB on the closing of the AG was examined by Braun et al. (2010) who found a modest impact.

Berends and Penaloza (2010) added an historical dimension to their study of the AG and showed that, between 1972 and 2004, the mathematics Black-White and Latino-White AGs increased. The authors attributed this phenomenon to the increase in segregation during that period.

Kelly (2009) studied the mathematics course taking of Black students and found that they were disproportionately enrolled in lower-track courses, a difference that could not be entirely explained by individual or family factors. Similar results were found by Long, Iatarola, and Conger (2009) in a study that focused on the need for remedial mathematics courses in Florida in relationship to the number and level of math courses taken by high schools students in that state.

Some studies have focused on teachers and their effect on mathematics scores. Hines (2008) found that students of teachers with low self-efficacy had lower mathematics test scores. In addition, Desimone and Long (2010) found that lower-achieving students had teachers who spent less time on instruction. On the other hand, Georges and Pallas (2010) found that teaching practices had little influence on mathematics scores and, at any rate, had uniform effects for all students.

Lee (2012) studied the effects of AGs on the possibility of obtaining a 2- or 4-year post-secondary degree, finding "large disparities between actual and desirable math achievement levels for college readiness at the national level" (p. 52).

While most research is focused on the problem of mathematics AG, a few, such as Stinson (2008), studied successes. That author conducted a participative study with four African American male students who were academically successful in mathematics.

The mathematics AG is often associated with educational inequity (Hines, 2008; Long et al., 2009). Ruiz (2011) stressed the social aspects of the mathematics AG, using her personal experience to discuss the importance of motivating Latino students in Algebra I. Most of the ELL students in the U.S. public school system are Latinos; thus, cultural and linguistic issues are often connected. Several studies have targeted the relationship between the language skills of Latinos and the mathematics AG (e.g., Abedi & Herman, 2010).

The most popular type of research on the subject of IAG is the statistical study of data from TIMSS (e.g., Chudgar & Luschei, 2009; Heuveline, Yang, & Timberlake, 2010; Wang & Zhu, 2003), or PISA (Perry, 2009). Hierarchical linear modeling is often employed for analysis of TIMSS data (Heuveline et al., 2010; J. Lee & Fish, 2010).

An interesting study was performed by Chudgar and Luschei (2009), who looked at differences between and within countries with respect to the SES of families. This study found that, in most cases, the schools are less important than the family situation in explaining student achievement. Similarly, Lee and Fish (2010) found that the international AG gap is due to school factors, but family factors explain differences between states in the U.S.

Perry (2009) did an in-depth statistical study that focused on equity and found that (1) academic selectivity in school admittance policies in compulsory education

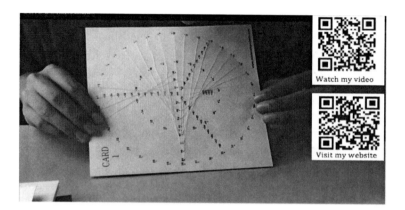

Figure 2. A student demonstrating his Level II project. (Please use your QR reader to scan the QR codes to watch his video and/or see his e-portfolio website.)

is strongly associated with inequitable outcomes, but not necessarily overall performance; (2) selective schooling does not always reproduce social status; (3) high levels of privatization and choice are not necessarily incompatible with educational equity, although they may diminish it; and (4) income inequality within the larger society does not appear to be strongly associated with equitable math achievement in OECD countries.

Heuveline et al. (2010) studied the relationship between family structure and mathematics achievement. As expected, children in single parent households scored lower. However, in the U.S. this gap was larger than in 13 other countries.

INTERVENTIONS

Several projects were implemented with the aim of reducing or even eliminating the AGs. These were implemented at various levels, including single schools (Beecher & Sweeny, 2008), school districts (Burris, Wiley, Welner, & Murphy, 2008; Lopez, 2010), and even larger geographical areas (Konstantopoulos & Chung, 2009; Smith, 2012). Common to all the successful interventions are the considerable amount of resources, the adoption of interactive whiteboard technology (Lopez, 2010), a complete restructuring of a school (Beecher & Sweeny, 2008), group counseling (Bruce, Getch, & Ziomek-Daigle, 2009), more advanced classes such as International Baccalaureate (IB) courses (Burris et al., 2008), class size reduction (Konstantopoulos & Chung, 2009), and summer programs (Smith, 2012).

The main objective of NCLB was to eliminate the AGs. Lee and Reeves (2012) performed a longitudinal study using hierarchical linear modeling of NAEP data to determine the impact of NCLB on the reading and mathematics AGs. Their results aligned with the previously mentioned research in that school resources were more influential than the instruments of reform law, accountability, data tracking and standards.

Can instructional practices reduce the mathematics or science AGs? To answer this question, Wenglinsky (2004) performed a hierarchical linear modeling study on a national sample. He found that instructional practices could make large differences even after the personal backgrounds of students were taken into consideration. Similar results were obtained by Crosnoe et al. (2010), Clarke et al. (2011), Santau, Maerten-Rivera and Huggins (2011) in science, and by Boaler and Staples (2008) in California. Other types of school interventions have met with success, such as "ethnic matching" of African American students with African American teachers (Eddy & Easton-Brooks, 2011).

However, supplementary programs were also found to have a positive effect (Lee, Olszewski-Kubilius, & Peternel, 2009). Similarly, the use of computers as both in-school and extra-school activities was able to narrow the mathematics AG, according to a national longitudinal study (Kim & Chang, 2010).

With the relatively recent influx of immigrants with low English language skills, an often used strategy in the closing of the mathematics AG is to act on the English language skills, after all almost all standardized tests are written in English (Kim & Chang, 2010; Santau et al., 2011). Sometimes, teachers receive English language learners (ELL) training or use special instructional practices targeted to ELLs (Pray & Ilieva, 2011). NCLB provides exclusions and deferrals for English ELL students.

Alson (2006) presented a personal case study, which, however interesting, has the limitation that it is not reproducible, even though most studies in education at a certain level share this limitation.

It seems that very few programs have been implemented to narrow the International AG (IAG). Tabernik and Williams (2010) studied the effect of teachers' professional development in Ohio on the international mathematics achievement gap.

Very little research has been done on whether project-based learning (PBL) can reduce or eliminate the AGs. Recently, Halvorsen et al. (2012) implemented a PBL series in low and high-SES schools in the subjects of social studies and reading and writing to learn content (content literacy). They found no statistically significant differences between high- and low-SES students at the end of the intervention. In other words, the researchers had, supposedly, closed the AG for these subjects. However, the study did not establish the presence of an AG before the intervention; it was simply assumed. There was no common pre-test across differing SES schools, only a post-test.

In their study, Lieberman and Hoody (1998) reported the results of the implementation in 40 schools of a framework that employed the environment as an Integrating Context for Learning (EIC). This approach provided "hands-on learning experiences, often through problem-solving and project-based activities" (p. 1). In addition to math and science, the academic subjects covered included social studies, reading and writing. The document states that EIC "holds great promise for helping 'close the achievement gap' in reading, writing, math, science, and social studies"

(p. 11); however, no data are shown to support this statement. Nonetheless, the study has shown improved academic performance in most schools that have implemented EIC.

In our discussion of interventions geared towards the elimination of the AGs, we need to mention the charter schools. Briefly, a charter school is a type of school that receives public funding, but operates independently from local school districts, even though it is subject to the same curriculum standards and state achievement testing as traditional public schools. Many have suggested that, due to the independence and flexibility of the charter schools, the movement is able to implement innovative academic activities and structures that can overcome the AGs (Read, 2008; Department of Education & WestEd, 2006; Ladner et al., 2010).

It is regrettable that the students who would most benefit from learning math and science are most often disinterested in these subjects. Technical, health, and engineering careers are wonderful opportunities for upward mobility because they do not usually require the presence of a network of connections as careers in law and management do (Sahin, Gulacar, & Stuessy, 2014). Hence, any means of eliciting the interest of the students in science and mathematics and thus their academic achievement should be fostered.

The Harmony charter schools have implemented a project-based STEM teaching called the STEM Students on the Stage (SOS)™ model to improve the mathematics and science achievement of students of all subgroups (Sahin & Top, in press; Sahin, Top, & Vanegas, 2014; Sahin et al., 2013; Sahin et al., 2014). Studies of the SOS model at HPS have shown that student are profoundly engaged, interested in STEM subjects and learning skills relevant to the workplace as well as getting ready for college and life. (Sahin & Top, in press; Sahin, Top, & Vanegas, 2014),

In the presence of promising preliminary results of PBL implementation and the results from research on the efficacy of PBL at Harmony Public Schools, we have reason to be optimistic.

CONCLUSION

During the last years, we have seen a certain decrease of the emphasis on the achievement gaps. However, there is also no indication that the AGs problem has been resolved. All but four states have obtained or requested a waiver from the U.S. Department of Education for failing to close the achievement gap as requested by NCLB. The public discourse on the achievement gaps has changed from the high hopes of ESEA and especially of its re-enactment as NCLB to the tacit and implicit admission of failure that these waivers denote. It is the understanding of the author that because of inherent contradictions build into the legislation aimed at resolving the achievement gaps, primarily NCLB and the more recent "Race To The Top" (RTTT), the AGs will not be solved within the current legislative framework (Indiogine & Kulm, 2014), even if localized interventions are able to mitigate if not resolve the achievement gaps.

REFERENCES

Abedi, J., & Herman, J. (2010). Assessing English language learners' opportunity to learn mathematics: Issues and limitations. *Teachers College Record, 112*(3), 723–746.

Adams, J. Q. (2005). Closing the performance gap in a 4th wave and post-modern society: Lessons from the field. *Mid-Western Educational Researcher, 18*(1), 14–18.

Alson, A. (2006). Attacking the achievement gap in a diverse urban-suburban community: A curricular case study. *Yearbook of the National Society for the Study of Education, 105*(1), 49–77.

Beecher, M., & Sweeny, S. M. (2008). Closing the achievement gap with curriculum enrichment and differentiation: One school's story. *Journal of Advanced Academics, 19*(3), 502–530.

Berends, M., & Penaloza, R. V. (2010). Increasing racial isolation and test score gaps in mathematics: A 30-year perspective. *Teachers College Record, 112*(4), 978–1007.

Boaler, J., & Staples, M. (2008). Creating mathematical futures through an equitable teaching approach: The case of Railside School. *Teachers College Record, 110*(3), 608–645.

Braun, H., Chapman, L., & Vezzu, S. (2010). The Black-White achievement gap revisited. *Education Policy Analysis Archives, 18*(21), 1–99.

Bruce, A. M., Getch, Y. Q., & Ziomek-Daigle, J. (2009). Closing the gap: A group counseling approach to improve test performance of African-American students. *Professional School Counseling, 12*(6), 450–457.

Burchinal, M., McCartney, K., Steinberg, L., Crosnoe, R., Friedman, S. L., McLoyd, V., & Pianta, R. (2011). Examining the Black-White achievement gap among low-income children using the NICHD study of early child care and youth development. *Child Development, 82*(5), 1404–1420.

Burris, C. C., Wiley, E., Welner, K. G., & Murphy, J. (2008). Accountability, rigor, and detracking: Achievement effects of embracing a challenging curriculum as a universal good for all students. *Teachers College Record, 110*(3), 571–607.

Carson, C. C., Heulskamp, R. M., & Woodall, R. D. (1993). Perspectives on education in America: An annotated briefing. *Journal of Educational Research, 86*(5), 259–310.

Chambers, T. V. (2009). The "receivement gap": School tracking policies and the fallacy of the "achievement gap". *Journal of Negro Education, 78*(4), 417–431.

Cholewa, B., & West-Olatunji, C. (2008). Exploring the relationship among cultural discontinuity, psychological distress, and academic outcomes with low-income, culturally diverse students. *Professional School Counseling, 12*(1), 54–61.

Chudgar, A., & Luschei, T. F. (2009). National income, income inequality, and the importance of schools: A hierarchical cross-national comparison. *American Educational Research Journal, 46*(3), 626–658.

Clarke, B., Smolkowski, K., Baker, S. K., Fien, H., Doabler, C. T., & Chard, D. J. (2011). The impact of a comprehensive Tier I Core Kindergarten Program on the achievement of students at risk in mathematics. *Elementary School Journal, 111*(4), 561–584.

Condron, D. J. (2009). Social class, school and non-school environments, and Black/White inequalities in children's learning. *American Sociological Review, 74*(5), 683–708.

Coulson, A. (2005). Private schools are closing the achievement gap. *School Reform News*, April.

Crosnoe, R., Morrison, F., Burchinal, M., Pianta, R., Keating, D., Friedman, S. L., & Clarke-Stewart, K. A. (2010). Instruction, teacher-student relations, and math achievement trajectories in elementary school. *Journal of Educational Psychology, 102*(2), 407–417.

Demerath, P., Lynch, J., Milner, H., Richard, I. V., Peters, A., & Davidson, M. (2010). Decoding success: A middle-class logic of individual advancement in a U.S. suburb and high school. *Teachers College Record, 112*(12), 2935–2987.

Desimone, L., & Long, D. A. (2010). Teacher effects and the achievement gap: Do teacher and teaching quality influence the achievement gap between Black and White and high- and low-SES students in the early grades? *Teachers College Record, 112*(12), 3024–3073.

Downey, C. J., Steffy, B. E., Poston, W. K., Jr., & English, F. W. (2009). *50 ways to close the achievement gap* (3rd ed.). Thousand Oaks, CA: Corwin Press.

Eddy, C. M., & Easton-Brooks, D. (2011). Ethnic matching, school placement, and mathematics achievement of African American students from kindergarten through fifth grade. *Urban Education, 46*(6), 1280–1299.

Georges, A., & Pallas, A. M. (2010). New look at a persistent problem: Inequality, mathematics achievement, and teaching. *Journal of Educational Research, 103*(4), 274–290.

Gill, W. W. A. (2011). Middle school A/B block and traditional scheduling: An analysis of math and reading performance by race. *NASSP Bulletin, 95*(4), 281–301.

Halle, T., Hair, E., Wandner, L., McNamara, M., & Chien, N. (2012). Predictors and outcomes of early versus later English language proficiency among English Language Learners. *Early Childhood Research Quarterly, 27*(1), 1–20.

Hallinan, M. T., & Kubitschek, W. N. (2010). School sector, school poverty, and the Catholic school advantage. *Catholic Education: A Journal of Inquiry and Practice, 14*(2), 143–172.

Halvorsen, A. L., Duke, N. K., Brugar, K. A., Block, M. K., Strachan, S. L., Berka, M. B., & Brown, J. M. (2012). Narrowing the achievement gap in second-grade social studies and content area literacy: The promise of a project-based approach. *Theory and Research in Social Education, 40*(3), 198–229.

Han, W. J. (2006). Academic achievements of children in immigrant families. *Educational Research and Reviews, 1,* 286–318.

Han, W. J. (2012). Bilingualism and academic achievement. *Child Development, 83*(1), 300–321.

Heilig, J. V., Williams, A., & Jez, S. J. (2010). Inputs and student achievement: An analysis of Latina/o-serving urban elementary schools. *Journal of the Association of Mexican American Educators, 4*(1), 55-67.

Heuveline, P., Yang, H., & Timberlake, J. M. (2010). It takes a village (perhaps a nation): Families, states, and educational achievement. *Journal of Marriage and Family, 72*(5), 1362–1376.

Hines, M. T. (2008). The interactive effects of race and teacher self efficacy on the achievement gap in school. *International Electronic Journal for Leadership in Learning, 12*(11).

Home School Legal Defense Association. (2001). *Home schooling achievement.* Purcellville, VA: Author.

Indiogine, S. E. P., Kulm, G. (2014). U.S. political discourse on math achievement gaps in light of Foucault's governmentality. In P. Liljedahl, C. Nicol, C. S. Oesterle, & D. Allan (Eds.), *Proceedings of the 38th Conference of the International Group for the Psychology of Mathematics Education and the 36th Conference of the North American Chapter of the Psychology of Mathematics Education* (Vol. 3) (pp. 369–375). Vancouver, Canada: PME.

Kelly, S. (2009). The Black-White gap in mathematics course taking. *Sociology of Education, 82*(1), 47–69.

Kim, S., & Chang, M. (2010). Does computer use promote the mathematical proficiency of ELL students? *Journal of Educational Computing Research, 42*(4), 285–305.

Konstantopoulos, S. (2009). The mean is not enough: Using quantile regression to examine trends in Asian-White differences across the entire achievement distribution. *Teachers College Record, 111*(5), 1274–1295.

Konstantopoulos, S., & Chung, V. (2009). What are the long-term effects of small classes on the achievement gap? Evidence from the lasting benefits study. *American Journal of Education, 116*(1), 125–154.

Lee, J. (2012). College for all: gaps between desirable and actual P-12 math achievement trajectories for college readiness. *Educational Researcher, 41*(2), 43–55.

Lee, J., & Fish, R. M. (2010). International and interstate gaps in value-added math achievement: Multilevel instrumental variable analysis of age effect and grade effect. *American Journal of Education, 117*(1), 109–137.

Lee, J., & Reeves, T. (2012). Revisiting the impact of NCLB high-stakes school accountability, capacity, and resources: State NAEP 1990-2009 reading and math achievement gaps and trends. *Educational Evaluation and Policy Analysis, 34*(2), 209–231.

Lee, S. Y., Olszewski-Kubilius, P., & Peternel, G. (2009). Follow-up with students after 6 years of participation in Project Excite. *Gifted Child Quarterly, 53*(2), 137–156.

Lieberman, G. A., & Hoody, L. L. (1998). *Closing the achievement gap: using the environment as an integrating context for learning.* San Diego, CA: State education; environment roundtable.

Long, M. C., Iatarola, P., & Conger, D. (2009). Explaining gaps in readiness for college-level math: The role of high school courses. *Education Finance and Policy, 4*(1), 1–33.

Lopez, O. S. (2010). The digital learning classroom: Improving English language learners' academic success in mathematics and reading using interactive whiteboard technology. *Computers & Education, 54*(4), 901–915.

Madrid, E. M. (2011). The Latino achievement gap. *Multicultural Education, 19*(3), 7–12.

Maloney, P., & Mayer, K. U. (2010). The U.S. educational system: Can it be a model for Europe? In J. Alber & N. Gilbert (Eds.), *United in diversity: Comparing social models in Europe and America* (pp. 328–358). New York, NY: Oxford University Press.

McMillen, B. J. (2004). School size, achievement, and achievement gaps. *Education Policy Analysis Archives, 12*(58), 1–27.

National Commission on Excellence in Education. (1983). *A Nation at Risk: The imperative for educational reform.* Washington, DC: U.S. Department of Education.

Neal, D. (1997). The effects of Catholic secondary school on student achievement. *Journal of Labor Economics, 15*(1), 98–123.

Pang, V. O., Han, P. P., & Pang, J. M. (2011). Asian American and Pacific Islander students: Equity and the achievement gap. *Educational Researcher, 40*(8), 378–389.

Perry, L. (2009). Characteristics of equitable systems of education: A cross-national analysis. *European Education, 41*(1), 79–100.

Pray, L., & Ilieva, V. (2011). Strategies for success: Links to increased mathematics achievement scores of English-Language learners. *Teacher Education and Practice, 24*(1), 30–45.

Reardon, S. F., & Galindo, C. (2009). The Hispanic-White achievement gap in math and reading in the elementary grades. *American Educational Research Journal, 46*(3), 853–891.

Riegle-Crumb, C., & Grodsky, E. (2010). Racial-ethnic differences at the intersection of math course-taking and achievement. *Sociology of Education, 83*(3), 248–270.

Robinson, J. P., & Lubienski, S. T. (2011). The development of gender achievement gaps in mathematics and reading during elementary and middle school: Examining direct cognitive assessments and teacher ratings. *American Educational Research Journal, 48*(2), 268–302.

Rowley, R. L., & Wright, D. W. (2011). No "White" Child Left Behind: The academic achievement gap between Black and White students. *Journal of Negro Education, 80*(2), 93–107.

Ruiz, E. C. (2011). Motivation of Latina/o students in Algebra I: Intertwining research and reflections. *School Science and Mathematics, 111*(6), 300–305.

Sahin, A., Willson, V., & Capraro, R. M. (2013, April 20). Charter school challenges and opportunities: Silver bullets, innovations, and divergent values. Paper presented at the 2013 annual meeting of the American Educational Research Association. Retrieved from the AERA Online Paper Repository.

Sahin, A., Willson, V., Top, N., & Capraro, R. M. (2014). Charter school system performance: How does student achievement compare? Paper presented at the 2014 annual meeting of the American Educational Research Association. Retrieved from the AERA Online Paper Repository.

Sahin, A., Gulacar, O., & Stuessy, C. (2014). High school students' perceptions of the effects of science Olympiad on their STEM career aspirations and 21st century skill development. *Research in Science Education.*

Sahin, A., Top, N., & Vanegas, S. (2014). *Harmony STEM SOS model increases college readiness and develops 21st century skills* (Whitepaper). Retrieved from http://harmonytx.org/Portals/0/HPS_Issue-1.pdf

Sahin, A., & Top, N. (In press). Make it happen: A study of a novel teaching style, STEM Students on the Stage (SOS)™, for increasing students' STEM knowledge and interest. *The Journal of STEM Education: Innovations and Research.*

Santau, A. O., Maerten-Rivera, J. L., & Huggins, A. C. (2011). Science achievement of English language learners in urban elementary schools: Fourth-grade student achievement results from a professional development intervention. *Science Education, 95*, 771–793.

Schwartz, A. E., & Stiefel, L. (2006). Is there a nativity gap? New evidence on the academic performance of immigrant students. *Education Finance and Policy, 1*(1), 17–49.

Simms, K. (2012). A hierarchical examination of the immigrant achievement gap: The additional explanatory power of nationality and educational selectivity over traditional explorations of race and socioeconomic status. *Journal of Advanced Academics, 23*(1), 72–98.

Smith, L. (2012). Slowing the summer slide. *Educational Leadership, 69*(4), 60–63.

Stedman, L. C. (1994). The Sandia Report and U.S. achievement: An assessment. *Journal of Educational Research, 87*(3), 133–147.

Stinson, D. W. (2008). Negotiating sociocultural discourses: The counter-storytelling of academically (and mathematically) successful African American male students. *American Educational Research Journal, 45*(4), 975–1010.

Tabernik, A. M., & Williams, P. R. (2010). Addressing low U.S. student achievement in mathematics and science through changes in professional development and teaching and learning. *International Journal of Educational Reform, 19*(1), 34–50.

Verdugo, R. R. (2011). The heavens may fall: School dropouts, the achievement gap, and statistical bias. *Education and Urban Society, 43*(2), 184–204.

Wagner, T. (2008). *The global achievement gap: Why even our best schools don't teach the new survival skills our children need–and what we can do about it.* New York, NY: Basic Books.

Wang, J., & Zhu, C. (2003). An in-depth analysis of achievement gaps between seventh and eighth grades in the TIMSS database. *School Science and Mathematics, 103*(4), 186–192.

Wenglinsky, H. (2004). Closing the racial achievement gap: The role of reforming instructional practices. *Education Policy Analysis Archives, 12*(64), 1–24.

S. Enrico P. Indiogine
Department of Learning, Teaching and Culture,
Texas A&M University

SECTION 2

DESCRIPTION OF STEM SOS MODEL

As you explore a brand-new project-based learning (PBL) method to prepare your students for the 21st century, Section II first helps you understand the differences between different PBL models, including the new STEM PBL model titled, STEM Students on the Stage (SOS)™. The next chapter presents a research study about the codification of the STEM SOS model and describes the STEM SOS model and its components. The final chapter in Section II discusses the way in which the STEM SOS model accomplishes PBL in a standards-focused world. After reading these chapters, you will have initial and broad understanding of the new STEM PBL model and how easy it is to implement.

NIYAZI ERDOGAN AND TODD DANE BOZEMAN

3. MODELS OF PROJECT-BASED LEARNING FOR THE 21ST CENTURY

INTRODUCTION

How students gain Science, Technology, Engineering, and Mathematics (STEM) content knowledge has been the focus of studies in the fields of neuroscience, psychology, anthropology and linguistics. Research from the 20th century suggested that for students, attaining knowledge in STEM content through experiential, hands-on and student-directed projects was likely to lead to greater achievement (Kolb, Boyatzis, & Mainemelis, 2001; Markham, Larmer, & Ravitz, 2003; Wehmeyer, Agran, & Hughes, 2000). As a result, Project-based Learning (PBL) has emerged as a preferred pedagogical method in STEM classrooms. Two factors in the 20th century increased the popularity of PBL within classrooms: (a) theory development and (b) the STEM education movement.

Theory Development

The first of two factors to influence the popularity of PBL involves theory development in the cognitive sciences. In 1954, Julian Rotter introduced new constructs for social learning theory when he proposed a model for understanding how people learned. Rotter suggested that learners' responses to external stimuli and desire to achieve rewards for successful mastery of content led to learning. Although Rotter moved the cognitive sciences away from behaviorism, the prevailing learning theory at the time, he still focused on external stimuli and exhibited a lack of understanding for internal cognition (Rotter, 1966). In 1977, Albert Bandura further broke away from behaviorism by asserting that social learning theory provided a better framework for studying cognition through examination of three general domains: (a) antecedent inducements or external stimuli acting on learners, (b) response feedback or learners' relation to environment, and (c) cognitive functions or learners' latent thought processes. Since Bandura's explication of social learning theory, researchers in the cognitive sciences have used social learning theory as a framework for many pedagogy studies, including studies on PBL. Today, social learning theory dominates 21st century cognitive models attempting to explain how students learn STEM content and how best to assist these students in achieving mastery of that knowledge (Bransford, Brown, & Cocking, 2000; Talbot-Smith, Abell, Appleton & Hanuscin, 2013).

A. Sahin (Ed.), A Practice-based Model of STEM Teaching, 31–42.

The STEM Education Movement

The second of two factors to influence the popularity of PBL in the 21st century relates to the STEM education movement of the late 20th and early 21st centuries. With the development of technology, rise of the Internet and transition from local to global perspectives, education stakeholders in the late 20th century recognized the importance of STEM education for developing the next generation of STEM leaders, researchers, and teachers (Augustine, 2005). As a direct result of this movement, students in today's STEM classrooms are held accountable to learning standards designed by cognitive scientists well-versed in social learning theory and are accustomed to solving problems as individuals or within collective learning venues. Therefore, PBL likely provides an optimal pedagogical method for assisting students in meeting standards for 21st century education (Markham, Larmer, & Ravitz, 2003).

In this chapter, we provide a discussion on PBL models for the 21st century. In our discussion we focus on (a) defining PBL, (b) identifying four elements within many PBL models and (c) discussing those elements from the context of three current PBL models. We conclude this chapter with a discussion on issues for PBL and potential solutions.

DEFINING PROJECT-BASED LEARNING

Project-based Learning is a pedagogical method containing several features, including: (a) authentic assessment and content, (b) challenging projects with complex tasks, (c) decision making and problem solving, (d) explicit objectives with individual and collective learning, (e) realistic products to real-world problems, (f) student directed and teacher facilitated and (g) time limited (Capraro & Slough, 2008; DeFilippi, 2001; Diehl, Grobe, Lopez, & Cabral, 1999; Jones, Rasmussen, & Moffitt, 1997; Moursund, 1999; Sahin, 2012; Smith & Dodds, 1977; Thomas, Mergendoller, & Michaelson, 1999). As multiple PBL models exist, defining PBL can prove to be quite difficult. Many models use different words to describe similar concepts, further complicating attempts to define PBL (see Figure 1). The definitions in Figure 1 come from two separate PBL models; however, despite their differences, the two models include similar features. For example, "various learning outcomes" in the Aggie STEM Center definition and "knowledge and skills" in the Buck Institute definition refer to what students gain through PBL. In addition, both definitions indicate that students participating in PBL go through a series of investigative processes. Finally, both definitions describe an "engaging" process for those students learning STEM content through PBL. Regardless of these similarities, no generally accepted definition currently exists for PBL.

In this chapter, we define PBL through four elements, identified as: (a) Initiation, (b) Management, (c) Deliverables, and (d) Assessment (see Figure 2). Specifically, we define PBL as a pedagogical method with initiation of learning combined with management between teachers and students to meet goals outlined by the STEM

Aggie STEM Center	Buck Institute
PBL is a well-defined outcome with an ill-defined task. PBL is the use of a project that often results in the emergence of various learning outcomes in addition to the ones anticipated. The learning is dynamic as students use various processes and methods to explore the project. The richness of the information is often directly related to the quality of the learning and level of student engagement. The information is often multifaceted and includes background information, graphs, pictures, specifications, generalized and specific outcome expectations, narrative, and in many cases, formative and summative expectations. (Capraro & Slough, 2008, p. 5)	Standards focused PBL is a systematic teaching method that engages students in learning knowledge and skills through an extended inquiry process structured around complex, authentic questions and carefully designed products and tasks. (Markham, Larmer, & Ravitz, 2003, p. 4)

Figure 1. Definition for PBL from two prominent PBL models.

education movement of the late 20th and early 21st centuries. Furthermore, we define PBL as a method in which students' deliverables and assessment are produced through social learning with an understanding of social learning theory.

CURRENT MODELS FOR PROJECT-BASED LEARNING

Just as different definitions for PBL exist, so too do models. In this section, we highlight PBL models from three different sources: (a) Harmony Public Schools, (b) Aggie STEM Center, and (c) Buck Institute. We focus attention on the similarities and differences of these models using the four elements from our definition for PBL.

Initiation

Initiation refers to the process for developing explicit objectives and standards, with individual and collective learning, to guide students' decision making and problem solving. The STEM education movement of the past century led to the development of standards-based education in many 21st century classrooms. However, in STEM classrooms using PBL, the development of objectives and standards should occur both before and after students enter the classroom. Initiation describes that part of PBL in which both teachers and students are actively involved in the development of objectives and standards. In this manner, students take ownership of challenging projects with complex tasks centered on authentic assessment and content (Barron et al., 1998; Blumenfeld et al., 1991).

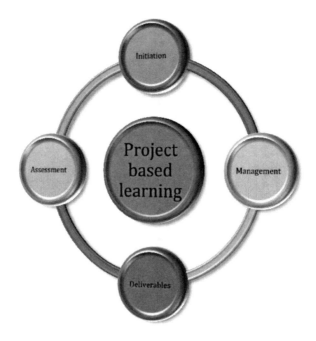

Figure 2. Four elements used to define project-based learning.

Initiation across three PBL models. In the Harmony STEM Students on the Stage (SOS)™ model, Initiation occurs through student customized approaches with a focus on incremental introduction of students to processes in PBL across two or three PBL levels (Sahin & Top, in press). In Level 1 PBL, teachers' and students' initiation occurs through their participation in PBL projects lasting no more than a week. Level 1 PBL prepares both teachers and students for Level 2 and Level 3 PBL, which can last as long as a full academic year. In contrast, Initiation in the Aggie STEM Center PBL model occurs with preparation of teachers to lead students in PBL. Initiation in the Aggie STEM PBL model focuses on ill-defined tasks given to students, which are constrained by teachers. In doing so, teachers are able to guide students in PBL and reduce the likelihood of simplistic solutions. Finally, Initiation in the Buck Institute PBL model focuses on driving questions to guide students' PBL. In the case of the Buck Institute PBL model, Initiation is characterized by the use of driving question to promote students' interest and direction while addressing real-world concerns. Each of these PBL models addresses Initiation from different perspectives. Specifically, the Harmony STEM SOS model focuses on the time requirement in PBL while the Aggie STEM Center PBL model centers on the relationship between teachers and students and the Buck Institute PBL model focuses on the use of driving questions to promote student

Figure 3. A student demonstrating her Level II project. (Please use your QR reader to scan the QR code to watch the video).

involvement. These differences suggest that many questions remain unanswered regarding how Initiation within PBL should be conducted.

Management

Management refers to the manner in which teachers and students engage in students' learning to generate realistic products for real-world problems. A result of the STEM education movement in the 20th century was greater emphasis on teachers' and students' sharing of responsibility for students' learning. In STEM classrooms using PBL, Management describes that part of PBL in which both student-directed and teacher-facilitated actions allow for individual and collective student learning. As a result, Management allows students to complete challenging projects with complex tasks in time-limited circumstances (Morgan & Slough, 2008).

Management across three PBL models. In the Harmony STEM SOS model, Management is overseen by teachers. In Level 1 PBL, teachers provide student groups (i.e., 3-4 students working together) with questions to answer during in-class research. In Level 2 and Level 3 PBL, teachers once again provide the majority of Management; however, students are provided options regarding teamwork, topics to address and work conducted outside the classroom environment. Management in the Aggie STEM Center PBL model is also overseen by teachers. In the Aggie STEM PBL model, ill-defined tasks are given to students; however, these tasks are constrained by teachers. In doing so, teachers are able to guide students in PBL and reduce the likelihood of simplistic solutions. Finally, as with the Aggie STEM model, the Buck Institute PBL model focuses on teachers in the Management of

PBL; Management is characterized by having teachers anticipate the needs of students and clarify students' expectations during PBL. For these three PBL models, Management remains the general domain of teachers. These examples of PBL models would suggest that for many schools, understanding the role of students in taking responsibility for their learning through PBL remains unclear.

Deliverables

Deliverables refers to those realistic products for real-world problems identified during Initiation. Social learning theory identifies explicit objectives with individual and collective learning as an important element in the mastery of content knowledge. In today's education policy environment, Deliverables are often confused with student achievement as measured on high-stakes tests. In STEM classrooms using PBL, Deliverables often present themselves as student-generated products evaluated through authentic assessment and are the end products of the decision-making and problem-solving process begun by both teachers and students during Initiation. Deliverables, therefore, provide students with opportunities to actively engage in student directed and teacher facilitated learning (Diehl, Grobe, Lopez, & Cabral, 1999).

Deliverables across three PBL models. In the Harmony STEM SOS model, Deliverables are identified by specific student products and the dissemination of those same products. Deliverables identified as student products in the Harmony STEM SOS model include: (a) results from the analysis of experimental data, (b) designs for practical solutions to worldwide problems and (c) technology-driven presentations of research results. In addition, Deliverables identified as dissemination include students' collaborative participation in school level discussions on results from research and participation in out-of-school competitions (e.g., Regional and State STEM fairs). Deliverables in the Aggie STEM Center PBL model are centered on students' learning conforming to local, state, and national standards. This focus on standards highlights the importance of standards-based education in the 21st century. Finally, as with the Aggie STEM PBL model, the Buck Institute PBL model focuses on standards-based education; however, the Buck Institute PBL model also identifies skill development within Deliverables for students' participation in PBL. For these three PBL models, Deliverables focus on student outcomes from their participation in PBL. However, each of these PBL models includes general or specific allusions to the importance of standards-based education in the 21st century.

Assessment

Assessment refers to the manner in which teachers and students evaluate the success of student-directed and teacher-facilitated decision making and problem solving. Social learning theory suggests that explicit objectives paired with problem solving

Figure 4. A student demonstrating his Level III computer project. (Please use your QR reader to scan the QR code to watch the video).

requires authentic assessment. In STEM classrooms using PBL, Assessment allows students to use formative and summative evaluation on the influences of authentic content in their generation of realistic products to real-world problems. Assessment, therefore, does not describe the end product of students' learning. Rather, Assessment runs through PBL, allowing teachers and students to continually evaluate students' work on challenging projects with complex tasks (Trauth-Nare & Buck, 2011).

Assessment across three PBL models. In the Harmony STEM SOS model, Assessment combines students' perceptions of learning with teachers' and content experts' feedback. In the Harmony STEM SOS model, Assessment is conducted using rubrics and exemplars to provide students with formative assessment during the early stages of the PBL. Assessment in the Harmony model concludes with teachers' and content experts' assessment of students' Deliverables in summative assessment during the later stages of the PBL. Assessment in the Aggie STEM Center PBL and Buck Institute PBL models follows the same path as the Harmony STEM SOS model. Each of these PBL models emphasizes both formative assessment driven by students' self-assessment with teachers' and content experts' input followed by summative assessment driven by teachers and content experts. This confluence on how Assessment is conducted highlights one aspect of PBL in which many researchers and practitioners are in agreement.

CURRENT ISSUES IN PROJECT-BASED LEARNING

In this section of the chapter, we provide a discussion on current issues in PBL. Current issues in PBL are centered on two needs: (a) development of STEM teachers and (b) measurement of student achievement. Education policy in general (e.g., professional development workshops on PBL, high-stakes tests, etc.) serves as the most common method for addressing both needs. However, as we shall soon see, policy may not provide an adequate method for fully addressing these needs, as PBL becomes a common pedagogical method in many STEM classrooms.

The development of STEM teachers requires time to properly train them in pedagogical methods aligned with authentic assessment for student-directed and teacher-facilitated learning. Recent studies on teacher retention suggest many teachers are either novice (i.e., less than three years of classroom experience) or highly experienced (i.e., more than 10 years of classroom experience). Consequently, many of these teachers lack either experience or current training in the Initiation of the decision making and problem solving associated with PBL (David, 2008). In addition, experienced teachers may lack those Management skills that allow students to engage in challenging projects with complex tasks. The lack of these skills on the part of experienced teachers most likely to provide school leadership can lead to negative attitudes towards PBL on the part of novice teachers. Also, some teachers fail to equate Deliverables as student-directed and teacher-facilitated outcomes; instead, many of these teachers equate Deliverables with teacher-directed and student-facilitated outcomes generated through individual students' mastery of inert content knowledge. Finally, most STEM teachers view Assessment as synonymous with high-stakes testing and not as the formative or summative assessment of students' realistic products to real-world problems. As a result, many teachers express feelings of inadequacy in assessing their students' mastery of STEM content knowledge. Although hardly exhaustive, these examples inform the importance for STEM teachers' development in using PBL for the 21st century.

The measurement of students' achievement will always be a concern for stakeholders in STEM education. Recent studies on achievement, however, suggested an overreliance on high-stakes testing to assess students' mastery of STEM content knowledge and a possible achievement gap in STEM education across ethnic or racial groups as measured by those tests. Consequently, many stakeholders (i.e., policymakers and parents) involved in STEM education fail to understand the need for the initiation of authentic assessment and explicit objectives with students' individual and collective learning. Many stakeholders fail to connect students' achievement with their completion of challenging projects with complex tasks. In addition, past education policy failed to address students' management of personal decision making and problem solving in their learning. This policy failure has led many stakeholders and students to classify management within PBL as a wholly teacher domain, resulting in a strict and hierarchical structure within many STEM classrooms. Also, stakeholders' perceptions of deliverables in STEM classrooms typically focus on end of course examinations and not on students' realistic products for real-world problems. Unfortunately, this leads many students in STEM classrooms to fail to connect STEM content knowledge with commonplace elements of their everyday lives. Finally, assessment of student achievement is almost universally associated with high-stakes testing and not the formative or summative assessment of students' realistic products to real-world problems.

As a result, many stakeholders lack an understanding of the importance in student-directed and teacher-facilitated learning for successful PBL. Some other issues in PBL can be listed as criteria for an acceptable project, function of projects in the curriculum, time limitations and carefully designed tasks (David, 2008). As with the examples for the development of STEM teachers, these examples are not exhaustive; however, they do highlight the importance in re-evaluating students' achievement in constructing STEM knowledge through PBL.

SOLUTIONS FOR CURRENT ISSUES IN PROJECT-BASED LEARNING

In the previous section, we highlighted just a few examples related to two current issues in STEM education: (a) development of STEM teachers and (b) measurement of student achievement. In this section of the chapter, we provide a discussion on our ideas for possible solutions to those issues. We begin this discussion by noting our belief that education policy serves as the most common method for addressing both issues. However, policy cannot provide solutions to meet all of the examples previously mentioned. We therefore offer these thoughts on possible solutions in using PBL within STEM classrooms.

As the development of STEM teachers requires time to properly train them in pedagogical methods aligned with authentic assessment for student-directed and teacher-facilitated learning, we contend more connections must be made between the universities in which teachers receive their initial training and the school districts where these same teachers will ultimately work with students. Because recent studies on teacher retention suggest that many STEM teachers are either novice (i.e., less than three years classroom experience) or highly experienced (i.e., more than 10 years classroom experience), the focus of this connection should include training in students' initiation of decision making and problem solving within PBL. In addition, with many experienced teachers lacking management skills that will allow students to engage in challenging projects with complex tasks, we believe steps should be taken to ensure experienced teachers receive specialized training in that area. Also, as teachers often fail to equate deliverables with student-directed and teacher-facilitated outcomes, the development of teachers should include information of the importance of learning outcomes which are generated through individual students' work in individual and collective learning venues. Finally, teachers' views of assessment as being synonymous with high-stakes testing rather than the formative or summative assessment of students' realistic products to real-world problems should be addressed through extensive time and contact with university personnel with expertise in PBL. Although hardly exhaustive, these solutions can help address the need for development of STEM teachers in PBL for the 21st century.

For all stakeholders, the measurement of student achievement in STEM classrooms will always be a concern. To address overreliance on high-stakes testing and the possible achievement gap in STEM education across ethnic or racial groups as measured by those tests, we believe more consideration should be given to authentic assessment in classrooms. Many stakeholders (i.e., policymakers and parents) involved in education fail to understand the need for authentic assessment and explicit objectives with individual and collective learning. We contend that explicit connections should be made between students' achievement and their completion of challenging projects with complex tasks. In addition, with the focus of past education policy on teachers' management of personal decision making and problem solving, we suggest school leaders take a more bottom up approach to students' learning. Such an approach can lead to the generation of student-directed and teacher-facilitated learning environments within STEM classrooms using PBL. Also, with the focus of deliverables on end of course examinations and other high-stakes tests, we argue for a shift towards a view of deliverables centered on realistic products for real-world problems. Finally, with assessment of student achievement almost universally associated with high-stakes testing and not the formative or summative assessment of students' realistic products, we believe stakeholders require more information regarding the successful learning of students using student-directed and teacher-facilitated learning often seen in STEM classrooms using PBL. As with the examples for the development of STEM teachers, these solutions are not exhaustive; however, they do highlight possible solutions for the measurement of students' achievement in PBL for the 21st century.

CONCLUSION

How students gain STEM content knowledge has long been the focus of stakeholders, including (a) parents, (b) teachers in STEM classrooms and (c) researchers in the cognitive sciences. As students enter the STEM classrooms of the 21st century – influenced by the development of technology, rise of the Internet, and transition from local to global perspectives – all stakeholders should consider the importance of learning theory and past STEM education movements when determining ways to develop the next generation of STEM leaders, researchers, and teachers (Augustine, 2005). With studies in the 20th century suggesting students' attainment of STEM knowledge in experiential, hands-on and student-directed projects leads to greater achievement (Kolb, Boyatzis, & Mainemelis, 2001; Markham, Larmer, & Ravitz, 2003; Wehmeyer, Agran, & Hughes, 2000), we conclude that PBL is a preferred pedagogical method in STEM classrooms. However, when implementing PBL within STEM classrooms, stakeholders must be vigilant to changes in learning theory and STEM education movements.

In this chapter, we provided a discussion on PBL models for the 21st century. In our discussion, we defined PBL as a pedagogical method with initiation of learning combined with management between teachers and learners to meet goals of the STEM education movement. We further defined PBL as a method in which learners' deliverables and assessment are produced through social learning. We used three

PBL models as exemplars for STEM classrooms using PBL in the 21st century with a focus on their use of (a) Initiation, (b) Management, (c) Deliverables, and (d) Assessment. We concluded this chapter with discussions of current issues with PBL in the 21st century and potential solutions to those issues as we move forward.

REFERENCES

Augustine, N. R. (2005). *Rising above the gathering storm: Energizing and employing America for a brighter economic future.* Washington, DC: The National Academies Press.

Bandura, A. (1977). *Social learning theory.* New York, NY: General Learning Press.

Barron, B. J., Schwartz, D. L., Vye, N. J., Moore, A., Petrosino, A., Zech, L., Bransford, J. D,. & Cognition and Technology Group at Vanderbilt (1998). Doing with understanding: Lessons from research on problem- and project-based learning. *Journal of the Learning Sciences, 7*(3-4), 271–311.

Blumenfeld, P., Soloway, E., Marx, R., Krajcik, J., Guzdial, M., & Palincsar, A. (1991). Motivating project-based learning: Sustaining the doing, supporting the learning. *Educational Psychologist, 26,* 369–398.

Bransford, J. D., Brown, A. L., & Cocking, R. R. (Eds.). (2000). *How people learn: Brain, mind, experience, and school: Expanded edition.* Washington, DC: The National Academies Press.

Caparro, R. M. & Slough, W. S. (2008). Why PBL? Why STEM? Why now? An introduction to STEM project-based learning: An integrated science, technology, engineering, and mathematics approach. In R. M. Capraro & S. W. Slough (Eds.), *Project-based learning: An integrated science, technology, engineering, and mathematics approach* (pp. 1–6). Rotterdam, The Netherlands: Sense Publishers.

David, J. L. (2008). What research says about project-based learning. *Educational Leadership, 65*(5), 80–82.

DeFillippi, R. J. (2001). Introduction: Project-based learning, reflective practices and learning. *Management Learning, 32*(1), 5–10.

Diehl, W., Grobe, T., Lopez, H., & Cabral, C. (1999). *Project-based learning: A strategy for teaching and learning.* Boston, MA: Center for Youth Development and Education, Corporation for Business, Work, and Learning.

Jones, B. F., Rasmussen, C. M., & Moffitt, M. C. (1997). *Real-life problem solving: A collaborative approach to interdisciplinary learning.* Washington, DC: American Psychological Association.

Kolb, D. A., Boyatzis, R. E., & Mainemelis, C. (2001). Experiential learning theory: Previous research and new directions. In R. J. Sternberg & L. Zhang (Eds.), *Perspectives on thinking, learning, and cognitive styles* (pp. 227–247). Mahwah, NJ: Lawrence Erlbaum Associates Publishers.

Markham, T., Larmer J., & Ravitz, J. (2003). *Project-based learning handbook.* Novato, CA: Buck Institute for Education.

Morgan, J. R. & Slough, S. W. (2008). Classroom management considerations: Implementing STEM project-based learning. In R. M. Capraro & S. W. Slough (Eds.), *Project-based learning: An integrated science, technology, engineering, and mathematics approach* (pp. 159–170). Rotterdam, The Netherlands: Sense Publishers.

Moursund, D. (1999). *Project-based learning using information technology.* Eugene, OR: International Society for Technology in Education.

Rotter, J. B. (1954). *Social learning and clinical psychology.* Upper Saddle River, NJ: Prentice-Hall Inc.

Rotter, J. B. (1966). Generalized expectancies for internal versus external control of reinforcement. *Psychological Monographs: General and Applied, 80*(1), 1–28.

Sahin, A. (2012). STEM project-based learning: Specialized form of inquiry-based learning. In R. M. Capraro, M. M. Capraro & J. Morgan (Eds.), *Project-based learning: An integrated science, technology, engineering, and mathematics (STEM) approach* (2nd ed.) (pp. 59–64). Rotterdam, The Netherlands: Sense

Sahin, A., & Top, N. (In Press). Make it happen: A study of novel teaching style, STEM students on the stage (SOS)™, for increasing students' STEM knowledge and interest. Journal of STEM Education: Innovations and Research.

Smith, B. & Dodds, R. (1977). *Developing managers through project-based learning.* Brookfield, VT: Gower.

Talbot-Smith, M., Abell, S. K., Appleton, K., & Hanuscin, D. L. (Eds.). (2013). *Handbook of research on science education.* New York, NY: Routledge.

Thomas, J. W., Mergendoller, J. R., and Michaelson, A. (1999). *Project-based learning: A handbook for middle and high school teachers.* Novato, CA: The Buck Institute for Education.

Trauth-Nare, A. & Buck, G. (2011). Assessment for learning: Using formative assessment in problem- and project-based learning. *The Science Teacher, 78*(1), 34–39.

Wehmeyer, M. L., Agran, M., & Hughes, C. (2000). A national survey of teachers' promotion of self-determination and student-directed learning. *Journal of Special Education, 34*(2), 58–68.

Niyazi Erdogan
Faculty of Education,
Balikesir University

Todd Dane Bozeman
College of Education
Texas A&M University

NAMIK TOP AND ALPASLAN SAHIN

4. MAKE IT HAPPEN: A STUDY OF A NOVEL TEACHING STYLE, *STEM STUDENTS ON THE STAGE* (SOS)™, FOR INCREASING STUDENTS' STEM KNOWLEDGE AND INTEREST

Science, technology, engineering and mathematics (STEM) education has become increasingly important to enhancing college readiness in mathematics and science, cultivating STEM interest among students, increasing the number of students majoring in STEM fields and preparing those students for the 21st century workforce. The purpose of this study was to investigate a new STEM project-based learning model developed by Harmony Public Schools (HPS). Using theoretical sampling, we interviewed 11 students (5 seniors, 5 juniors, and 1 sophomore). Interview transcripts were analyzed using grounded theory coding and constant comparative analysis. As a result of the analysis, a new STEM education model titled "STEM Students on the Stage" (SOS)™ emerged. Study findings suggested that students who received instruction in the STEM SOS model increased their conceptual understanding of STEM subjects, reported greater interest in both STEM and in pursuing higher education, developed greater self-confidence and enhanced their technology, communication, life/career and collaboration skills. Findings are discussed in the context of STEM education and its effects on students' interest in STEM careers.

INTRODUCTION

In recent years, science, technology, engineering, and mathematics (STEM) education has become a critical priority for countries due to its important role in global competitiveness (Sahin, Gulacar, & Stuessy, in press; Sahin, Ayar, & Adiguzel, 2014; Sahin, 2013). Numerous reports have highlighted the links between a well-rounded K-12 STEM education, preparing the next generation's scientists, leaders and innovators, and countries' economic leadership (National Academy of Sciences, National Academy of Engineering, and Institute of Medicine, 2007; President's Council of Advisors on Science and Technology, 2010). Research also shows that STEM jobs typically pay higher salaries and provide more job opportunities than other professions (Terrell, 2007). A recent report also indicated a demand for STEM employees. The U.S. Department of Labor announced that more than 1.2 million STEM employees will be needed by 2018; however, data shows that there is a shortage in meeting this need in terms of numbers and quality (Lacey & Wright, 2009). Therefore, providing

A. Sahin (Ed.), A Practice-based Model of STEM Teaching, 43–61.

STEM education in a way that will effectively teach STEM content and cultivate students' interest in STEM is very important (Mahoney, 2010).

Different approaches to STEM education to address the need for well-prepared STEM workers have been implemented in K-12 settings. Some of the research-based methods to interdisciplinary STEM education are Design-Based Science (DBS) (Fortus, Krajcikb, Dershimerb, Marx, & Mamlok- Naamand, 2005), Math Out of the Box™ (Diaz & King, 2007), Learning by Design™ (LBD) (Kolodner et al., 2003), and Integrated Mathematics, Science, and Technology (IMaST) (Satchwell & Loepp, 2002). These approaches involve inquiry-based learning in which students work collaboratively to complete a project using their existing knowledge and then present their findings (Laboy-Rush, 2011). Each approach has a four- or five-step process, with each step accomplishing a specific process-based objective. The project-based learning strategy has also been found to be an effective STEM education program (Laboy-Rush, 2011). These approaches have been implemented because of the models' integration of cooperative learning, research, testing of theories and production of artifacts (Meyrick, 2011). Harwood and Rudnistsky (2005) found that such teaching methods increase students' involvement and engagement and "can stimulate students as well as enable them to recognize links between their lessons and tasks performed by engineers in the real world" (p. 54). In this study, we investigate a new model that incorporates components of several active learning strategies, including project-based learning and inquiry-based learning.

STEM Teaching in the U.S. and The Novel Teaching Style, STEM Students on The Stage (SOS)™

U.S public education has some chronic problems, including a lack of college readiness in mathematics and science among high school graduates (Diaz & King, 2007), lagging behind on international tests (e.g., TIMSS, PISA), a shortage of postsecondary STEM majors (NRC, 2011; Schmidt, 2011) and a lack of preparation for the 21st century workforce (NRC, 2011). To address these problems, integrated STEM education and project-based learning have been utilized (e.g., Fortus, Krajcikb, Dershimerb, Marx, & Mamlok-Naamand, 2005). These approaches are based on research showing that completing collaborative projects with real-world connections and building products with real-world applications can increase student interest in STEM (Fortus et al., 2005). Harmony Public Schools (HPS) has developed their own STEM curriculum, which incorporates project-based and inquiry-based learning and is titled, "STEM Students on the Stage (SOS)™" through a Race to the Top grant funded by the U.S. Department of Education with the goal of not only increasing students' STEM knowledge and interest, but also producing self-motivated and self-regulated learners (Harmony STEM Program, 2013).

According to the Harmony STEM Program Handbook (2013), the STEM SOS model aims "to maintain the focus on standards-based and student-centered teaching while enriching and extending the learning of students through PBL projects. The goal is to promote not only collaborative skills and student ownership of learning, but also to promote student success in state and national standards" through student projects: Level I, II, and III (p. x). According to the curriculum, all students have to complete a level I project followed by either a regular level II or advanced level III project.

Level I.   Students are assigned two Level I projects per semester for each core subject (Mathematics, Science, ELA, and Social Studies). Projects are conducted in classes with a group of 3-4 students aligned with the curriculum's scope and sequence within a week. Students are provided training and necessary documentation to complete the project at the beginning of the school year. Teachers provide timely guidance and feedback for completion of the projects. The final product consists of a report of their work with a digital presentation of the project. Core content teachers conduct assessments using rubrics for each project separately.

Level II.   Apart from the Level I project, students are also required to complete one interdisciplinary STEM SOS project focused on either mathematics or science. Social Studies and ELA components also have to be part of those projects. Projects are assigned at the beginning of the year out of 25-30 possible mathematics and science projects. These are year-long projects. The Level II projects have student handouts and teacher guides. Teachers provide students with guidance, timely feedback and documentation, including rubrics for the successful completion of the projects. Upon completion, students present their findings and products through a video presentation and website.

Level III.   Level III projects are for students who enjoy the challenge of creating and conducting their own research and product. These projects are interdisciplinary and integrate technology in each step towards project completion. Although most of the level III projects are optional and students can choose from a pre-existing list of projects, students can still develop with their own project ideas. The content is rigorous and students receive extra credit upon completion. Projects are completed using the given materials within a certain time period and their scope, driving questions, expectations and guidelines are decided in collaboration with students' teachers. Students' Level II and level III projects are presented at the campus-wide STEM festivals, science fairs, STEM exhibitions and other STEM-related competitions.

   The purpose of this study was to investigate the components of successful STEM engagement in a high school that implements the STEM Students on the Stage model. The overarching research question to which we sought an answer was: How does learning in the STEM Students on the Stage (SOS)™ model occur and what benefits do students gain in the end?

METHOD

Setting

The setting for this study was the Harmony Public Schools, a network of high-performing K-12 public charter schools located across Texas including all metropolitan areas, which focus on providing science, computer technology, engineering, and mathematics education (STEM) to traditionally underserved students (HPS, 2014). HPS schools serve more than 24,000 students of diverse backgrounds: 56% receive free or reduced price lunch and slightly more than 80% are nonwhite (45% Hispanic, 19% African American, and 16% Asian).

Participants

The sample was collected from one of the Harmony high schools in the Houston area. Eleven students agreed to participate in the study. The sample was comprised of 5 seniors, 5 juniors, and 1 sophomore student. All students were enrolled in one of the following courses: Pre Advanced Placement Physics, Chemistry, or Advanced Placement Physics. Three different teachers taught the courses.

Procedure

A broad two-part research question was formulated examining how learning in the STEM SOS model occurs and what benefits students obtain from it. The grounded theory method was used to examine these questions and to develop a substantive theory.

The grounded theory method is a set of flexible analytical procedures that inspires researchers to remain close to their studied world. In addition to synthesizing and indicating processual relationships, the need for developing an integrated set of theoretical concepts helps us esteem the grounded theory method (Charmaz, 2010). We recognize our position within the studied world, locating ourselves within our research interest in codifying the STEM SOS model and disclosing student gains through the model.

Samples were collected from one of the Harmony Public Schools in which the STEM SOS model was implemented in a pilot study during May of the 2012-2013 school year. The model was officially launched in all HPS campuses in the 2013-2014 school year. The students interviewed were all volunteers and provided informed consent. The sample was identified through an iterative process over a two-semester period, based on the interaction of data collection and analysis enabled via theoretical sampling throughout the study (Holt & Tamminen, 2010). We reached theoretical saturation with 11 individual interviews (out of 15). Four interviews were removed from the data for not contributing to advanced theoretical saturation. Theoretical sampling was utilized in the present study, which was grounded on

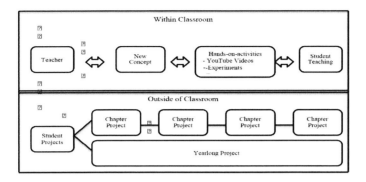

Figure 1. STEM SOS Model from students' perspectives.

emerging concepts and associated with figuring out new people, to advance or refine theoretical saturation – not merely to fill gaps in the data (Charmaz 2005).

For data analysis, we followed the grounded theory coding and constant comparative analysis. Initially, each student interview was open-coded using action codes (Charmaz 2010). We then applied focused coding by constantly comparing each initial code with similar ones in order to develop categories and sub-categories from the raw data. While the categories were being produced, we performed axial coding by relating categories, via the combination of inductive and deductive thinking. We present a series of diagrams that illustrate the relationships among categories during these coding processes. The analytical process provided the emerging substantive theory of the model and student gains in the STEM SOS model.

RESULTS

The findings revealed two core categories including the (1) STEM SOS model (see Figure 1) and (2) Impact on student gains (see Figure 5).

For students, the STEM SOS model has two critical parts: (1.a) Teacher-directed teaching or Teacher lecture and (1.b). Student Projects. Student responses showed that the teacher lecture part has three important components: (1.a.a) Lecturing or teaching the theory part, (1.a.b) Hands-on activities part, and (1.a.c) Student-teaching part. In addition, the interviews revealed that two fundamental areas of student gains (2.a) Academic and (2.b) 21st century skills were a function of the novel teaching style, STEM SOS Furthermore, the first area of student gains (Academic) has three sub-categories: (2.a.a) STEM interest, (2.a.b) Knowledge, and (2.a.c) Research interest in higher education, and the second area of student gains (21st Century Skills) has five sub-categories: (2.b.a) Self-confidence, (2.b.b) Technology Skills (2.b.c) Life and Career Skills, (2.b.d) Communication Skills and (2.b.e) Collaboration Skills.

SOS MODEL

Teacher-Directed Teaching

Lecturing part. Teachers in the STEM SOS model begin new lessons by lecturing about a new concept to lay the foundation for upcoming material. Student 1 stated that during the "Initial lecture, he introduces the ideas, he introduces the chapter or whatever the subject area is." This part includes direct lecturing of the concept as well as asking students questions and checking for understanding, as indicated by Student 4.

> One of the things that I see from him (Science Teacher) is he is not just standing behind the lecture podium [and] talking. He is teaching, he is interacting with students. He is making them laugh. He is making them understand things. He doesn't just talk to you like most teachers do. He does a great job.

Teacher-directed lecturing is different from typical lecturing because the teacher is not only lecturing, but is also actively listening to students' responses and checking for understanding. This was emphasized by Student 10:

> During lectures Mr S. talks to us one-on-one and in groups. He comes to each group about every ten minutes and checks whether we have any questions.

> Teachers don't just lecture, but also explain any formula or theory step by step and/or with an example from daily life and with hands-on experiments or videos. The way he teaches is good because instead of making you memorize things, he shows you how everything is connected. He shows us how every law is connected to one another.

Moreover, one of the important parts of teacher-directed lecturing is giving students many opportunities to be involved. Teachers incorporate a variety of different activities into lectures, including hands-on experiments, YouTube videos and student teaching.

> Except when the teacher is doing the initial lecture, he doesn't do much talking, which is good. During the initial lecture, he introduces the main idea and the chapter or whatever the subject area it is. Then we have videos, we have demos and student teaching. He is not just sitting behind the desk during class. He is working proactively to make sure that we learn the material. (Student 4)

Hands-on activities. Hands-on activities are central to instruction in the STEM SOS model and increase student involvement. Student 9 described the benefits of the SOS model for students' involvement, stating:

> [SOS] teaching is very hands on and the teacher puts effort into making it fun and enjoyable for us. Most other teachers [in other Physics classes], they just lecture and you don't spend as much time paying attention and you drop off, but with the hands-on projects you stay on topic.

Figure 2. Students demonstrating their projects at the STEM EXP0 2011. (Please use your QR reader to scan the QR code to watch the video)

Teachers incorporate experiments, YouTube videos and hands-on activities to explain theories and show the relevance of content to real life. Student 2 stated, "I presented in school [festival and classroom], we presented in the STEM expo, and ISWEEEP, and repeating it so many times really helps it to stick in your head."

Student teaching. The final component of the teacher-directed lecturing is student teaching. This works by teachers assigning projects to a student or group of students for each chapter before they begin instruction in that content area. The teacher asks the student groups to teach and conduct the experiment that explains the content or concept. One student described this process, stating, "So suppose we were learning about sound waves and that is what my demonstration is about the teacher allows us to come in and we present in front of the whole class like the Bernoulli principle or something else." Student 4 described another benefit of student teaching:

> Let's say he makes us do an experiment like a rollercoaster back there and after we complete it, after he teaches us how to construct it and how all the formulas work, then he says pick a day on the calendar. So, okay that day, you are going to teach the class. Teach what? Everything you just learned. Instead of regurgitating, you are actually going to take what you have learned from what you built or what you made and teach people about it.

Therefore, students act like teachers and this helps both the students teaching the lesson and their classmates learn the content. Students also benefit in other ways, including developing greater self-confidence and more positive attitudes towards science subjects.

Student Projects.   There are two types of student projects. The first type of project is presented during each chapter, as mentioned in the previous section. Students are assigned a short-term project that is related to the content they learn during each chapter. An individual student or group of students is assigned to prepare an experiment including hands-on activities, experiments and/or a video. Part of their responsibility is to present their experiment while the related content is being taught. The second type of project is a yearlong project. Students choose their project from a list that is posted on the Harmony Schools' Physics webpage at the beginning of the year. One student stated, "At the beginning of the year there was a list and I randomly chose, but I ended up liking it a lot because it is more interactive and I am an interactive person. So it went with me and I wouldn't have changed it or I am pretty sure even if I looked inside of each one, I would have picked this one" (Student 3). Students are required to prepare a video presentation, which includes a picture of materials used in the experiment, short video episodes of experiments, related graphs, tables, and conclusions. Student 3 described this process, stating, "We make science videos. And we take videos of the experiment and record them here or anywhere. And then we put it together as a video. Would you like to see a sample?" As their teachers check students' products and provide feedback, students go back and revise their products. Students develop ownership of their projects because they spend a significant amount of time completing them during school and after school.

Students are also required to upload the videos they make to the Harmony YouTube Channel and create a brochure explaining their project. Another requirement is to design their own website where they can present everything they did while they worked toward completion of the project. This yearlong project is usually an individual effort; however, students may collaborate with their classmates to complete it. Students find many opportunities to present their projects before an audience. For example, whenever their school has a visitor such as Congressmen, the mayor or educators from other institutions, students display their projects. Students also present their findings and products during the STEM EXPO and ISWEEEP competitions. Science demos change students' way of looking at science; through participation in these activities and projects, students develop a better understanding of science and it is often perceived as less intimidating, as was expressed by Student 2:

> I said science was not always my biggest thing, but participating in demos lets you know that it is not just listening and drawing or writing down your equations or writing down the words that the teacher said. You can get hands on, you can figure out something and you can learn about it and apply it to everyday life. And it is one of those things that you see on TV or you see someone else to do and you are like wait a minute, it is not magic, it is all basically science, it is Physics, it is Chemistry, it is any of those things.

IMPACT ON STUDENT GAINS

The second core category is the impact of the STEM SOS model on student gains, which include both academic and 21st century skills. Students provided extensive information about their gains in these areas during the interviews. The information provided during interviews revealed two categories: academic and 21st century skills (see Figure 5).

Academic.

In this category, students discussed the important role of the STEM SOS model in their academic skills development. Student 5 stated, "I think I developed how to study the right way, how to learn, how to approach the problem and then how to apply it in real life." This statement clearly indicates that students began to learn how to conduct academic research. Students also became aware of the connections between academic knowledge and its real-life applications. Student 2 stated, "You can apply what you learn to many things and whatever you do in the future." Student 4 added, "So in the real-world environment, it helped me develop something very useful." This category led us to develop three sub-categories: STEM interest, knowledge, and research interest in higher education.

STEM interest.   Student responses revealed that they developed STEM interest through the STEM SOS model. In this subcategory, students' responses showed that they started enjoying scientific experiments because they became more fun for them. Student 2 stated this explicitly:

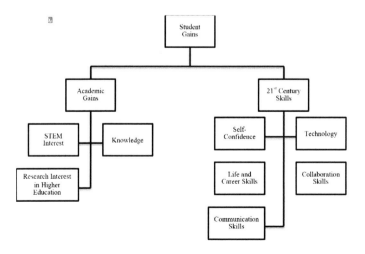

Figure 3. Student gains from student interviews.

Figure 4. A student presenting her chapter project for her e-portfolio. (Please use your QR reader to scan the QR codes to watch her demonstration and/or to see her website)

This is fun. It is cute and I can come up with ideas even think I can bring someone and change the color and … it when with the carbon dioxide hand in the air it fades away so it was really cool.

Another student also discussed developing STEM interest through the STEM SOS model, stating, "Science demo are like one of those, it is fun, you learned it and it is not so hard that you are stressing about it."

Many students mentioned that they had not previously considered themselves to be good at science, but developed a greater interest in it through the STEM SOS model. Student 3 stated, "I have never really been great at science, but I have learned that when you really focus on it, it becomes more interesting." Student 2 also described how they became more interested in science:

I always said science was not my biggest thing, but being in demos (student projects) made me realize that it is not just listening and drawing or writing down your equations or writing down the words that the teacher said. You can get hands on, you can figure out something and you can learn about it and apply it to everyday life.

Knowledge/Conceptual Understanding. All students reported that they learned a great deal through the STEM SOS model. Specifically, students indicated that they increased their conceptual understanding of science concepts through demos and by conducting experiments. Student 11 stated, "I will never forget that principle because I have learned it, I saw it, and I experienced it. It will stay with me forever." This student quote demonstrates how lifelong learning occurs in the STEM SOS model.

Another student described how the emphasis on visual learning in the STEM SOS model increased their conceptual understanding, stating: "So visual learning and letting you know what it is all about it helps you understand everything about it." The STEM SOS model also helps students learn how to adjust their presentations according to the audience. In this regard, Student 3 explained, "I am definitely learning how to simplify physics for myself and for other people to make it easier for them to understand because if I simplify it for them, I'll be learning too." Student 2 also stressed the extent to which they learn during the class with the following statement:

So it is just in class you learn more, you get to know how to calculate things that kind of stuff. And in the Physics demo it is little heads up that you will learn a little bit of it and that way you just like oh yeah I remember this I know this.

Student 4's statement also illustrates their confidence in the gains in their academic knowledge and conceptual understanding: "Instead of regurgitating, you are actually going to take what you have learned and understood from what you built or what you made and teach people about it."

Students also explained that they became more aware of their environment through the STEM SOS model. In this regard, participation in the STEM SOS model helped them pay attention to their environment and think about the physical things occurring in their daily lives. Student 3 stated, "You learn what happens. You never realize it, you know when the car moves there is something you are learning what is happening beneath the wheels and it is interesting to learn that."

Research interest in higher education. The last subcategory of the impact of the STEM SOS model on academic gains is research interest in higher education. In this category, students discussed their interest in conducting research in higher education. Student 6 describes this interest in the following statement:

I guess definitely it helps you to gain a group of friends who have the same interests as you. Like when you go to college and you find a study group it's really nice. I feel like after doing this you know when you find somebody who has the same interests as you.

As mentioned in the previous subcategory, students reported that they gained a great deal of information through the STEM SOS model. In this category, they also discussed their plans to continue applying their knowledge in higher education. Student 7 stated, "Hopefully I can carry all these skills over not only to higher education, but also to graduate school and my career." Student 10 also expressed his research interest in the following statement, "I feel more comfortable like I can already do [research] by myself or with other students. I can create study groups and always feel like teacher. I like having back and forth communication, it really helps you".

21ˢᵗ Century Skills. Apart from academic gains, findings also showed the impact of the STEM SOS model on students' social and emotional functioning. Students started to believe that they could achieve something such as presenting in front of a group of people, communicating with other students and understanding the benefits in daily life. Generally, students discussed gains in five areas of 21st century skills: self-confidence, technology skills, life and career skills, communication skills and collaboration skills.

Self-Confidence. In this subcategory, students explained that before they were taught with the STEM SOS model, they were not accustomed to preparing a presentation, presenting before a large group or communicating their findings to others. After instruction in the STEM SOS model and completion of projects, students reported greater confidence in giving presentations to others. Student 2 stated, "You know it feels nice to know something and it gives you confidence and you feel like wow, I know this." The same student expressed that he learned how to "present better, and get over my fear. [Previously] I didn't know how to speak in public. I have now had experiences speaking in public and this just encourages me and improves my public speaking ability." Through the STEM SOS model, students who were nervous about public speaking improved their skills and increased their confidence. In this regard, Student 1 stated:

> We had this one thing called news testing. They had cameras and were recording us. You know being nervous in front of people, I was like I don't know how I look like in the camera, and you know stuff like that. So I learned how to speak in front of the camera and be able to relate what I have to say.

Students also reported that they needed to develop their confidence and communication skills for higher education and felt that the STEM SOS model helped them achieve that. In this regard, Student 6 stated:

> [STEM SOS] built my confidence because I'm okay with speaking to a crowd of people as long as I know what I'm speaking about. And it really helped me because I know that in order to go into the medical field you have to bring more to the table, you can't just go to college and be like oh okay I want to study this, you have to be determined and confident in what you're doing. And I feel like it really built my confidence up and helped me to study because until this day, if I don't understand the teacher, I'll still go home and I'll study myself and I'll get it.

Technology Skills. As a result of making YouTube videos, websites, and video presentations, students also developed technology skills through the STEM SOS model. Many students reported that they did not know how to work with technological tools before participating in the STEM SOS model. For example, Student 2 stated, "Making your web sites you need to learn how to go and link things. [For instance] I learned from someone how to link a picture. I didn't know how to do that."

Because almost every step of project completion involves technology, students develop a variety of technology skills. Student 3 stated, "When I go home, I am usually working on editing videos and putting them together." This statement indicates that students are working with technological tools at school and home. Student 9 stated, "I learned how to build [a] website." Student 4 reported that although she had previously worked as an intern for a technology company, she learned more technological skills through the STEM SOS model. To this end, Student 4 stated:

Even though I have prior knowledge in these things, I took my knowledge that I am gaining in Apple and different sources and from here, putting them all together and literally testing them out right here, which is great because then I don't have to worry about this in another project for another company.

Life and Career Skills. Quite significantly, students developed valuable life and career skills through STEM SOS In this regard, STEM SOS helped them look at the world in a scientific way and discover things that might assist them in their lives and careers. Student 5 stated, "This helps you in your real life, for example, in a kitchen or while driving." They also learned time management skills through STEM SOS, as was described by Student 7:

In my daily life the management skills [I gained by completing science demos by the due date] has helped a lot. I am able to better manage my time. That helped with my college applications and I guess in general, I am just able to manage my time more wisely.

Students also developed an interest in helping others such as people who are disadvantaged or unhealthy. This shows how they became aware of the benefits they could provide through what they learned during class, after school hours, and STEM Expos not only for themselves, but also for others. Student 1 expressed this desire to help others:

Since I want to go into social work, I want to go to families and homeless people so I can notice different things about know whether a child has been abused or the homeless man is doing illegal things or not. Noticing different things about the person helps you see whether they are healthy or not.

Another student even discussed passing the knowledge they gained through the STEM SOS model on to their future, children stating, "It is always nice to learn so I can teach my children." Quite clearly, students believed that the things they learned through STEM SOS will be used in their personal lives and careers.

Communication skills. As seen in the previous categories, students acquired skills in different fields such as content knowledge, self-confidence, social skills, etc. Many students underscored the importance of the STEM SOS class environment by comparing STEM SOS classes with their other classes. Student 4 described communication in the traditional classroom environment in the following statement:

When the other teacher is speaking until almost the bell rings, there is no communication other than from the teacher to you and you are reading a book alone. You don't have any communication with your classmates, with the professor or the teacher, so it was extremely boring. You just heard information and if you didn't catch it, you just didn't catch it. It just flew by. It wasn't a very good environment.

In contrast, in the STEM SOS class environment, students engage in frequent communication with their peers and teachers, and develop their communication skills. Student 5 summarized the communication process:

We work in groups a lot of the time and we have to talk. Otherwise, he puts people in different groups, but not everybody is on the same page so basically we have to talk a lot if you want to understand the topic.

Students are also required to present their projects at science festivals in their schools and international conferences, such as I-SWEEEP. This helps students learn how to communicate their findings to others such as teachers, professors, graduate students, and other participants. Student 7 stated:

It was actually kind of intimidating talking to professors at first. I didn't know what to expect, but now I'm able to talk to them one on one with understanding. As well as when visitors come here we have to present projects and I'm able to present it so that they understand it.

Student 9 stated, "I did develop communication skills and learn how to present topics to people." Students perceived the development of communication skills as very important. Student 3 indicated this in the following statement, "Just communication skills in general is a huge thing" and "I feel like having back and forth communication with the teacher really helps you." These statements clearly show the importance of STEM SOS for developing students' communication skills.

Collaboration skills. The last category of the impact of 21st century skills is collaboration. In the STEM SOS model, students are required to study and collaborate with other students. Students reported that the STEM SOS model helped them learn how to get along with other students and work to complete projects and how to get help from more experienced students. The following expression by Student 6 demonstrates this growth: "We were able to learn from each other." Student 6's statement revealed the level of collaboration among students as follows:

I guess because you are not doing it only by yourself, you have other people doing it and it's a good club to meet people from other grades and make friends. Most of the people in here are seniors and they all know me and we all speak even though I'm a 10th grader. It's just really nice.

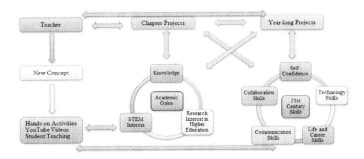

Figure 5. A grounded theory of STEM SOS and its components and benefits for students.

After a time, the collaboration among students increased. They started to willingly help each other, not only on scientific studies, but also when somebody was out sick or needed additional help. The extent of collaboration went beyond school borders, which improved the school climate. Student 5 stated:

We're nice to each other and we help each other out like if their partner is sick or they have a cold and they need somebody to fill in for them, then you can find somebody who would be willing to help you out.

Overall, all these components of the STEM SOS model helped students develop their academic and 21st century skills.

DISCUSSION

Because the STEM SOS is a novel model that was developed to improve K-12 STEM education, we wanted to examine its effectiveness among students. After performing the coding process (open, focused, and axial coding), student interviews revealed that hands-on-activities, including YouTube videos and experiments, and student teaching from Chapter and Year-Long Projects are the main components of the STEM SOS teaching in the suggested grounded theory. The effective implementation of these components in the STEM SOS model not only produced benefits in two primary areas: Academic, and 21st Century Skills, but also helped circulate the sub-components of these two gains. That is, through the STEM SOS model, students improved their knowledge/conceptual understanding, STEM interest, and research interest in higher education and developed self-confidence, technology, life and career, communication and collaboration skills and these skills continued to improve circularly.

To elucidate the whole process of developing the grounded theory of the STEM SOS model, teachers initially act as role models by teaching new content in an original way. One of the discussions among teachers is whether they can prepare their students for standardized testing by using active teaching methods such as project-based learning when standardized testing is the primary metric for schools' success (Needham, 2010). Teachers using the STEM SOS model overcame this problem by beginning instruction with active lectures. Research has shown that one problem with traditional lectures is that most students' attention begins to wander after 15 minutes (Dowd & Hulse, 1996); however, the STEM SOS model solves this problem by engaging students with YouTube videos, hands-on activities and student teaching. In this regard, one student stated, "Except when he is doing the initial lecture, he doesn't do much talking, which is good. During the initial lecture, he introduces the ideas, he introduces the chapter and whatever the subject area is. Then we have videos, we have demos, and we have student teaching" (Student 4). Indeed, the literature says that students learn best when they are at the center of instruction and take responsibility for their own learning (e.g., Blumenfeld et al., 2011), which are two central components of project-based learning (Pearson, Barlowe, & Price, 1999). This helps students create connections between concepts and their real-life applications without having to memorize numbers or formulas: "The way he teaches [is] good because instead of making you memorize things, he shows you how everything is connected, and he shows us how every law is connected to one another (Student 10). This is parallel with research on situated cognition indicating that learning is enhanced if the context for learning closely resembles the real-life context in which the materials learned would be used (Collins & Duguid, 1991).

Chapter and year-long projects are central to the STEM SOS model. Because students perceive project completion as a privilege, they develop ownership of their projects and take responsibility for their learning. This might STEM from students' admiration of their charismatic science teachers during classes in which they complete hands-on activities and mind-on experiments. Students also receive extra credit for anything additional they do for their projects. Therefore, they try their best to do something different and new; thus, learning happens concurrently. Also, completion of projects requires many personal and interpersonal skills and technology use. Because research has found that high school graduates are not ready for college curriculum (e.g., Anderson, 2013) and college graduates are not ready for the workforce in terms of necessary skills (e.g., Grassgreen, 2014), developing personal, interpersonal, and technology skills has become more important than ever. At Harmony Schools, students are required to make a video presentation of their assignment by taking pictures of each step of the experiment and materials, recording the important episodes of experiment and putting them in order in the movie. They also have to insert any graphic that will show the change in measures at the time of, for instance, collision as well as the collision of the cars. They have to collaborate and get help from other students during completion of some projects without any formal requirement. In addition, they have to make a website of the experiment and upload the video presentation to the Harmony YouTube page. What's more, students have to present their products not only in the classroom, but also to audiences during school STEM festivals, ISWEEEP competitions, and STEM expos. Thus, it is not surprising to see that students develop self-confidence, technology, life and career, communication, and collaboration skills that are necessary for the 21st century workforce (Pacific Policy Research Center, 2010). As they receive positive feedback from participants and viewers, they also become more motivated, self-confident, better presenters and experts in the content they present. Accordingly, this positively changes their attitudes towards science; they may develop STEM interest as is suggested by the social learning theory of Albert Bandura, (1977). This is congruent with research findings in which student attitudes toward STEM education proved to be a major factor in increasing student interest in STEM subjects (e.g., Mahoney, 2010). Also, we learned that students primarily cultivate STEM interest during beginning of their high school years (Archer, DeWitt, & Wong, 2013: Maltese & Tai, 2011) and see daily life connections with hands-on activities (Myers & Fouts, 1992). Therefore, the role of chapter and yearlong projects seem to be very central to the STEM SOS model.

Teachers play an extremely important role in the STEM SOS model, not only teaching the content and making instruction engaging and fun, but also providing assistance and feedback to students throughout the project completion process. Teachers' friendly approach towards their students enhances students' learning and students' attitudes towards science during chapter and year-long project completion process. This helps explain why many students, especially female students, who chose STEM majors reported that they were inspired and influenced by their science teachers (Microsoft Corporation, 2011).

The elements described as important components of the STEM SOS model (e.g., creation of YouTube videos, student teaching from chapter and yearlong projects, and hands-on-activities) suggest the fundamental components of a successful STEM SOS model can be emulated in other contexts.

CONCLUSION

This research study described the STEM SOS model and explored how it helped students grow academically and develop their skills for the 21st century workforce. The emerging theory suggests that there are two core elements of the model: teacher-led teaching and student-directed and completion of chapter and yearlong projects. The study findings suggest that the STEM SOS model results in benefits for students' academic and 21st century skills. If students are to gain academic knowledge, develop STEM interest, research interest in higher education and 21st century skills, then this model should attract the attention of parents, educators, students, and policymakers to improve the quality of STEM education and increase the number of students in the STEM pipeline. So far the STEM SOS model seems to be accomplishing this goal because the Harmony schools' STEM matriculation percentage is higher than the national average (66 vs. 33) (Sahin, 2013).

REFERENCES

Anderson, L. (2013). *Less than half of high school graduate are prepared for college, says maker of SAT.* Retrieved from http://www.boston.com/mt/yourcampus/college-bound-boston/2013/09/less_than_half_of_high_school.html

Archer, L., DeWitt, J., & Wong, B. (2013). Spheres of influence: what shapes young people's aspirations at age 12/13 and what are the implications for education policy? *Journal of Education Policy, 29*(1), 58–85.

Blumenfeld, B. C., Soloway, E., Marx, R. W., Krajcik, J. S., Guzdial, M., & Palincsar, A. (2011). Motivating project-based learning: Sustaining the doing, supporting the learning. *Educational Psychologist, 26*(3-4), 369–398.

Charmaz, K. (2005). Grounded theory in the 21st century: applications for advancing social justice studies. In N. Denzin & Y. S. Lincoln (Ed.), *The Sage handbook of qualitative research* (pp. 507–535). Thousand Oaks, CA: Sage.

Charmaz, K. (2010). Grounded theory: Objectivist and constructivist methods. In W. Luttrell (Ed.), *Qualitative educational research: Readings in reflexive methodology and transformative practice* (pp. 509–535). New York, NY: Routledge.

Collins, A., Brown, J. S., & Newman, S. (1991). Cognitive apprenticeship: Teaching the crafts of reading, writing, and mathematics. In L. B. Resnick (Ed.), *Motivation, learning and instruction: Essays in honor of Robert Glaser* (pp. 453–494). Hillsdale, NJ: Lawrence Erlbaum Associates.

Diaz, D., & King, P. (2007). Adapting a post-secondary STEM instructional model to K-5 mathematics instruction. In *ASEE Annual Conference & Exposition*, Honolulu, HI.

Fortus, D., Krajcik, J., Dershimer, R. C., Marx, R. W., & Mamlok-Naaman, R. (2005). Design-based science and real-world problem-solving.*International Journal of Science Education,27*(7), 855–879.

Grasgreen, A. (2014). *Are college graduates prepared for the workforces? Only university administrators seem to think so.* Retrieved from http://www.slate.com/articles/life/inside_higher_ed/2014/02/gallup_higher_education_poll_college_graduates_aren_t_prepared_for_the_workforce.html

Harwood, J., & Rudnitsky, A. (2005). *Learning about scientific inquiry through engineering.* Proceedings of the 2005 ASEE Annual Conference, Portland, OR.

Holt, N. L., & Tamminen, K. A. (2010). Improving grounded theory research in sport and exercise psychology: Further reflections as a response to Mike Weed. *Psychology of Sport and Exercise,11*(6), 405–413.

Harmony STEM Program. (2013). *Part II: Harmony public schools (HPS) project-based learning initiative.* Retrieved from https://docs.google.com/document/d/1Iwk06YS2fXhvRwtj_LP41v4ctDRuUFyQg2BaKA6owls/pub

Dowd, S. B., & Hulse, S. F. (1996). *Instructional techniques in the radiological sciences.* Albuquerque, NM: The American Society of Radiologic Technologists.

Kolodner, J. L., Camp, P. J., Crismond, D., Fasse, B., Gray, J., Holbrook, J., Puntambekar, S., & Ryan, M. (2003). Problem-based learning meets case-based reasoning in the middle-school science classroom: Putting Learning by Design™ into practice.*The Journal of the Learning Sciences,12*(4), 495–547.

Laboy-Rush, D. (2011). Integrated STEM education through Project-Based Learning. *Retrieved from http://rondoutmar.sharpschool.com/UserFiles/Servers/Server_719363/File/12-13/STEM/STEM-White-Paper%20101207%20final[1].pdf*

Lacey, T. A., & Wright, B. (2009). Occupational employment projections to 2018. *Monthly Labor Review*, 82–123.

Mahoney, M. (2010). Students' attitudes toward STEM: Development of an instrument for high school STEM-based programs. *Journal of Technology Studies, 36*(1), 24–34.

Maltese, A. V., & Tai, R. H. (2011). Pipeline persistence: Examining the association of educational experiences with earned degrees in STEM among U.S. students. *Science Education, 95*(5), 877–907.

Meyrick, K. M. (2011). How STEM education improves student learning. *Meridian K-12 School Computer Technologies Journal, 14*(1), 1–6.

Microsoft Corporation. (2011). *STEM perceptions: Student and parent study.* Retrieved from http://www.microsoft.com/en-us/news/press/2011/sep11/09-07MSSTEMSurveyPR.aspx

Myers, R. E., & Fouts, J. T. (1992). A cluster analysis of high school science classroom environments and attitude toward science. *Journal of Research in Science Teaching, 29*(9), 929–937.

National Academy of Sciences, National Academy of Engineering, and Institute of Medicine. (2007). *Rising above the gathering storm: Energizing and employing America for a brighter economic future.* Washington, DC: The National Academies Press.

National Research Council. (2011). *Successful K-12 STEM education: Identifying effective approaches in science, technology, engineering, and mathematics.* Washington, DC: NAP.

Needham, M. E. (2010). *Comparison of standardized test scores from traditional classrooms and those using problem-based learning* (Doctoral dissertation). Retrieved from ProQuest Dissertations and Theses.

Pacific Policy Research Center. (2010). *21ˢᵗ century skills for students and teachers.* Retrieved from http://www.ksbe.edu/spi/PDFS/21%20century%20skills%20full.pdf

Pearson, M., Barlowe, C., & Price, A. (1999). Project-based learning: Not just another constructivist environment. In *HERDSA Annual International Conference.* Retrieved from http://www.herdsa.org.au/wp-content/uploads/conference/1999/pdf/PearsonM.PDF

President's Council of Advisors on Science and Technology. (2010). *Prepare and inspire: K-12 education in science, technology, engineering, and math (STEM) for America's future.* Washington, DC. Retrieved from http:// www.whitehouse.gov/sites/default/files/microsites/ostp/pcast-stem- ed-final. pdf

Sahin, A., Ayar, M. C., & Adiguzel, T. (2014). STEM related after-school program activities and associated outcomes on student learning. *Educational Sciences: Theory & Practice, 14*(1), 13–26.

Sahin, A. (2013). STEM clubs and science fair competitions: Effects on post-secondary matriculation. *Journal of STEM Education: Innovations and Research, 14*(1), 5–11.

Satchwell, R. E., & Loepp, F. L. (2002). Designing and implementing an integrated mathematics, science, and technology curriculum for the middle school.*Journal of Industrial Teacher Education,39*(3), 41–66.

Sahin, A. Gulacar, O., & Stuessy, C. (In Press). High school students' perceptions of the effects of science Olympiad on their STEM career aspirations and 21st century skill development. *Research in Science Education.*

Schmidt, W. H. (2011, May). *STEM reform: Which way to go?* Paper presented at the National Research Council Workshop on Successful STEM Education in K-12 Schools. Retrieved from http://www7. nationalacademies.org/ bose/ STEM_Schools_Workshop_Paper_Schmidt.pdf

Terrell, N. (2007). STEM occupations: High-tech jobs for a high-tech economy. *Occupations Outlook Quarterly,* 26–33.

Alpaslan Sahin
Harmony Public Schools
Namik Top
Texas A&M University

OZGUR OZER, ISMAIL AYYILDIZ AND NICKOLA ESCH

5. PROJECT-BASED LEARNING IN A WORLD FOCUSED ON STANDARDS

INTRODUCTION

The old school instructional model involves passive teaching of facts and reciting them out of context. This is no longer sufficient to prepare students to survive in today's world. By recently emerging standards such as Common Core, NGSS, and 21st century standards, students are asked to become independent workers, critical thinkers and lifelong learners. The experience of thousands of teachers across all grade levels and subject areas confirms that Project-based Learning (PBL) is an effective way to develop the deep learning competencies required for success in 21st century world (Larmer & Mergendoller, 2012). On the other hand, schools have experienced a host of challenges with the implementation of PBL due to contradictory expectations of accountability and testing, both of which are major issues driving the instruction in the classrooms. Teachers often find PBL implementation impractical since it requires a great deal of time (Ladewski, Krajcik, & Harvey, 1994). The lack of professional development, resistance to instructional shift, standards-based testing and lack of resources emerge as some other common threats (David, 2008). Harmony's STEM SOS model proposes a new approach blending standards-focused learning with inquiry-based learning and project-based learning activities by addressing those issues. The model breaks down the PBL activities into three levels, starting with Level I, which is teacher-facilitated, and culminating at Level III, which is student-driven and more complex. This leveling provides a transitional stage for students to move towards taking full responsibility of their own learning (Sahin & Top, 2014). Moreover, technology and 21st century skills are practiced at every level of the PBL implementation. In this chapter, the challenges of PBL implementation will be discussed and the STEM SOS model will be presented to address those challenges.

WHY PROJECT-BASED LEARNING?

Project-based Learning as a Model

As the title suggests, project-based learning (PBL) is a model that organizes learning around projects. Projects are complex tasks, based on challenging questions or problems, which involve students in design, problem solving, decision making or

A. Sahin (Ed.), A Practice-based Model of STEM Teaching, 63–73.

investigative activities; give students the opportunity to work with relative autonomy over extended periods of time; and culminate in realistic products or presentations. Other defining features may include authentic content, authentic assessment, teacher facilitation but not direction, explicit educational goals, cooperative learning, reflection and incorporation of college and career readiness skills.

The New Generation Seeks Meaningful Experiences and Authenticity

We often hear the question "Why do we need to do this?" in today's classrooms. More than ever, students find school boring and meaningless. In PBL, students engage in meaningful inquiry that is of personal interest to them. The real-world focus of PBL activities motivates students and enhances the value of their work. The learners decide how to approach a problem and what activities or processes they must execute to complete the task. Since students are actively involved in the project, they retain the content knowledge much longer than knowledge obtained through traditional instruction. Students who gain content knowledge through PBL are more capable of applying what they have learned to new situations (Boss, 2013).

PBL activities incorporate a good deal more student autonomy, choice, unsupervised work time and responsibility than do traditional instruction and projects. Projects are realistic and not school-like and embody characteristics that provide a feeling of authenticity to students. These characteristics can include the topic, tasks, roles that students play, context within which the work of the project is carried out, the collaborators who work with students on the project, the products that are produced, the audience for the project's products or the criteria by which the products or performances are judged. PBL incorporates real-life challenges where the focus is on authentic (not simulated) problems or questions and where solutions have the potential to be implemented.

New Standards Promote Deep Learning.

Recently emerging standards such as Common Core, NGSS, and 21st Century Skills ask for more than basic knowledge and skills. Remembering the facts no longer enough to be successful in college and the workforce. The Common Core and other current standards emphasize real-world applications of content and the development of the 21st century competencies such as critical thinking, communication in a variety of media and collaboration skills. Additionally, success in standardized testing requires more than basic knowledge and skills. Traditional teaching methods that rely primarily on rote memorization do not help students gain these skills (Barron & Darling-Hammond, 2008). In PBL, students not only understand content more deeply, but also learn how to take responsibility, solve problems, work collaboratively, communicate ideas, and be creative innovators (Boss, 2013).

Students Want to See Technology in the Classroom.

Today, students use technology almost every single minute of their lives. PBL is a perfect fit to address technology needs of students, allowing teachers and students to use tech tools to find resources and information, create products, collaborate and communicate more effectively.

STANDARDS-FOCUSED ENVIRONMENT AND CHALLENGES FOR PBL

Although PBL is admired, it is not an established instructional method in the majority of schools. Challenges in its implementation pose a threat to its existence and the promise it holds.

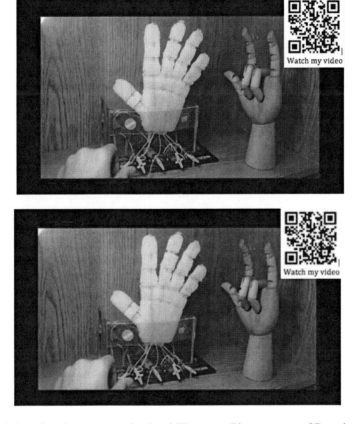

Figure 1. A student demonstrating his Level III project. (Please use your QR reader to scan the QR code to watch the video).

Is It Going to Be on the Test?

Teachers and school administrators strive on a daily basis to maximize student achievement. Regardless of whether achievement is defined as meeting the minimum standards on a state assessment or adequate growth on a national norm-referenced test, there is an assessment tool that checks student learning against certain learning standards. Success on these assessments is closely linked to various issues such as grade promotion, teacher evaluation, school ratings, performance pay, school choice, college acceptance, etc.

Teachers are unwilling to be trained in, prepare for and teach skills or strategies such as PBL, discovery learning and 21st century skills which will not be tested (Marx, Blumenfeld, Krajcik, & Soloway, 1997). Curriculum specialists invest in resources and professional development that will cover standards in the state curriculum framework and, moreover, focus on tested items.

Time Limit

Project-based learning activities take longer than traditional lessons (Ladewski, Krajcik, & Harvey, 1994). Students need more time for research, formulating questions, discussions, writing reports, preparing presentations and building products.

Teachers under pressure to adhere to a mandated pacing guide may be unable to create openings in the calendar for PBL activities that may take a week or two. It is also difficult to accurately plan for each stage of PBL, since learning is driven by the student and the amount of time that each student or group needs to complete a state can vary greatly.

Lack of a Common Structure

Project-based learning has many definitions and interpretations and a common structure for PBL does not exist. The structure may also vary based on the subject. A science PBL unit will be much different from an ELA version. Other traditional teaching methods such as independent practice, direct teaching and questioning have particular structures that are easy to implement. This lack of common structure creates ambiguity for curriculum directors, administrators and teachers. Duration of activities, resources, and evaluation practices can vary; it is difficult to come to a consensus.

Space and Resource Limitations for Completing Work

PBL activities may require access to resources which are not available at the time of the activity. Some of PBLs necessitate research in the library, Internet access, surveying people and construction of artifacts. The variety of the projects makes it extremely difficult for the teacher to gather materials, provide access to all resources and make accommodations for each project.

The Interdisciplinary Collaboration

Project-based learning encourages collaboration among teachers. Commitment, coherence and availability of common planning time are necessary for an interdisciplinary project to be successful. Some of the conflicts include issues such as teachers not feeling accountable, difficulty of grading and a lack of alignment to curriculum.

Lack of Background Knowledge and Skills

Project-based learning is student-driven, with students expected to have the background knowledge and skills necessary to complete the project. Students who do not have a strong foundation of knowledge on the topic on which they are working or who have to deal with material higher than their reading and comprehension level will experience difficulty in building new learning upon a weak foundation. Other skills students may lack, which are needed during project work, include research skills, communication, collaboration, critical thinking, creativity and technology literacy skills.

Student Drive / Motivation

Progress on PBL projects is driven by the individual student. Teachers as facilitators can become frustrated with students or groups of students who do not make adequate progress. Tracking of students becomes more challenging when students complete steps at varying paces. Teachers find it hard to hold students accountable for a calendar that is not strictly set by the classroom teacher.

Classroom Management and Engagement

An effective PBL requires student independence and ownership of one's learning experience (Sahin, 2012). Often, teachers report difficulties associated with maintaining a balance between the need to secure order in the classroom and the need to allow students to work on their own (Marx et. al., 1997; Sahin, 2012). There is a possibility of only a few students in a group being engaged at all times (Marx et. al., 1997).

STEM SOS MODEL

Dichotomy or Continuum: The Answer is Standards-focused PBL.

Standards and state accountability are two main driving forces in classroom instruction. Every educator is a believer in deep learning activities, but the question is "Do we have time for that?" PBL promotes deep learning, but it requires a large amount of time.

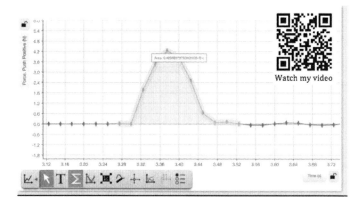

Figure 2. A digital presentation for Level I investigation (Please use your QR reader to scan the QR code to watch the video).

In many cases, PBL is only introduced to a selected group of students by school districts. Usually, experienced fellow teachers implement the program with a select group of students who seem to have strong foundations and skills.

The Harmony SOS model successfully blends standard-based teaching with inquiry- and project-based teaching. It also addresses the challenges mentioned above with a unique implementation of standards-focused PBL approach. In standards-based PBL, the significant content is derived from curriculum standards (Markham, Larmer, & Ravitz, 2003).

The Harmony approach is to maintain the focus on standards-based teaching while enriching and extending the learning of students through PBL projects and inquiry-based investigations. The goal is to promote not only collaborative skills and student ownership of learning, but also student achievement and success with respect to state and national standards. Every student is exposed to the STEM SOS model at Harmony Schools.

STEM SOS Model

The STEM SOS model at Harmony attempts to capture the true essence of the PBL experience without compromising the integrity of the curriculum for its students. Students experience PBL projects at various levels.

Level I is a short-term project that students experience within the context of the curriculum and that targets 21st century skills. The project primarily focuses on one or two standards that will be tested by state. Level I projects are integrated into district scope and sequence documents; that being the case, teachers don't see them as out of context projects.

Level II and Level III projects are semester-long interdisciplinary projects and allow the application and development of these critical skills. Level II and III projects are initiated in science and math courses with a STEM prompt in which students begin investigations during the first quarter of the course and complete by the end of the semester. Students also need to meet cross-curricular requirements to complete the project.

Technology is integrated into every phase to enable students to progress and complete projects successfully while learning life skills. The scope of the STEM SOS model for middle and high school students is outlined below.

Building Foundations for Real PBL Experience: Level I Projects/Investigations

Level I investigations are curriculum-based learning experiences that serve as essential activities in the course. These activities may be a part of the lesson; usually the "Elaborate" phase of a lesson is designed according to the 5E instructional model. Within the context of Level I, the students learn how to plan an investigation, implement it, analyze data and report/present their findings and conclusions. Additionally, the students learn how to collaborate, engage in self-evaluation and work as responsible citizens in the classroom. These investigations may serve as an "entry event" for a student to design a long-term Level III project.

No additional work is required of the teacher other than monitoring and guiding students towards successful learning outcomes. These activities will be completed in class during the school year according to the district curriculum-pacing guide; therefore, teachers are not under the pressure of time limitations. Since these activities may serve as a spark to student inquiry, student presentations and discussion of real life applications are an integral part of classroom instruction.

Table 1. SOS Model Scope of the Project.

	Essential Project (Level I)	Ambitious Project (Levels II & III)
Duration	One week long	Most of the semester
Breadth	Mostly one topic Covers 1 or 2 standards	Multiple disciplines Multiple standards
Technology	Limited Photo gallery or digital ppt.	Extensive Website / Digital Story Video
Teacher Role	Facilitator One Teacher	Provides support, if necessary Multiple teachers
Audience	Classroom or school Class Presentations	Experts and Community STEM Festival presentations
Environment	Both in class and out of class	Out of class

Enriching Curriculum with Long-term Projects (Level II or III)

Level II and Level III are semester-long projects that students begin during the first quarter of the course and complete by the end of the first semester. The projects conform to all attributes of PBL. Students are required to complete either a Level II or Level III project in addition to the curriculum-based Level I investigations. Level II and Level III projects provide opportunities for students to engage in meaningful inquiry into their personal interests at greater depth.

Level II is intended for students who have a difficult time developing project ideas and driving questions on their own. Level II scaffolds students into the first phase of the project by providing a choice of thought-provoking activities that will allow them to generate driving questions that they can investigate on their own. Level II aims to prepare students who need more support and structure for Level III projects.

Level III applies to students who create and develop their project from start to finish on their own with little support from the teacher.

In Level II, the teacher provides the list of "Study" activities for student selection and also provides the time, space, and supervision for the student to complete the laboratory activities. In both Levels II and III, the teacher guides and mentors the students in a timely manner through various phases of the project. Teachers arrange a timeline to meet students for afterschool PBL time to provide support and feedback.

Both Level II and Level III projects are interdisciplinary; projects start with a science or math topic and students find social studies and ELA connections to their ideas. Since the students take the initiative, the project does not require collaboration among teachers. Primarily, students mostly work on their STEM piece in the first quarter with the support of a STEM teacher; they then connect other disciplines in the second quarter. If necessary, students take initiative to ask support from their social studies and ELA teachers as well.

A framework of the Harmony Public Schools SOS model for middle and high school is shown below (see Appendix I & II).

CONCLUSION

First, we discussed the dilemma between goals of PBL implementation and expectations of the current testing and accountability system. PBL promotes deep learning activities with less focus on breadth of learning, but this is contradicted by current testing and accountability systems. Challenges with PBL implementation add to the dilemma. Therefore, it is very likely that schools have provided PBL experience to only a select group of students who perform at a higher level than that which testing standards require.

The STEM SOS model has been studied in terms of how it helps students and teachers to develop the necessary skills for the 21st century workforce while excelling in standard-based tests. The emerging model aims to build foundations and skills for more ambitious projects with Level I activities in a teacher-facilitated and structured environment. Level II has a semi-structure in which the teacher provides start-up activities with supervision and guidance; the students then produce more driving questions and come up with a final product. Level III activities are fully student-driven projects with little teacher support. Students produce digital products at every level of implementation.

The STEM SOS model has been embraced by Harmony students and parents. The model presents PBL as a strong companion (not alternative) to more traditional teaching methods.

REFERENCES

Barron, B., & Darling-Hammond, L. (2008). *Teaching for meaningful learning: A review of research on inquiry-based and cooperative learning.* Retrieved from http://www.edutopia.org/pdfs/edutopia teaching-for-meaningful-learning.pdf

Boss, S. (2013). *PBL for 21st century success.* Buck Institute of Education, Project-based Learning Toolkit Series.

Grant, M. (2002). Getting a grip on project-based learning: Theory, cases and recommendations. *Meridian: A Middle School Computer Technology Journal, 5.*

Ladewski, B. G., Krajcik, J. S., & Harvey, C. L. (1994). A middle grade science teacher's emerging understanding of project-based instruction. *The Elementary School Journal, 94*(5), 498–515.

Larmer, J., & Mergendoller, J. (2010). *8 essentials for project-based learning.* Retrieved from http:// www.bie.org/tools/freebies/Project-based Learning for the 21st Century

Markham, T., Larmer, J., & Ravitz, J. (2003). *Project-based learning: A guide to standards-focused project-based learning for middle and high school teachers.* Novato, CA: Buck Institute for Education.

Marx, R. W., Blumenfeld, P. C., Krajcik, J., & Soloway, E. (1997). Enacting project-based science: Challenges for practice and policy. *Elementary School Journal, 97*(4), 341–358.

Sahin, A., & Top, N. (2014). Making it happen: A study of a novel teaching style, *STEM Students on the Stage* (SOS)™, for increasing students' STEM knowledge and interest. Manuscript submitted for publication.

Sahin, A., Top, N., & Vanegas, S. (2014). *Harmony STEM SOS model increases college readiness and develops 21st century skills* (Whitepaper). Retrieved from http://harmonytx.org/Portals/0/HPS_ Issue-1.pdf

Sahin, A. (2012). STEM project-based learning: Specialized form of inquiry-based learning. In R. M. Capraro, M. M. Capraro, & J. Morgan (Eds.)., *Project-based learning: An integrated science, technology, engineering, and mathematics (STEM) approach* (2nd ed., pp. 59–64). Rotterdam, The Netherlands: Sense

Solomon, G. (2003). *Project-based learning: A primer.* Retrieved from http://www.techlearning.com/ db_area/archives/TL/2003/01/project.php

John Smith
Institute of Higher Education
University of Toronto

APPENDIX I

High School –PBL Framework

Levels	Content/ Courses	# of Projects	Allotted Time	Structure	Tech. Integration
Level I	English	1 Project Each Semester	1 week	Group work (3-4 students per group)	Digital Photo Gallery Presentation (optional)
	Math	1 Project Each Semester	1 week	Group work (3-4 students per group)	1 Digital Photo Gallery Presentation per semester
	Social Studies	1 Project Each Semester	1 week	Group work (3-4 students per group)	Digital Photo Gallery Presentation (optional)
	Science	2 Projects Each Semester	1 week	Group work (3-4 students per group)	1 Digital Photo Gallery Presentation per semester
Level II	Math/ Science with integrated ELA, Social Studies,& Technology	1 Inter-disciplinary Project each Year	1st Semester	Individual or group of no more than three members	Presentation through video, website and brochure + (STEM Digital Story Contest)
OR Level III	Math/ Science with integrated ELA, Social Studies,& Technology	1 Inter-disciplinary Project each Year	1st Semester	Individual or group of no more than three members	Presentation through video, website and brochure + (STEM Digital Story Contest)

APPENDIX II

Middle School- PBL Framework

Levels	Content/ Courses	# of Projects	Allotted Time	Structure	Technology Integration
Level I	English	1 Project each Semester	1 week	Group work (3-4 students per group)	Digital Photo Gallery Presentation (optional)
	Math	1 Project each Semester	1 week	Group work (3-4 students per group)	1 Digital Photo Gallery Presentation per year
	Social Studies	1 Project each Semester	1 week	Group work (3-4 students per group)	Digital Photo Gallery Presentation (optional)
	Science	1 Project each Semester	1 week (may be done in small increments throughout a period of two weeks)	Group work (3-4 students per group)	1 Digital Photo Gallery Presentation per year
Level II*	Math/ Science / Engineering	1 Holistic Project each Year	1st Semester	Individual or group of no more than three members	1 Video Presentation + (STEM Digital Story Contest)

Level-II of middle school shows similar approach with Level-III of high school.

SECTION 3

COMPONENTS OF STEM SOS MODEL

Section III focuses on the components of the STEM SOS model so that readers will gain an in-depth understanding of the model. The first chapter in this section describes how technology is infused in each and every step of the STEM SOS model. Then, the chapter outlines how the interdisciplinary nature of the STEM SOS model embraces all teachers and provides continual collaboration opportunities among students and between teachers. Next, you will see how different types of assessments are incorporated in the model. Another strong component of the model involves the tracking system built for teachers' tasks and students' products. The following chapter explains how the tracking and rewarding systems are tackled. The success of the model largely STEMs from its strong investment in teacher professional development as well as having a systematic support system, as explained in the Professional Development chapter. The STEM outreach chapter summarizes Harmony students' outreach endeavours whereby they showcase their best products and develop 21st century skills in a variety of venues. The STEM SOS model provides learning opportunities for all students, regardless of demographic background and socioeconomic status, due to the model's mission and curriculum materials.

BULENT DOGAN AND BERNARD ROBIN

6. TECHNOLOGY'S ROLE IN STEM EDUCATION AND THE STEM SOS MODEL

This chapter outlines the benefits of technology in STEM education, including how it can support students' development of the 21st century skills of critical thinking, problem-solving and social skills, and some of the uses of technology for STEM activities. In addition, the STEM SOS model's technology integration is defined, specifically, what is expected from middle and high school STEM projects, technology needed to create these projects, academic competitions in which students are encouraged to participate and training of teachers and students through the model.

INTRODUCTION

Technology is an indispensible component of any science, technology, engineering, and mathematics (STEM) or project-based learning (PBL) activity. Technology may contribute to the design and implementation of the STEM activities in multiple ways. However, two patterns emerge when technology use is analyzed for STEM education: 1) direct integration and embedding of technology into STEM activities; and 2) using technology as a tool or facilitator to enrich STEM PBL (Akgun, 2013).

In direct integration, technology is embedded into science, engineering and math activities. In this approach, learners use technology to find solutions to problems in a creative and challenging manner. In this way, the use of technology encourages students to become innovative and to develop creative thinking skills while they work on their projects.

Technology can also serve as a great tool to facilitate PBL projects. For example, learners can use word-processing, spreadsheets and databases to perform tasks during the project. In addition, collaboration tools such as wikis, blogs, discussion forums and other online applications such as Google Drive and Dropbox support learners working together in small groups or teams. Students can also participate in virtual worlds or simulations mediated through various technology applications.

Benefits of Technology in STEM Education

Advances in computer and network technologies may facilitate and provide constructivist and cooperative learning environments, thus paving the way for cooperative activities and constructivist learning (Bottino & Robotti, 2007; ChanLin, 2008). This can be achieved through PBL pedagogy since it involves a hands-on,

A. Sahin (Ed.), A Practice-based Model of STEM Teaching, 77–94.

minds-on, experiential approach centered on an authentic problem in which the students take ownership (Pelech, 2008). In addition, most PBL activities align with constructivist teaching practices such as students taking autonomy in the classroom; conducting work in groups; initiating, sustaining and concluding thoughts; and utilizing an overall student-centered approach in which the teacher plays the role of facilitator or coach (Pelech, 2008; Vermette & Foote, 2001).

Project-based Learning has been reported to greatly benefit students. For instance, students learning through PBL retain content longer and have a deeper understanding of what they are learning (Penuel & Means, 2000; Stepien, Gallagher, & Workman, 1993). In specific content areas (e.g., math, economics, language, science and other disciplines), PBL has been shown to be more effective than traditional methods or teaching (Beckett & Miller, 2006; Finkelstein, Hanson, Huang, Hirschman, & Huang, 2011; Mergendoller, Maxwell, & Bellisimo, 2006). On high-stakes tests, PBL students perform as well as or better than traditionally taught students (Geier et al., 2008; Parker et al., 2011). For example, in a study conducted with 10th grade Biology students, pre- and post-tests were used to determine students' academic achievement and performance skills before and after the treatment. Students in this experiment earned significantly higher scores than those instructed with traditionally designed Biology instruction (Sungur, Tekkaya, & Geban, 2006).

The benefits of PBL are clearly shown in the literature, and technology may further increase or reinforce these benefits. Technology-rich PBL projects help students develop certain forms of literacy and skills such as technological literacy, critical thinking, problem-solving and social skills (Mioduser & Betzer, 2008; Tlhapane & Simelane, 2010). Technological literacy is defined as "one's ability to use, manage, evaluate, and understand technology" (ITEEA, 2011). In a study of high school students, Mioduser and Betzer (2007) documented that students involved in project-based learning activities showed a significant gain in formal content knowledge and technological knowledge, as well as an increase in their positive attitudes toward using technology in their classroom work.

Technology also fosters student-directed scientific inquiry of problems in a real-world setting (Barak & Dori, 2005). When students participate in PBL projects, they learn from each other through cooperative learning and group interaction and develop scientific knowledge through the various group actions involved in investigation and exploration (ChanLin, 2008). Overall, research indicates that the use of technology as a tool in PBL may increase student achievement, interest and motivation as well as improve students' attitudes (ChanLin, 2008; Cobbs & Cranor-Buck, 2011; Harada, Kirio, & Yamamoto, 2008; Hayden, Ouyang, Scinski, Olszewski, & Bielefeldt, 2011).

How Technology is used for STEM PBL Education

Numerous technology tools can be used in PBL activities that focus on STEM. For instance, mind mapping tools, concept mapping tools, and graphic design software may be used to develop critical thinking skills through STEM projects (Jonassen & Carr,

2000). Computer technology may also be utilized as a tool for collecting information, organizing it and presenting it to the class (ChanLin, 2008). Online resources can be utilized to support PBL courses (Watson, 2002). In addition, students conducting research, interacting with peers, teachers and the community and displaying their understanding of knowledge through web-based presentations are just some examples of the many ways technology can be used with PBL projects (ChanLin, 2008).

THE STEM SOS MODEL & TECHNOLOGY

The STEM Students on the Stage (SOS)™ model addresses the increased need for students to acquire 21st century skills. "Through PBL, students are exposed to deep learning experiences that are inquiry based, student-centered, and integrated into the curriculum" in the SOS Model (HPS, 2014, p. 1).

Students may experience PBL projects at various levels in the STEM SOS model. Level I is a short-term project that primarily targets 21st century skills within the context of the curriculum. Level I investigations are curriculum-based learning experiences that are essential activities in a course. These activities are part of the lesson, usually, the "Elaborate" phase of a lesson designed according to the 5E Instructional model, which consists of engagement, exploration, explanation, elaboration, and evaluation (Bybee et al., 2006). During the "Elaborate phase", Bybee et al. (2006) indicated that teachers challenge and extend students' conceptual understanding and skills, allowing students to develop deeper and broader understanding, gain more information, and increase their skills through new experiences, as well as apply their understanding of the concept by conducting additional activities. Within the context of Level I, students learn how to plan an investigation, implement it, analyze data and report/present their findings and conclusions. Additionally, students learn how to collaborate, engage in self-evaluation and work as responsible citizens in the classroom. In Level I, the teacher provides the time, space and supervision for the student to complete the laboratory activities.

Level II and Level III of the STEM SOS model focus on interdisciplinary projects and allow the application and development of 21st century skills (Sahin & Top, in press; Sahin, Top, & Almus, 2014). These are semester-long projects that students begin during the first quarter of a course and complete by the end of the first semester. Students complete the Level II project in addition to the curriculum-based Level I investigations, with Level II projects providing opportunities for students to engage in meaningful inquiry at greater and more personal depth.

Students who have a difficult time constructing project ideas and driving questions on their own may receive help from the teacher. The "explore" and "engineering connections" activities, as well as the Level I projects, scaffold students into the first phase of a project (HPS, 2014). They provide a choice of thought-provoking activities that allow students to generate driving questions, which they can investigate on their own. However, students in Level II are asked to create and develop their project from start to finish on their own, or with a partner, and with some support from the teacher. In Level II, the teacher provides structure via checkpoint deadlines as increments of work are completed. In both Levels I and II, the teacher guides and mentors the students in a timely manner through various phases of the project. This timeline aids students and teachers in keeping track of time and allows for efficient completion without unnecessary stress at the end of the year.

The STEM SOS Model includes training for students in the following technology components:

- Chromebooks and Google Services: for project creation and productivity
- Creating Digital Stories: as final video presentations and collaboration
- Building Websites: to showcase completed work and collaboration
- Designing and Publishing Project Brochure: to share information

Chromebooks and Google Services

In the STEM SOS model, students are provided access to Chromebooks to be used as personal computers in their PBL projects. In addition, all students are provided an email account through Harmony Public School's Gmail domain. Through this email system, students have access to Google services, including Gmail for communication, YouTube for storage of digital stories, Google Docs for office applications, Google Drive for data and file storage and Google Sites for website development. The Google account provided by the school allows students to seamlessly use their Chromebooks with PBL projects and digital presentations as this account is integrated with the Chromebook Operating System.

Digital Storytelling in the STEM SOS Model

Digital storytelling is the process of using various multimedia components, such as still images, text audio narration and music, to create a short, purposeful video on an educationally meaningful topic. An original script, often in the author's own voice combined with the multimedia components, is an essential part of this process (Dogan, 2014). Topics for digital stories can range from personal reflections to instructional subjects. A digital story typically runs for 3 to 5 minutes. A variety of software can be used for creating digital stories, ranging from easy-to-use software such as Microsoft Photo Story 3, iMovie, and Windows Movie Maker to more complex programs such as Photoshop Elements and Final Cut Express (Lambert, 2010; Robin & McNeil, 2012).

Many educators believe that creating digital stories facilitates the development of virtually all of the skills students in K-12 are expected to have in the 21st century. A majority of 21st century skills such as media literacy, technology literacy, information literacy, visual literacy, creativity and problem-solving can be gained when students actively participate in the process of digital storytelling (Jakes & Brennan, 2005; Robin, 2008). In addition, student motivation and engagement levels have been reported to increase with the use of digital storytelling (Banaszewski, 2005; Pauli, 2002; Salpeter, 2005). In a study of senior high school students, Yang and Wu

(2012) reported that students who participated in digital storytelling outperformed traditionally taught students in areas such as critical thinking, understanding of course content and enthusiasm for exploring new material, skills that are widely accepted to be "important in preparing students for an ever-changing 21st century" (p. 339). It has also been reported that students generally enjoy learning through digital stories as they deeply explore the subjects they present in their digital story (Dogan, 2012, 2014). Many teachers endorse the idea that one of the best features of digital storytelling is that it motivates users to learn more about the subject (Dogan, 2014). Examples of digital stories created by students can be viewed at http://www.distco.org/gallery.

At all project levels (Level I, II, & III) for middle and high school, students are expected to complete a digital story as part of their final video presentation in the STEM SOS Model. Digital stories allow students to not only acquire skills, but also actively engage in the process of PBL projects. They also serve as a final artifact and end product with which students can showcase their work and share it on many different digital platforms. Upon completion of the projects, students are directed to upload their digital stories to their YouTube channels as well as to their Google Drive for sharing and storage purposes.

Some of the sample digital stories created for PBL in the SOS Model can be found online at the following sites:

- High School Math: Balloon Race, https://www.youtube.com/watch?v=-K4zod4Qrws (Figure 1)
- High School Science: Computer Vision, https://www.youtube.com/watch?v=iXfInHQYl4c
- Middle School Science: Best Bacteria Killer (Toothpaste) https://www.youtube.com/watch?v=mbdQFy8QlLo

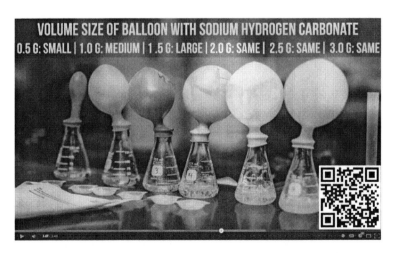

Figure 1. A digital story on a PBL science project created by a high school student. (Please use your QR reader to scan the QR code to watch the video).

Website Development through Google Sites

Google Sites is a free and easy-to-use website development system that works through a Google account. Google Sites allows users to make information accessible to people who need quick and up-to-date access. According to Google (2011), "People can work together on a Site to add file attachments, information from other Google applications (like Google Docs, Google Calendar, YouTube and Picasa), and new free-form content." Users can collaborate and edit a site's content together in a manner similar to editing a document and can have control over who has access to the system. Sites can be private or set to display as public pages so that they can be shared through the Internet.

In addition to creating digital stories, high school students in Level II and III are required to create websites using Google Sites. Through Google Sites, students compile all of their PBL work in one place where it can be presented to their audience in a convenient platform. Communication between students and teachers throughout the project occurs via these Google sites, specifically created for this purpose. Since Google Sites is integrated with students' Google accounts and can be used seamlessly on Chromebooks, it is a natural choice as a website development system for the SOS Model.

Some of the example websites created by students in Google Sites are shown below:

- Physics project about center of mass: https://sites.google.com/site/balancingprojects2014/
- 3D design for an Engineering project (https://sites.google.com/site/hse2013jaina25/my-pbl-project) (Figure 2)
- Gaming for Biology project (https://sites.google.com/site/hsa2012hung12/) (Figure 2)
- Biology project about protein synthesis: https://sites.google.com/site/proteinssynthesis/
- Algebra project: Uni Dog: https://sites.google.com/site/unitdog2014/
- Geometry project: String Design https://sites.google.com/site/stringdesigns2014/
- Chemistry project about chromatography https://sites.google.com/site/chromatography2014/home
- Computer Science project about binary systems: https://sites.google.com/site/hsa2013yaseem33/

Designing and Publishing Project Brochures

Students following the STEM SOS Model are asked to create a project brochure to be used during a science fair, an academic competition, exhibition or a presentation. The brochure includes information on the PBL project, a Quick Response (QR) code to easily share the links to both the digital story and website (Google Site). Students may use Google Docs or Microsoft Word to create their brochures. Once the students

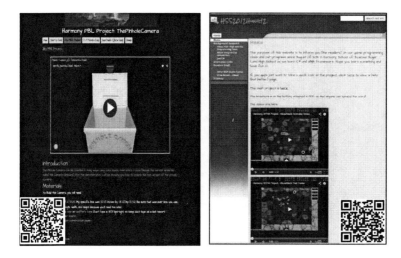

Figure 2. Student websites created with Google sites. (Please use your QR reader to scan the QR codes to watch the video).

design their project brochures, they are asked to upload the brochure file to their websites so that they can share it with their audience. A sample project brochure is shown in Figure 3.

Technology Training for Students

Training materials such as written and video tutorials are provided to students in the STEM SOS Model. Since students are required to complete certain tasks within a specific time frame for their PBL projects, the technology training materials are made available to them through the Harmony PBL Resource website at http://pbl. harmonytx.org/. The majority of the training materials focus on how to use digital storytelling software with PBL projects and how to create a website using Google Sites.

TECHNOLOGY INTEGRATION IN HIGH SCHOOL PROJECTS

High School Level I PBL Projects

High school students in Level I complete one PBL project each semester in English, math, and social studies and two projects each semester in science. Similar to the middle school Level I, upon completion of PBL projects in math and science, students are required to produce a digital story involving photos and captions only (digital photo gallery presentations). Producing digital photo gallery presentations in Social Studies and English is optional at this level (see Table 1).

Figure 3. Sample student PBL project brochure.

The digital gallery presentations are evaluated through a digital storytelling rubric (DISTCO, 2014) at this level. In addition, teachers evaluate the content of the video presentations for grading purposes. Several digital storytelling software programs, including Microsoft Photo Story 3, Windows Movie Maker, Animoto, iMovie or WeVideo, can be used at this level. In addition to easy-to-use Photo Story 3 software, more advanced digital storytelling software, such as Windows Movie Maker, is suggested for high school students. However, similar to the implementation in middle school, WeVideo is preferred as the primary software in the SOS Model due to its seamless integration with Gmail, Google Drive, and Chromebooks. WeVideo is cloud-based software that can be used without the need for software installation or physical storage space in Chromebooks.

The digital photo gallery presentations created in Level I by high school students are kept in students' Google Drive folders for future access and reference. Students

Table 1. PBL Framework and Technology Integration for High School PBL.

Grade	Levels	Content/ Courses	# of Projects	Allotted Time	Structure	Technology Integration
High School	Level I	Science	2 Projects each Semester	1 week	Group work (3-4 students per group)	2 Digital Photo Gallery Presentations per semester
		Math	1 Project each Semester	1 week	Group work (3-4 students per group)	1 Digital Photo Gallery Presentation per semester
		English Language Arts/Social Studies	1 Project each Semester	1 week	Group work (3-4 students per group)	Digital Photo Gallery Presentation (optional)
	Level II OR Level III	Math/ Science with integrated ELA, Social Studies, & Technology	1 Inter-disciplinary Project each Year	1st Semester	Individual or group of no more than three members	Presentation through Digital Story, Project Website (through Google Sites) and Project Brochure + Participation in DISTCO PBL Contest, and STEM WEB Contest

are also encouraged to enter academic competitions with their PBL projects (see Academic Competition Section for more information).

High School Level II & III PBL Projects

In addition to the Level I project described above, each student completes one interdisciplinary PBL/STEM-type project-based on math or science content (See Table 1). These projects also contain integrated social studies and English Language Arts (ELA) components. The projects at this level can be completed individually or in groups. Students begin the project work in the first semester and continue the work through the second semester.

Upon completion of the project, students are expected to present their findings through a digital story consisting of video, images, sound clips, background music and narration in their own voice. In addition to the digital stories created at this level, students are required to develop websites through Google Sites to showcase their work.

Project assessments are completed in each of the content areas (math, science, social studies, ELA, and technology) by the respective teachers. In addition, the DISTCO digital storytelling rubric (DISTCO, 2014) is used to evaluate digital stories created at this level.

In addition to easy-to-use Photo Story 3 software, more advanced digital storytelling software, such as Windows Movie Maker, is recommended for high school students at this level. However, WeVideo is preferred as the primary software tool for creating PBL digital stories at this level; this decision was based on the following factors: ease of use, seamless integration of WeVideo with Gmail and Google Drive, being an Internet-based software without the need of installation and the ability to work with Chromebooks.

High school students at this level upload their digital stories to their YouTube channels to be used in their Google Sites as well as kept in their Google Drive folders for future access. Students are required to submit their work to the DISTCO PBL and STEM WEB contest along with their PBL projects (see Academic Competition Section for more information).

TECHNOLOGY INTEGRATION IN MIDDLE SCHOOL PROJECTS

The STEM SOS Model includes a middle school component with two levels that are similar to the high school component. In Level I, students are required to produce a "digital story" involving photos and captions only, also called a "digital photo gallery presentation" upon completion of PBL projects in math and science. Digital photo gallery presentations are not required for projects completed in English Language Arts and social studies. Typically, Level I projects are completed within several weeks as part of the curriculum. In Level II, students complete one interdisciplinary and holistic PBL project during the first semester of the academic year; that same project is also used as a student's science fair submission. Unlike Level I projects, Level II students are required to produce a digital story with images, music, and narration (voiceover recorded by the student) upon completion of the PBL projects. To obtain more information on middle school projects, you can refer to the Harmony PBL resource website located at http://pbl.harmonytx.org/

ACADEMIC COMPETITIONS IN THE SOS MODEL

Students participate in several technology-related contests during project development or after they have completed their projects. These competitions allow students to present their findings and showcase their products. Students in the STEM SOS Model participate in following academic competitions:

Distco PBL

DISTCO, a long-running "Digital Storytelling Contest" for K-12 students and teachers (http://www.distco.org), in partnership with Harmony Public Schools (HPS) created a special STEM-related competition. Known as DISTCO PBL, this competition supports strategies to achieve program goals of the STEM SOS Model. One of the goals of the program is to extend the current PBL curriculum in HPS. DISTCO PBL accepts cross-disciplinary, multi-sensory, technology-enabled video projects integrating STEM with Social Studies, and English Language Arts.

Through this partnership, students and teachers in the HPS system are trained on the technologies (such as video production, technical skills, submission/retrieval of the PBL projects along with training on the DISTCO project) that students will use to develop their PBL products. Digital Storytelling Contest (DISTCO) PBL is an annual competition and PBL projects created in Level II & III in the SOS Model are automatically accepted to the contest. The DISTCO system hosts students' PBL digital stories for future review and access.

DISTCO PBL accepts digital stories in three categories, Middle School Science, High School Math, and High School Science, from December-March every year (Figure 8). Submitted stories are evaluated by DISTCO judges based on the digital story rubric (DISTCO, 2014), and the top projects are checked for their content by faculty from the Science Department at HPS. Winners are typically announced in an award ceremony held in May.

Figure 4. DISTCO PBL and STEM WEB contest flyer. (Please use your smartphone to see the websites).

STEM Web Contest

High School Students in Level II and III in the STEM SOS Model participate in the STEM WEB contest. Students submit their Google Sites link to the contest. Specifically, the Google Sites include information about the student's school and a summary of their project, digital story, and project brochure. Students may submit their websites between December and March (Figure 4). After the submission, the websites along with the digital stories are checked and approved. If they are rejected, students are asked to update their site and resubmit it. Public voting begins in April and winners are announced in May in the STEM WEB contest.

Figure 5. STEM festival activities.

STEM Festivals and ISWEEEP

STEM Festivals are organized at the school level using the STEM SOS Model. These are project competitions where students showcase their PBL projects in a science fair setting and share their PBL projects with the public through their display boards, digital stories, project brochures and websites (Figure 5). Campuses in Harmony Public Schools are encouraged to organize their own STEM Festival every year.

Students are also encouraged to join regional, statewide, and international STEM and PBL contests, one of which I-SWEEEP, the International Sustainable World Energy, Engineering, and Environment Project. I-SWEEEP is a science fair competition organized by Harmony Public Schools with the support of leaders of industry and higher education institutions (Figure 6). It is the largest science fair event of its kind in the world and is open to high school students at the international level. More information can be found at: http://isweeep.org/.

Figure 6. ISWEEP public day exhibition.

TECHNOLOGY TRAINING OF TEACHERS IN THE STEM SOS MODEL

Teacher Development is one of primary program objectives of STEM education in the United States (United States Government Accountability Office, 2012). Teachers should have the necessary knowledge and skills to successfully teach and facilitate STEM projects. Therefore, proper training of teachers in STEM delivery and STEM PBL is key to any STEM teaching model.

In the STEM SOS Model, training teachers to use the technologies that are part of STEM PBL projects plays an important role. Specifically, teachers are trained through the following means:

- District and School-wide Professional Development Programs
- PBL Technology Training
- The Harmony PBL Resource Website

District and School-wide Professional Development Programs

These professional development programs are typically provided at the beginning of the school year and are intended to provide a general overview of the STEM PBL activities and the roles of teachers in these activities. As part of these programs, teachers receive training in technology components and expectations in the delivery of STEM PBL using the STEM SOS Model. More detailed training in this area is provided through PBL technology training sessions throughout the year.

PBL Technology Training

In the STEM SOS model, PBL Technology training sessions for teachers are offered in every quarter of the school semester. Depending on the tasks identified in each quarter of the school year, teachers receive training in the areas requiring the use of technology. These quarter-based sessions involve training modules on how to create and design a website through Google Sites, how to use digital storytelling and video editing software, including Microsoft Photo Story 3, Windows Movie Maker, WeVideo and iMovie, and how to design and publish a project brochure. For example, the topic of Quarter 1 Middle and High School Level I PBL technology training for teachers was "How to create a Digital Gallery Presentations using PowerPoint and WeVideo."

Harmony PBL Resource Website

The Harmony PBL Resource Website (http://pbl.harmonytx.org) serves as a central platform for administrators, teachers, students, science coaches, curriculum specialists and department heads in the Harmony System regarding the Harmony PBL initiative and its required activities. The website contains specific information on the PBL initiative launched in the 2013-2014 school year and made possible through a U.S. Department of Education "Race to the Top" grant. In addition, the website serves as an internal communication tool for the participants using the STEM SOS model.

The information is divided into following subtopics and a separate section is devoted to each of them:

- PBL Middle School: Middle school-related PBL tasks and project requirements
- PBL High School: High school-related PBL tasks and project requirements
- PBL Performance: A list showing the ranking of Harmony Public School campuses based on their PBL project preparation Progress Report
- PBL Teacher Resources: The training schedule, video recordings of training sessions and other training resources and materials
- Central Office PBL reports: A list of PBL teachers and their progress on completion of PBL projects with their students.

CONCLUSION

The PBL-based STEM SOS model is rich in technology-infused activities that can benefit teachers who utilize it. Many of the teachers who go through training and professional development sessions gain knowledge and skills that help them implement PBL projects with students. Prior to the use of the STEM SOS model, teachers traditionally used technology as an aid in science classes or with PBL projects, mostly to instruct and allow students to conduct online research on the PBL topic. However, teachers are now required to make a more active use of technology during instruction through hands-on activities. For example, YouTube videos are used when teachers incorporate experiments in their instruction and during hands-on activities to explain theories and show the relevancy of content to real-world conditions.

Because the development of websites and presentation videos are major technology components in the STEM SOS model, teachers learn about these technologies along with their students, so that they can coach their students while they work on the technology components of their projects. It is not surprising that some teachers have changed their teaching style as a result of their experience with the STEM SOS model and its technology components; for example, several teachers have started implementing flipped-classroom approaches for their science classes so that they can conduct more hands-on activities within their classrooms.

Educators such as Ottenbreit-Leftwich, Glazewski, Newby and Ertmer (2010) have conducted research that indicates that teachers who believe that technology can be a valuable component in the educational process are more likely to integrate it into their instructional practice. Later studies, such as those by Ertmer, Ottenbreit-Leftwich, Sadik, Sendurur, and Sendurur (2012), further explored teachers' beliefs about the usefulness of technology and suggested that a "teachers' own beliefs and attitudes about the relevance of technology to students' learning were perceived as having the biggest impact on their success" (p. 423).

Overall, our experience has shown that teachers who participate in the PBL-based STEM SOS model greatly benefit from this process, not only by increasing their technology skills, but also by successfully integrating technology into their instruction. This success ultimately changes their belief and attitudes about technology and helps shape their teaching practices for the 21st century.

REFERENCES

Akgun, O. (2013). Technology in STEM project-based learning. In R. M. Caparro, M. M. Capraro & James R. Morgan (Eds.), *STEM project-based learning: An integrated science, technology, engineering, and mathematics (STEM) Approach* (2nd ed.). Rotterdam, Netherlands: Sense Publishers.

Banaszewski, T. M. (2005). *Digital storytelling: Supporting digital literacy in grades 4 – 12* (Master's Thesis). Georgia Institute of Technology. Retrieved from http://techszewski.blogs.com/techszewski/files/TBanaszewski_DS_thesis.pdf

Barak, M., & Dori, Y. J. (2005). Enhancing undergraduate students' chemistry understanding through project-based learning in an IT environment. *Science Education, 89*(1), 117–139.

Beckett, G. H., & Miller, P. C. (2006). *Project-based second and foreign language education: Past, present, and future*. Charlotte, NC: IAP.

Bottino, R. M., & Robotti, E. (2007). Transforming classroom teaching & learning through technology: Analysis of a case study. *Educational Technology & Society, 10*(4), 174–186.

Bybee, R. W., Taylor, J. A., Gardner, A., Van Scotter, P., Powell, J. C., Westbrook, A., & Landes, N. (2006). *The BSCS 5E instructional model: Origins and effectiveness*. Colorado Springs, CO: BSCS.

ChanLin, L. J. (2008). Technology integration applied to project-based learning in science. *Innovations in Education and Teaching International, 45*(1), 55–65.

Cobbs, G. A., & Cranor-Buck, E. (2011). Getting into GEAR. *Mathematics Teaching in the Middle School, 17*(3), 160–165.

DISTCO. (2014). *Digital storytelling evaluation rubric*. Retrieved from http://www.distco.org/wp-content/uploads/2011/10/Digital-Storytelling-Rubric-DISTCO-2014.pdf

Dogan, B. (2010). Educational use of digital storytelling: Research results of an online digital storytelling contest. In D. Gibson & B. Dodge (Eds.), *Proceedings of Society for Information Technology & Teacher Education International Conference 2010* (pp. 1061–1066). San Diego, CA: AACE. Retrieved from http://www.editlib.org/p/33494

Dogan, B. (2014). Educational uses of digital storytelling in K-12: Research results of a digital storytelling contest (DISTCO) 2013. In M. Searson & M. N. Ochoa (Eds.), *Society for Information Technology & Teacher Education International Conference 2014* (pp. 520–529). Jacksonville, FL: AACE. Retrieved from http://www.editlib.org/p/130802

Ertmer, P. A., Ottenbreit-Leftwich, A. T., Sadik, O., Sendurur, E., & Sendurur, P. (2012). Teacher beliefs and technology integration practices: A critical relationship. *Computers & Education, 59*(2), 423–435.

Finkelstein, N., Hanson, T., Huang, C. W., Hirschman, B., & Huang, M. (2011). Effects of problem based economics on high school economics instruction. *Society for Research on Educational Effectiveness*. Retrieved from http://ies.ed.gov/ncee/edlabs/regions/west/pdf/REL_20104022.pdf

Geier, R., Blumenfeld, P. C., Marx, R. W., Krajcik, J. S., Fishman, B., Soloway, E., & Clay-Chambers, J. (2008). Standardized test outcomes for students engaged in inquiry-based science curricula in the context of urban reform. *Journal of Research in Science Teaching, 45*(8), 922–939.

Google. (2011). *Google sites overview*. Retrieved from http://www.google.com/sites/overview.html

Harada, V. H., Kirio, C. H., & Yamamoto, S. H. (2008). *Collaborating for project-based learning in grades 9-12*. Columbus, OH: Linworth Publishing.

Hayden, K., Ouyang, Y., Scinski, L., Olszewski, B., & Bielefeldt, T. (2011). Increasing student interest and attitudes in STEM: Professional development and activities to engage and inspire learners. *Contemporary Issues in Technology and Teacher Education, 11*(1), 47–69.

HPS. (2014). *PBL initiative information booklet.* Houston, Texas: Harmony Public Schools. Retrieved from https://sites.google.com/a/harmonytx.org/pbl/booklet

ITEEA. (2011). *Technologically literate citizens.* Retrieved from http://www.iteaconnect.org/TAA/TAA_Literacy.html

Jakes, D., & Brennan, J. (2005). *Capturing stories, capturing lives: An introduction to digital storytelling.* Retrieved from http://www.jakesonline.org/dstory_ice.pdf

Jonassen, D. H., & Carr, C. S. (2000). Mindtools: Affordable multiple knowledge representation for learning. In S. P. Lajoie (Ed.), *Computers as cognitive tools, Volume 2: No more walls.* Mahwah, NJ: Lawrence Erlbaum Associates.

Lambert, J. (2010). *Digital Storytelling Cookbook.* Berkeley, CA: Center for Digital Storytelling. Retrieved from http://www.storycenter.org/cookbook.pdf

Mergendoller, J. R., Maxwell, N. L., & Bellisimo, Y. (2006). The effectiveness of problem-based instruction: A comparative study of instructional methods and student characteristics. *Interdisciplinary Journal of Problem-Based Learning, 1*(2), 49–69.

Mioduser, D., & Betzer, N. (2008). The contribution of Project-based-learning to high-achievers' acquisition of technological knowledge and skills. *International Journal of Technology and Design Education, 18,* 59–77.

Ottenbreit-Leftwich, A. T., Glazewski, K. D., Newby, T. J., & Ertmer, P. A. (2010). Teacher value beliefs associated with using technology: Addressing professional and student needs. *Computers & Education, 55*(3), 1321–1335.

Parker, W., Mosborg, S., Bransford, J., Vye, N., Wilkerson, J., & Abbott, R. (2011). Rethinking advanced high school coursework: Tackling the depth/breadth tension in the AP "US Government and Politics" course. *Journal of Curriculum Studies, 43*(4), 533–559.

Paull, C. N. (2002). *Self-perceptions and social connections: Empowerment through digital storytelling in Adult Education.* Berkeley, CA: University of California.

Pelech, J. (2008). *Delivering constructivism through project-based learning (PBL).* Institute for Learning Centered Education. Retrieved from http://jpacte.learningcentered.org/Articles/Winter2008/Pelech.pdf

Penuel, W. R., & Means, B. (2000). *Designing a performance assessment to measure students' communication skills in multi-media-supported, project-based learning.* Paper presented at the Annual Meeting of the American Educational Research Association, New Orleans.

Robin, B. (2008). The effective uses of digital storytelling as a teaching and learning tool. In J. Flood, S. B. Heath, & D. Lapp (Eds.), *Handbook of Research on Teaching Literacy Through the Communicative and Visual Arts* (Vol. 2) (pp. 429–440). New York, NY: Lawrence Erlbaum Associates.

Robin, B., & McNeil, S. (2012). Lessons from the Trenches: What educators should know about teaching digital storytelling. In *Society for Information Technology & Teacher Education International Conference* (Vol. 2012) (pp. 1433–1440). Retrieved from http://www.editlib.org/p/39783

Sahin, A., Top, N., & Almus, K. (2014). *Teachers' reflections on STEM students on the stage (SOS)™, model* (Whitepaper). Retrieved from http://www.harmonytx.org/Portals/0/HPS%20Issue-2.pdf

Sahin, A., & Top, N. (in press). Make it happen: A study of a novel teaching style, *STEM Students on the Stage* (SOS)™, for increasing students' STEM knowledge and interest. *The Journal of STEM Education: Innovations and Research.*

Salpeter, J. (2005). Telling tales with technology: Digital storytelling is a new twist on the ancient art of the oral narrative. *Technology & Learning, 25*(7), 18–24.

Stepien, W. J., Gallagher, S. A., & Workman, D. (1993). Problem-based learning for traditional and interdisciplinary classrooms. *Journal for the Education of the Gifted, 16*(4), 338–357.

Sungur, S., Tekkaya, C., & Geban, Ö. (2006). Improving achievement through problem-based learning. *Journal of Biological Education, 40*(4), 155–160.

Tlhapane, S. M., & Simelane, S. (2010). Technology-enhanced problem-based learning methodology in geographically dispersed learners of Tshwane University of Technology. *Knowledge Management & E-Learning: An International Journal (KM&EL)*, *2*(1), 68–83.

United States Government Accountability Office. (2012). *Science, technology, engineering, and mathematics education: Strategic planning needed to better manage overlapping programs across multiple agencies.* Washington, D.C. Retrieved from http://www.aura-astronomy.org/news/EPO/GAOReportStem.pdf

Vermette, P., & Foote, C. (2001). Constructivist philosophy and cooperative learning practice: Toward integration and reconciliation in secondary classrooms. *American Secondary Education, 30*(1), 26–37.

Watson, G. (2002). *Using technology to promote success in PBL courses.* Retrieved from http://technologysource.org/article/using_technology_to_promote_success_in_pbl_courses/

Yang, Y. T. C., & Wu, W. C. I. (2012). Digital storytelling for enhancing student academic achievement, critical thinking, and learning motivation: A year-long experimental study. *Computers & Education, 59*(2), 339–352.

Bulent Dogan
North American University
Bernard Robin
University of Houston

ROBERT THORNTON AND KERI BELL

7. THE INTERDISCIPLINARY NATURE OF STEM SOS

PERSPECTIVES FROM ENGLISH LANGUAGE ASRTS AND SOCIAL STUDIES

The interdisciplinary elements of the STEM SOS model are crucial to enabling the overall success of that model. The heightened focus on the scientific method across many content areas encourages the implementation of rigor and skills-based inquiry by teachers in English Language Arts (ELA) and Social Studies. In turn, both teachers and students routinely think about and discuss how their subjects relate to others during the course of yearlong student projects, an experience that increases the relevance of learning for students. Once students see the larger context of their learning experience, they become more engaged, goal-oriented and aware of how their learning will translate into a career in the future. Teachers who apply the STEM SOS model will notice that it encourages the implementation of established best practices in instruction. In fact, the model overcomes issues commonly experienced when trying to implement interdisciplinary instruction. Success in implementing the model is often assisted by the creation of an effective interdisciplinary school culture.

INTRODUCTION

During the past few decades, we have witnessed many shifts in the global workforce. Not only has specialization within fields grown, but the demand for highly trained, STEM-oriented workers has also increased. In light of these paradigm shifts, the world of education has tried to react accordingly with new models for educating the workforce of tomorrow. Often, what is lost in these new, highly-specialized models is the interdisciplinary element. After all, despite the increase in specialization, the world is growing more interconnected, not less, and therefore the four core subject areas should overlap more than ever before. The STEM SOS model equips schools and teachers with the opportunity to instill a STEM-awareness in their students that transcends subject areas (Sahin, Top, & Almus, 2014; Sahin, Top, & Vanegas, 2014).

Concurrent with the changes described above, several other shifts within education have also taken place, such as increased accountability and revised curriculum standards. These shifts have forced teachers in ELA and Social Studies to focus more on academic skills and less on the socialization function that these two fields have long performed at the secondary level. This shift towards academic readiness

A. Sahin (Ed.), A Practice-based Model of STEM Teaching, 95–109.

and skill-based instruction has embedded the scientific method within effective ELA and Social Studies classrooms. Secondary students are no longer just absorbing the analytic work of professor-sages, but are asked to create and defend their own theses using evidence from a wide variety of sources. Participation in the STEM SOS model helps ELA and Social Studies teachers accomplish this through an increase in student engagement that occurs naturally due to the inherent relevance of their studies. Instead of spending large amounts of class time attempting to attain unmeasurable goals, the model allows students to experience what people in these fields actually do. Experts in the fields of literary criticism, historical research and contemporary issues are expected to engage others within their disciplines, to weigh many sources of evidence and to present their findings to broad audiences. Therefore, the STEM SOS model expects the same from students on a lesser scale, one more appropriate to the secondary classroom. In aligning with common elements of the Advanced Placement (AP) skill sets in English and Social Studies and by containing the rigor necessary to achieve standards mastery on state tests, the model achieves college readiness in a way that is measurable and effective. This trait then enables educators to feel confident that they are creating a world in which all students, regardless of whether they enter STEM or liberal arts fields, have a degree of STEM-awareness that helps them solve the pressing concerns of the 21st century. English Language Arts and Social Studies teachers who participate in the model will also be pleased to discover that success within the model requires drawing on the established "best practices" of their fields.

INTERDISCIPLINARY ASPECTS OF ELA & SOCIAL STUDIES STEM SOS PROJECTS [LEVEL I]

The notion of inquiry-based projects in ELA and Social Studies is not new; after all, the PBL model has been enthusiastically implemented across the country. The influence of the PBL model on the STEM SOS model has been discussed in further detail in previous chapters. What is important to note here is that when a school implements the STEM SOS model across the four core content areas, the common approach engrains the scientific method into the ELA and Social Studies projects in a way that lends itself to interdisciplinary instruction by the ELA or Social Studies teacher. By examining a project in each field, we can see how the student is guided through rigorous, skills-based inquiry by the teacher, as well as interdisciplinary aspects essential to the project's success.

During a 6th grade unit on persuasive texts, English Language Arts students complete what is called the *"See Something, Say Something (S⁴)"* project. Early in the unit, students read and analyze a variety of persuasive texts (e.g., public service announcements, articles, advertisements and editorials), finding and annotating persuasive techniques as they appear. With partners, students are asked to determine *which* techniques they find to be *more, or most*, effective and to explain how and why they came to those conclusions. Each pair is also asked to consult with another pair of students in order to gain exposure to a wider variety of persuasive methods. Prior to creating the "scenario," the teacher asks students to write and discuss responses to the following questions – making sure to pull everyone together for a short, whole-class discussion:

- *What compels someone to speak their mind?*
- *Why do we waver for some things but stand our ground for others?*
- *What causes people to intervene or tell someone about a concern . or simply walk away and mind their own business?*

As the teacher explains the objective of a PSA, i.e., to persuade and teach the audience or community about an issue that is important to the developer, he or she presents the primary task to students:

As engaged users and consumers of media, and as digital citizens of the 21st century, we use media to inform ourselves, to help shape our opinions, to interact with and within our communities, and to make our voices heard (Media Smarts). In an effort to make our physical and digital school community a safe place for everyone, the 6th grade class has been chosen to create persuasive PSAs to be played in the cafeteria before and after school for the entire student body.

The teacher creates a scenario that is similar to what someone with a degree in marketing might encounter in the business world. At this point, the teacher explains the goals of advertisements, commercials, and infomercials – to create a 'tipping point' – or the point at which a sufficient number of people have been persuaded by the message to create a new and irreversible development. If a message is meaningful

Figure 1. A student demonstrating his Level II project. (Please use your QR reader to scan the QR codes to watch his video and/or see his e-portfolio website).

to enough people, it has the power to spark something within a community and instigate change. After this explanation, students engage in discussions with other group members about potential topics for their PSA and effective persuasive methods that might be incorporated into their PSA. Students conduct research on their chosen issue to glean a better perspective and then synthesize their findings while maintaining focus on their desired outcome: to convince their classmates and school community of the importance of being respectful, savvy consumers of digital media. Students create a one-minute Public Service Announcement, as well as an outlet or "community hotline" to serve as a safe place for students to voice their concerns about issues they encounter when participating in technological communities with their peers (the hotline/mailbox will house complaints, concerns and suggestions that students may want to report or share anonymously, improving and supporting the cyber community of students). The creation of the PSA and hotline reinforces students' understanding of content knowledge (how and why authors employ persuasive techniques) as well as their use of digital literacy and 'netiquette' when participating in social media and other technological requirements in school.

In Figure 2, it is clear that the students spend a great deal of time engaged in thoughtful discussion and inquiry with other students while mastering content standards, utilizing 21st century skills and synthesizing knowledge from multiple fields.

During tenth grade World History, students complete a project commonly referred to as the "U.N. Seminar" project. At the start of the project, the teacher finds a creative way to announce an upcoming, on-campus seminar to be hosted by the U.N. Students will be asked to present information to a special U.N. committee, seeking their expert advice on how to help government deal with issues related to indigenous people. In doing so, the teacher is trying to create a scenario that is similar to one that an anthropologist or historian who specializes in this field

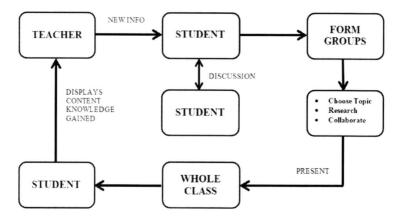

Figure 2. Map of ELA Level I project.

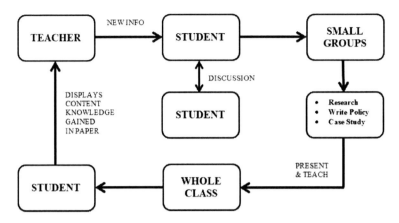

Figure 3. Map of SS Level I project.

might encounter in their career. The teacher then gives the students a brief lecture addressing different historical explanations for why some groups of people were eventually able to govern other groups of people and their territories. Following the lecture, students participate in small group discussions centered on the different explanations presented. At this point, the teacher provides students with research from the U.N. regarding current issues faced by indigenous people and asks them to develop a series of recommendations to the U.N. In addition, students must perform a case study for which they research an indigenous group and seek to show how their recommendations would be successful in helping government appropriately respond to the issues they face. By the time groups present their findings to their classmates, they themselves are the experts mentioned in the original announcement of the project.

As seen in Figure 3, the bulk of the project involves students' interacting and teaching other students. Most importantly, students are forced to draw upon the knowledge they have gained across content areas to perform proficiently while constantly implementing 21st century skills. The research they encounter involves varied topics such as the environment, education, health, culture and economics. The ability to discuss and present recommendations regarding any of these topics requires the students to consider catalysts, variables and constants in a methodical fashion. The initial focus of different historical explanations for the current status quo is kept in the background until the students write their individual papers, in which they demonstrate the content standards they have mastered.

INTERDISCIPLINARY SUCCESS IN YEARLONG STEM SOS PROJECTS [LEVEL II]

While interdisciplinary instruction within one classroom is certainly commendable, the true standard for interdisciplinary success is providing students with assignments that flow seamlessly from one classroom to another, between multiple teachers. This is the intended goal behind the interdisciplinary tasks in the Level II STEM SOS projects. After choosing their level II project tasks within their Math or Science classrooms, students are expected to approach and work closely with their ELA and Social Studies teachers to complete several interdisciplinary tasks, as seen in Figure 4.

During the first interdisciplinary component, Task 7, students take their knowledge of the project chosen in their Math or Science classroom into their ELA and Social Studies classes in order to explore the project from different angles. During this process, student choice and a willingness to collaborate with their teachers are the priority. In ELA, students must choose a genre or literary form that best enables them to reflect upon and analyze their experience when completing their project (for a full list of project options for the ELA connection, see Appendix A). In Social Studies, they must make a connection between their project and a topic in their social studies course (for a full list of project options for the Social Studies connection, see Appendix B). In both cases, the students must work closely with their ELA and Social Studies teachers. When done successfully, the ELA and Social Studies teachers serve as consultants or sounding boards for the students' ideas. Because both the ELA and the Social Studies teachers will grade these components in their classes, they have a vested interest in helping the students complete their tasks. The actual finished product is then posted to the students' project websites (Task 8) and ultimately referenced in their final project videos (Task 12).

To better highlight the interdisciplinary success in level II projects, a real experience reported by a teacher should be examined. In this experience, the student approached his Social Studies teacher after class and asked if he could set up a time to meet and discuss the Social Studies connection to his project. After working out a

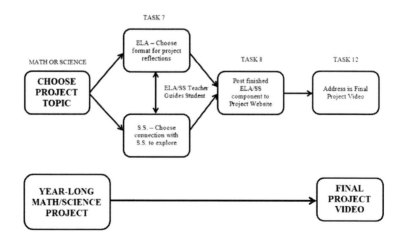

Figure 4. Map of ELA/SS in level II projects.

ten-minute window convenient for both parties, the teacher asked the student to bring a brief explanation of his project, his ELA connection choice and some brainstormed questions that might help them discover a connection. When the meeting took place, the teacher reported that the student was prepared and conducted the interaction in a professional manner. The student wanted to collect data with which he could compare common cultural explanations for phenomena that he was analyzing. Needless to say, his Social Studies teacher was delighted. Perhaps the best part was that the student did not merely want the teacher to explain the connection; rather, the student had prepared a series of questions to ask the teacher, enabling the Social Studies teacher to assist the student through a conversation, without any additional preparatory work.

INCREASED RELEVANCE LEADS TO INCREASED STUDENT ENGAGEMENT

There are several ways in which the skills and processes learned when completing the projects described above are directly relevant to students. First, and probably most distant in students' minds, is that the processes develop the 21st century skills necessary for our highly specialized and increasingly STEM-focused economy. Secondly, this project model moves students towards college readiness by developing skills related to collaboration, time management and approaching experts within their educational communities. Finally, and perhaps most immediate in students' minds, are the projects' connections to real-world dilemmas and the numerous paths of inquiry provided. This increase in relevance directly leads to an increase in student engagement for a variety of reasons that will now be discussed.

Participation in the STEM SOS model helps ELA and Social Studies teachers create both a relevant learning environment and an engaged classroom. Research shows that students are more likely to be engaged if they "know why something is important, personally relevant, and worthy of their attention" (Saphier, 2008, p. 20). In a world increasingly oriented towards STEM, being able to include interdisciplinary connections within the ELA and Social Studies classrooms helps this cause. The real-world scenario, which is the starting point for all STEM SOS projects, requires students to apply educational skills from numerous disciplines. This element opens up each project to student choice in a way that creates novelty in every student's project. As students chart their own path, they gain a feeling of ownership and pride in their work. In fact, students often comment on how they feel like adults when completing these projects. Most real-world problems require interdisciplinary solutions and collaboration with experts. When students are asked to approach their ELA or Social Studies teachers to gain information to help them complete a Math or Science project, it is not unlike a college student conducting research and meeting with a professor in a related field to gain further insight. The skill of knowing one's own schedule well enough to setup and attend a meeting creates a sense of professionalism that will serve students well in college and the workforce.

The STEM SOS model also gives teachers the necessary platform to positively affect students' emotional states, as their range of emotions can be directly related to their level of engagement. Each project provides opportunities for high-energy engagement through vibrant group discussions and teacher-led demonstrations. On the other hand, by creating time for students to reflect upon and make connections to past learning, calm, purposeful, yet low-pressure opportunities also arise. In fact, the STEM SOS model provides the opportunity for teachers to implement many commonly recommended principles for increasing student engagement, such as purposeful framing of learning, periodic breaks for processing learning, adjusting the learning experience to the student and being mindful of the students' skill-level before starting projects.

INTERDISCIPLINARY INSTRUCTION AS A PATH TO BEST PRACTICES

In the paragraphs above, the argument was made that the STEM SOS model presents students with unique interdisciplinary experiences within ELA and Social Studies classrooms during level I projects and across Math or Science classrooms during level II projects. In order to accomplish this task, the classroom teachers involved find themselves implementing commonly held best practices in instruction by necessity. What follows is an analysis of that path using *The Skillful Teacher* as a guide, a widely referenced book that summarizes decades of educational research into a set of skills. Of particular interest will be the section related to creating more effective and enduring learning experiences (Saphier, 2008) and the section that presents a variety of teaching models.

Teachers are often encouraged to ensure the cognitive impact of the learning experience within the classroom. The STEM SOS model urges teachers to create situations that are analogous to those that professionals in these fields might experience in real life. This allows teachers to practice what is commonly referred to as "application in setting" (Saphier, 2008). By doing so, the students are forced to utilize interdisciplinary knowledge, as mentioned above. This process creates an opportunity for the teacher to encourage students' metacognition by isolating the critical attributes of learning that went into each stage of the project, another critical element of cognitive impact. This active participation in the learning experience generates levels of engagement in students that are critical for enduring learning (Saphier, 2008). Other elements often argued as critical to enduring learning experiences that the STEM SOS model also provides include goal-setting opportunities, open-minded thinking, consistent guidance, logical sequence and chances for cumulative review. The latter serves as a particularly useful side effect of the interdisciplinary elements of the STEM SOS model.

Teachers often encounter presentations on a variety of "models of teaching" that create different roles for both the teacher and the student (Saphier, 2008). The STEM SOS model as a whole creates settings in which many of these models can be implemented. The interdisciplinary elements act as the catalyst for the implementation of these commonly held best practices in teaching.

Figure 5. A student demonstrating his Level II project. (Please use your QR reader to scan the QR codes to watch the video and/or see his e-portfolio website).

To begin, the task-oriented yearlong projects and the multi-day/weeklong projects both ensure a progressive layering of concepts. This model of gradually increasing the complexity of concepts from step to step allows ample room for formative assessment and reflection on learning on the part of the student (Saphier, 2008). The interdisciplinary elements enter these projects at appropriate times in order to increase the complexity of knowledge gained by the student. Each step in the project is logically connected to the preceding one and requires the student to employ and fine-tune their analytic skills on a regular basis. This analysis, which is in and of itself a common model of teaching, usually asks the students to use past knowledge to create new knowledge or to use inductive thinking, another frequently referenced model. The interdisciplinary elements embed inductive thinking into the skeletal framework of each project in the STEM SOS model. Other models for teaching routinely implemented by educators within this model include the use of sharing learning experiences with others, acquiring responsibility for one's own learning through planning and group investigation (Saphier, 2008).

HOW THE SOS MODEL OVERCOMES COMMON LIMITATIONS OF INTERDISCIPLINARY PBLS

The implementation of any new method for instruction usually meets with some degree of resistance and growing pains as teachers, students and administrators learn and adapt to the new method. Interdisciplinary instruction, as a model, has routinely been said to be great in idea and very difficult in implementation. Some limitations of interdisciplinary PBLs have included time constraints for planning and executing within one classroom and the coordination time required between teachers across different classrooms. In addition, students often possess different skill and content levels and teachers may find this and the lack of a day-to-day classroom routine to be challenging (Capraro, 2012). It can be argued, however, that the STEM SOS model can overcome these common limitations.

Frequently, educators seem to point to the finite amount of time in class with students, as they often feel as though they do not have enough time to employ all of their great ideas. The STEM SOS model attempts to deal with this in several ways. At Level I, the projects are intended to be completed within five class periods and teachers are encouraged to spread these class periods out in order to relieve the pressure of planning for a weeklong project in their classroom. Teachers are provided with materials for projects, including rubrics, handouts and presentation materials, and a specific protocol exists that allows the teachers to modify these provided materials for their students if necessary. Therefore, the teacher is not starting from scratch, but rather adapting a project idea to fit their classroom. At Level II, the projects are broken down into a series of tasks with time windows spread out across the entire school year. This coordination is done by administration and instructional coaches who ensure compliance by individual teachers. Removing much of the *planning* burden from teachers allows them to focus on improving projects across disciplines during staff and department meetings. In essence, the STEM SOS model's tight structure, combined with the degree of intellectual freedom allowed within that structure, is conducive to instinctual rather than planned interdisciplinary learning.

Establishing habits in learning through classroom routines is often the bedrock of a well-managed classroom. The fact that after the first day of a STEM SOS project, the teacher often steps into the background can be unnerving. In addition, students participating in the projects may be in advanced classes in Math or Science and mainstream classes in Social Studies and English, or vice versa, making it very difficult to craft a project that appropriately suits their needs. The STEM SOS model overcomes this at Level I by containing the interdisciplinary elements within a content-area classroom. At Level II, the project is chosen based on the level of the Math or Science classroom and is designed to take up limited classroom time in Social Studies and ELA. By turning the Social Studies and ELA teachers into experts whom the students contact during the project, the burden of including coordinated lessons across content areas is shifted from the teacher to the student. At both levels, then, the classroom experience is dramatically shifted from the traditional, teacher-driven learning experience to a clear, student-centered endeavor. The learning curve for this is generally quick; teachers often report uneasiness at first, but after the first experience, usually report positive student feedback and confidence that their students participated in a meaningful learning experience. Over time, as teachers share these experiences with other teachers, this reluctance to step off the stage is generally overcome.

CREATING AN INTERDISCIPLINARY SCHOOL CULTURE

There are several things a school system can do to encourage the creation of an interdisciplinary school culture. First, time and space must be created for teachers to work together across disciplines and within content areas. This can be done through many different methods such as common planning periods, PLCs or professional development sessions. Second, department chairs and instructional coaches working with each other across disciplines can assist in detecting weaknesses in communication between the parties involved, as well as identifying common issues with projects. This constant feedback process positively reinforces a shift towards a more interdisciplinary school culture. Third, and possibly most importantly, administrators and teachers alike must learn to trust their students and hold them accountable; these two shifts in mentality go hand in hand. The core belief of the STEM SOS model is that when learning is facilitated by a teacher and controlled by the student, the experience is bolstered and the learning is more enduring. Teachers must learn to let certain students run with interesting ideas even if they do not meet their original assumptions about the project's path and destination. At the same time, administrators must communicate specific expectations for learning outcomes, and teachers must hold their students accountable for reaching those learning outcomes via whatever path the students choose to take. In short, creating an interdisciplinary school culture involves creating a goal-oriented, yet open-minded approach to learning for all participants.

REFERENCES

Capraro, M. M., & Jones, M. (2012). Interdisciplinary STEM project-based learning. In R. M. Capraro, M. M. Capraro & J. Morgan (Eds.), *Project-based learning: An integrated science, technology, engineering, and mathematics (STEM) approach* (2nd ed.). Rotterdam, The Netherlands: Sense.

Media Smarts. *Digital literacy fundamentals.* Retrieved from: http://mediasmarts.ca/digital-media-literacy-fundamentals/

Sahin, A., Top, N., & Almus, K. (2014). *Teachers' reflections on STEM students on the stage (SOS)™ model (Whitepaper).* Retrieved from http://www.harmonytx.org/Portals/0/HPS%20Issue-2.pdf

Sahin, A., Top, N., & Vanegas, S. (2014). *Harmony STEM SOS model increases college readiness and develops 21st century skills* (Whitepaper). Retrieved from http://harmonytx.org/Portals/0/HPS_Issue-1.pdf

Saphier, J. (2008). *The skillful teacher: Building your teaching skills* (6th ed.). Acton, MA: Research for Better Teaching.

Morison, S. E. (1936). *Harvard College in the seventeenth century.* Cambridge, MA: Harvard University Press.

Baldwin, R. G. (1996). Faculty career stages and implications for professional development. In D. Finnegan, D. Webster & Z. F. Gamson (Eds.), *Faculty and faculty issues in colleges and universities* (2nd ed.). Boston, MA: Pearson Custom Publishing.

Robert Thornton
Harmony Public Schools

Keri Bell
Harmony Public Schools

APPENDICES

APPENDIX A: THE ENGLISH/LANGUAGE ARTS CONNECTION OF THE LEVEL II PBL

- Students will select at least one of the options below to complete during the process of developing their Level II project, or will obtain ELA teacher-permission to pursue a different option.
- Teachers/campuses should determine specific assessment criteria for their students' projects.

ELA Project Options

1. **Journal**: This assignment provides students with a platform to consistently reflect on all aspects of their project throughout the entire project experience.

   a. Students should have 10 journal entries spanning at least 9 weeks of school.
   b. Students should write the date and entry # at the top of each new entry.
   c. Entries must be a minimum of 7-8 complete, grammatically correct sentences.
   d. Entries may be on a variety of topics, including but not limited to:

      i. The process of developing your project idea
      ii. The process of obtaining background research
      iii. The experience of seeking assistance from a teacher or another peer
      iv. Your thoughts on diagrams or visuals
      v. our plans for project revisions
      vi. Details and outcomes of each experiment
      vii. Daily successes or frustrations
      viii. How this project might assist with future career goals

2. **Argumentative Essay**: This style of essay requires students to investigate a topic; to collect, generate, and evaluate evidence; and to establish a position on the topic in a concise manner (*Purdue Online Writing Lab*).

   a. Essay must be a minimum of 800 words (typed in MLA format).
   b. Essay must contain:

      i. An interesting introduction, including a clear, concise thesis statement.

         1. Make sure to include why your topic is important (why readers should care).
         2. Make sure your thesis is *arguing* a claim about your topic/project, and supporting the claim with reasons.

    ii. Clear and logical transitions between paragraphs, as well as in the body of your essay.

    iii. At least three body paragraphs that include supporting *evidence*.

    iv. Evidence

    v. A conclusion that doesn't *restate* the thesis directly, but instead re-examines it in light of the evidence provided.

3. **Narrative Essay**: This style of essay requires students to *tell a story of a personal experience (Purdue Online Writing Lab)*.

    a. Essay must be a minimum of 800 words (typed in MLA format).

    b. Essay must:

        i. Include all the parts of a story (introduction, plot, characters, setting, climax, and conclusion).

        ii. Have a purpose (the *thesis* of your story---your reason for narrating this tale).

        iii. Be written from a clear point of view.

        iv. Use clear and concise language throughout the essay.

        v. Be organized! (Let your introduction set the tone for the rest of your essay)

4. **Newspaper**: This assignment requires students to be creative, identify the parts of a news story, and identify the differences between newspaper and other media sources.

    a. Newspaper must:

        i. Have a title

        ii. Contain at least two visuals, including captions.

        iii. Contain a minimum of 7 articles.

            1. Consider having a variety of articles (headline/feature, editorial, opinion, etc.)

            2. Each article must:

                a. Contain a relevant, interesting title, located at the top (along with the date).

                b. Contain a minimum of 10-12 grammatically correct sentences.

                c. Clearly support your field of study (stay on topic).

                d. Investigate the "5 Ws" (*who, what, when, where, why).*

*Students may also choose to produce an online newspaper.

5. **Interview**: This assignment is designed to help students grow in their fields of study by giving them the opportunity to have a conversation with someone who has done similar studies.

a. For the interview, you must:

   i. Identify someone who is considered to be "knowledgeable" on your topic (someone from whom you can deepen your project knowledge).

     *Consider local professionals in your field of study, teachers, or college students majoring in your field of study.
     *Consider recording your interview (to assist you when writing your report), and take notes on each question.
     *Make sure to thank your interviewee.

   ii. Include a brief statement explaining your rationale for selecting this person.

   iii. Include a minimum of 10 thoughtful, probing questions that clearly demonstrate your desire to learn more about your field of study.

   iv. Write a short report explaining what you learned and how it will aid you in your field of study.

     1. Begin by describing the interview circumstances and relevant project details.
     2. Summarize your interviewee's responses to each question.
     3. Write a short biography of the person you interviewed based on the interview conducted.
     4. Conclude with a list of relevant lessons you learned for growth in your field of study.
     5. Attach the final list of questions you took to the interview.

     * Bradley Dilger, Western Illinois University

APPENDIX B: THE SOCIAL STUDIES CONNECTION OF THE LEVEL II PBL

○ Students will select at least one of the options below to complete during the process of developing their Level II project, or will obtain SS teacher-permission to pursue a different option.

○ Teachers/campuses should determine specific assessment criteria for their students' projects.

Social Studies Project Options

1. **Historical Connection:** Students should be encouraged to examine the historical connections to a math or science problem. They can do this by exploring an event in the past that might be related to the discovery, or an effect of the discovery on an event that had happened as a result. For example, if a student is investigating air presser, they can include how air pressure is related to the discovery of flight. (From the discovery of hot air balloons in the 18th century, all the way through space travel).

2. **Economic Influence:** Students can connect a scientific discovery with its economic impact. For example they can explain the discovery of radio waves, and the impact that has had on business and trade. Or explain how a new product has revolutionized an industry (GM Foods) or has caused the destruction of an existing economy.

3. **Political influence:** Students could investigate the role politics plays in their topic of choice. They can trace the influence governments have on funding particular research programs or how much funding is directed towards developing new scientists. Conversely, students could explore how science influences politics, such as the discovery of "greenhouse gases."

4. **Geographical influence:** Students can look at how their topic can be observed in the natural world, and investigate if geography is an influence. As volcanoes, geysers and hurricanes all have geographical influences students can make these connections and explain how these forces affect all of us.

5. **Effect of change on Society:** Students can show how the topic of their project has influenced the way we live. Students investigating the development of computers, and show how this technology has revolutionized our whole world. Or how discoveries in the medical fields have changed the life expectancy, and what impact this has on culture.

6. **Legal impact:** Students can also look at how scientific and mathematical discoveries have impacted our legal system. The discovery of steam power directly led to the Gibbons Vs. Ogden Supreme court case, which decided several aspects of federal power in the United States.

PAM SRINIVASAN

8. ASSESSMENTS IN STEM SOS

This chapter describes the multi-tiered Harmony Public Schools assessment model for measuring student growth and progress through the completion of STEM SOS projects. An overview of the Harmony STEM SOS Model project is presented described to enable an understanding of the various components of the assessment framework in relation to student products and learning outcomes (Sahin & Top, In press; Sahin, Top, & Vanessa, 2014).

INTRODUCTION

The current curricula for science, math, and technology for secondary schools reflect an increasing emphasis on deeper or more rigorous content and higher-order cognitive processing. Many teachers struggle to simultaneously develop and implement instruction at the mandated curriculum level and meet the needs of diverse learners in the classroom. Student achievement is dependent on the alignment between the written, taught and tested curriculum (Squires, 2012).

While there are a variety of assessment and evaluation tools available for the teacher to monitor student progress in these areas, it can be challenging to determine whether assessment tools truly evaluate student progress in content and process and whether assessment is aligned with the curriculum and learning at each phase. According to Demers (2000), there is a need in science for assessment that evaluates students on their ability to demonstrate their understanding of the scientific process in a meaningful, hands-on fashion. He discusses performance-based assessment tools such as task questions and rubrics that evaluate students' understanding of content as well as mastery of the scientific process. A research study by McMillan and Lawson (2001) of the assessment practices of secondary teachers found a wide range of practices; performance-based assessment and higher-order cognitive processing were primarily used as assessments by teachers of higher-ability students while, conversely, teachers of lower-ability students emphasized recall knowledge and homework and placed less emphasis on academic achievement and higher order thinking.

The Harmony assessment model for STEM projects is a work in progress, but a deliberate attempt has been made to align that assessment to the curriculum and instruction within each course. Opportunities for growth and improvement during learning are built into the architecture of assessment. The shift towards student ownership of learning and self-assessment is another distinct feature of the Harmony assessment model.

A. Sahin (Ed.), A Practice-based Model of STEM Teaching, 111–120.

FOUNDATIONS FOR HARMONY STEM SOS

The foundation for the Harmony STEM projects is based on the eight essential criteria for meaningful project-based learning (PBL) experiences outlined by the Buck Institute for Education (Larmer & Mergendoller, 2010). These essentials are summarized below and are inherent to the project at all phases, including assessment.

1. *Significant content:* The project focuses on important knowledge and concepts derived from the standards and targets essential understanding in the course; further, students should find the content to be significant in terms of their own lives and interests. A well-designed PBL is an effective vehicle for understanding content more deeply than is possible with traditional methods such as lectures and textbooks.
2. *A Need to Know:* Teachers activate students' need to know content by launching a project with an "entry event" that engages student interest and initiates questioning. At Harmony, this entry event may occur within the context of the course. The PBL experience adds meaning and the need to know what is being taught; with a compelling student project, the reason for learning relevant material becomes personal and purposeful to the student.
3. *A Driving Question:* Students create a driving question on which they focus their efforts. A good driving question captures the heart of the project in clear, compelling language and allows students to understand why they are undertaking a project as well as the sequence of activities that ensue from their personal challenge. At Harmony, the student's crafting of the question is customized and coached by the teacher, based on student capability.
4. *Student Choice and Voice:* Students' choices and voices make the project meaningful to them. The more voice and choice is given to the student, the greater is the ownership of learning. At Harmony, teachers design projects to the extent of student choice that fits their students.
5. *21ˢᵗ Century Skills:* Collaboration is central to the PBL learning experience. Students work in teams of three or four to plan and conduct tasks related to their project. Each team regularly takes time to review their progress. The project provides students with opportunities to build valuable 21ˢᵗ century skills such as collaboration, communication, critical thinking and the use of technology, all of which will serve them well in both the workplace and in life.
6. *Inquiry and Innovation:* Project work becomes more meaningful to students as they conduct real inquiry in which they follow a trail that begins with their own questions and leads to a search for resources and the discovery of answers, which ultimately leads to generating new questions, testing ideas and drawing their own conclusions. With real inquiry comes innovation – a new answer to a driving question, a new product and a new solution to a problem.
7. *Feedback and Revision:* As students develop their ideas and products, student teams review and critique one another's work, referring to rubrics and exemplars. The mentoring process of monitoring and feedback is formalized and structured

so that all student teams have guidance from their teacher throughout the duration of the project. Through the mentoring process, students learn that first attempts do not typically result in high-quality work and that revisions are a frequent feature of the real world. Teachers arrange for experts or adult mentors to provide feedback, which is especially meaningful to students because of the source.

8. *Publicly Presented Product:* At Harmony, student teams have ample opportunities to present their findings and solutions to a range of audiences, including peers, parents, representatives from the community and government organizations and professionals from various industries. Students answer questions and reflect on how they completed the project, the next steps they might take and what they gained in terms of knowledge, skills and pride. When students present their work to a real audience, they connect to real life through their PBL projects.

The Project-based Learning initiative, launched during the 2013–2014 school year, directly addresses the increased need for students to acquire 21st century skills. The Harmony approach is to maintain the focus on standards-based and student-centered learning while enriching and extending that learning through STEM projects. The goal is to promote not only collaborative skills and student ownership of learning, but also student achievement and success with respect to state and national curriculum standards.

To meet these challenging goals and foster student success at every level, the Harmony program customizes and individualizes the STEM experience for its students while incorporating research from successful PBL programs into the programs' design and structure. Technology is integrated into every phase to enable students to progress and complete projects successfully while learning life skills (Sahin, Top, & Vanegas, 2014; Sahin & Top, 2014).

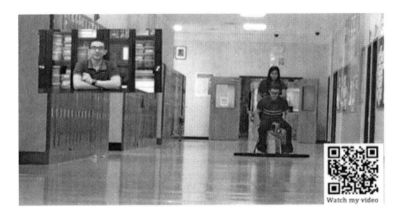

Figure 1. A student demonstrating how a hovercraft works. (Please use your QR reader to scan the QR code to watch the movie).

113

The design of the project incorporates several levels. The first level is curriculum-based and all students complete Level I projects within their coursework. Level I projects allow students to learn the skills necessary to successfully complete individual projects and also provide the scaffolding element that students sometimes need in their growth towards independent learning. Levels II and III provide the opportunity for student choice, interest and inquiry.

ASSESSMENTS IN HARMONY STEM SOS

Since the STEM program at the middle school and high school levels is multi-tiered in its design, the assessment model follows a similar structure. A summary of the Harmony Public Schools STEM program is outlined in table 1 prior to a discussion of the various components in the assessment.

Level I projects occur within the context of coursework in the core subjects and are assessed as part of the grading cycle by the respective teachers. The Level I project constitutes an authentic and alternate assessment within the grading cycle, measuring complex skills far beyond mere content knowledge. The project provides several opportunities for a formative assessment of science process, technical and scientific inquiry skills.

Students are expected to submit a Level I investigative report for their projects via Google Drive as Google documents. Templates for the completion of the investigations and report are downloadable from the project website. In Level I, students are expected to learn the content and processes necessary for successfully conducting long-term individual projects. As a result, the assessment emphasis is on the investigative report that shows evidence of student growth in content and inquiry process. Rubrics used for grading Level I projects are available for students and parents; students learn to use the rubric to evaluate their own projects before

Table 1. Harmony Level I STEM

Level I	Content/Courses	# of Projects each Semester	Time	Work Structure
High School	English	1 Project	1 week	Small Group
	Math	1 Project	1 week	Small Group
	Social Studies	1 Project	1 week	Small Group
	Science	2 Projects	1 week	Small Group
Middle School	English	1 Project	1 week	Small Group
	Math	1 Project	1 week	Small Group
	Social Studies	1 Project	1 week	Small Group
	Science	1 Project	1 week	Small Group

Investigation Report – Grading Rubric (Chemistry Level I)						Name: Class:

COMPONENT	Excellent = 4 out of 4 criteria (4 pts)	Good (3 pts)	Satis-factory (2 pts)	Needs Work (1 pt)	No Attempt (0 pts)	Total
1. Title, Purpose and Question	• Title is relevant and representative of purpose, • Purpose clearly identified and stated • Includes question to be investigated • Variables are clearly articulated					
2. Experimental Design/Plan	• Plan is based on sound reasoning • Step by step process is articulated logically • Diagrams or flow charts are provided as necessary • Includes safety precautions based on a review of MSDS and safety regulations					
3. Materials, Procedure and Safety	• Materials and equipment listed • Description of altered or added procedures as per the plan • Reasons for the change in procedures • Description of altered or added safety as per the plan					
4. Data/ Observations	• Data presented in tables with labels and units • Significant figures in measurement visible • Qualitative observations written clearly • Graphs provided as necessary					
5. Calculations	• Step by step work is shown • Significant figures are used in computation • Final results are shown with correct units and significant figures • Percent error calculations are shown					
6. Analysis and Conclusions	• Outcome of investigation discussed clearly • Actual data is used to support discussion • Inferences based on observed data is articulated • Error is analyzed using scientific reasoning					
7. Application and Extension	• Relevance to personal experience discussed (What did I learn?) • Relation to real life is identified (Where do I see this concept in real life?) • Applications of the concept learned (Where can I use this?) • Extension of the concept described (Given this, what is the next step?)					
8. Lab Protocols	• Report submitted as directed • On time • Directions and safety protocols were followed • Stations were cleaned and tidied					
9. Report Format	• No errors in spelling, punctuation, grammar • Report is written/typed neatly as specified • Details and specifics are included • Well organized					
10. Collaboration and Contribution	• All members participate equally in design • All members participate in investigation • All members participate in discussion • Oral presentation clear and well presented					
Total Points for Investigation (Maximum 40 points)						

Figure 2. Sample rubric for investigation report.

submission and also to evaluate peer projects. A sample rubric used to assess a Chemistry Level I investigation is shown.

In addition to the investigative report, students also create a digital presentation. Students select which type of digital presentation they would like to create, including: a photo story, photo gallery, and video or movie presentation. Training videos for development and uploading of the digital product are also available to students as they develop their digital skills. The digital product provides ample opportunity for students to learn and develop their technology skills. Informal formative assessment is implemented for the digital portion for Level I as students' skill sets are extremely diverse at this time. Monitoring and coaching are provided as needed for students to learn and master technology skills.

The weight of the project in the grading cycle is predetermined by each teacher. Students and parents are informed of the weight of the project before the start of the project. That weight may vary across coursework and grading cycles. For example, the Level I project in Chemistry may count as a lab grade for the quarter while the Level I project in Geometry may count as a test grade for the semester. Also, the Level I project in Chemistry may count as a lab grade in the first quarter, but may

Figure 3. A student demonstrating her Level II project. (Please use your QR reader to scan the QR code to watch her demonstration and/or see her website).

count as two lab grades in the second quarter. In middle school, the Level I project in Science may count as a lab grade and, in Math, may count as a quiz grade. This customization and variation is done to ensure that the assessment matches students' effort and the complexity of the tasks involved.

The timelines and deliverables for Level I projects are discussed in class so that student groups understand the expectations. Although the suggested timeline for completion of each Level I project is about one week, the actual amount of class time may vary slightly based on students' ability.

Harmony Level II and III STEM

Level II and Level III projects begin early in the school year and continue throughout the year. These are individual projects and students choose their topic of interest from one of two areas in high school: Science or Math, and from one of three areas in middle school: Science, Math, or Engineering. The only difference between a Level II and a Level III project is the extent of student-driven inquiry. Level III projects are completed by high school students almost entirely independently with very little support and guidance from the teacher. Middle school students only complete Level II projects. The assessment structure for Level II and III projects is the same since both types of yearlong projects have essentially the same design. The intent of this differentiation and customization in the Harmony STEM project model is to accommodate the needs of Harmony students who vary widely in their inquiry skills. For Level II projects, students select a topic of interest from the provided list of activities and inquiry questions. This allows them to develop a framework for exercising their choice and voice instead of trying to develop their project from the limitless options in the real world. The Level II project also helps in vertical articulation of support for struggling middle school students as they move to high school.

The grading weight of a Level II or III project is anywhere from 10% to 20% of the course grade and is predetermined by the Math or Science teachers. As soon as students choose their topic area, they are assigned to their Math or Science teacher for coaching and mentoring.

Since the project begins at the start of the school year and proceeds through various phases throughout the school year, managing it is very important. To help students pace themselves through the project and to avoid a frenzy at the end of the year, a checklist of tasks with accompanying due dates is provided to students and parents; this checklist also helps teachers monitor student progress in the project. Steps for students to improve their project and for catching up are built into the task list. This measure is necessary to accommodate student growth and progress. The assessment follows the same pattern. Students are graded on an improved product during the "makeup" step, which helps them strive to create a better product. A sample Level II or III Project task list from the website for high school Science or Math is shown below:

Details and a step-by-step guide for completing each task are available online through instructions and training videos. Students meet periodically with their teacher to discuss progress and troubleshoot any difficulties with project completion. Communication between students and teachers throughout the project occurs via a Google site specifically created for this purpose. The communication history also provides a valuable record and tool for assessment of project growth.

Assessment of projects is completed in Math/Science content areas by the respective teachers using rubrics. Like the Level I projects, students complete an investigative report as well as a digital presentation, story, or gallery and the rubric used for evaluating the investigative report is identical to the one used for Level I. Students develop an understanding of this rubric through repeated use. In Level II/III, the investigative reports and digital products are assessed using different rubrics. A portion of the rubric used to evaluate a digital story at the middle school is shown.

Harmony students complete their STEM projects by the end of the third quarter so that they are ready to participate in events and contests to exhibit their projects and gain a real-world perspective from the judges, who offer advice and suggestions relating to their projects. Students also exhibit their projects online so viewers can provide feedback.

Some of the events in which Harmony students participate are:

- Harmony Schools Share and Shine (School-based and districtwide)
- T-STEM activities statewide

FIRST GRADING PERIOD (1st Quarter):
TASK 1: Create your e-portfolio (Google Site) and Choose your Project (Graded by Science or Math Teacher)
TASK 2: Present Background research and maintain your project materials (Graded by Science or Math Teacher)
TASK 3: Creating "About My School" page (Graded by Science or Math Teacher)
TASK 4 & TASK 5 : Creating "My PBL Project" page (Graded by Science or Math Teacher)
TASK 6: Post "investigation part" to your PBL Page (Graded by Science or Math Teacher)
SECOND GRADING PERIOD (2nd Quarter):
TASK 7: Choosing the ELA and SS (Social Studies) components of your project (Graded by ELA and SS Teacher)
TASK 8: Posting the ELA component and SS connection. (Graded by ELA and SS Teacher)
TASK 9 & TASK 10: PBL Video Presentation (Digital Story) (Graded by Science or Math Teacher)
TASK 11: Designing and Publishing Project Brochure (Graded by Science or Math Teacher)
TASK 12: Movie Presentation - ELA component and SS Connection (Graded by ELA and Social Studies Teacher)
THIRD GRADING PERIOD (3rd Quarter):
This quarter will be a make-up period, teachers will grade previous tasks from 1st and 2nd quarter again, so that the students will have chance to improve and update their projects. The students who are falling behind may work on completing the missing tasks.
TASK 13: "My School" Page (Graded by Science or Math Teacher) This task is make-up for TASK 3.
TASK 14: "My PBL Project" Page (Graded by Science or Math Teacher) This task is make-up for TASK 4 and TASK 5.
TASK 15: Video Presentation (Graded by Science or Math Teacher) This task is make-up for TASK 9 and TASK 10.
TASK 16: Homepage and Brochure (Graded by Science or Math Teacher) This task is make-up for TASK 11.
TASK 17: "ELA component" and "SS connection" Page (Graded by ELA and Social Studies Teachers) This task is make-up for TASK 8.
TASK 18: Movie Presentation - ELA component and SS connection (Graded by ELA and Social Studies Teachers) This task is make-up for TASK 12.

Figure 4. Sample level II or III project task.

- INTEL - ISEF Regional and State Science Fairs
- International I-SWEEEP Olympiad organized by Harmony Public Schools
- Google Science Fair
- DISTCO Digital Story Contest
- Robotics contests – EARLY, LEGO, BEST, and USFIRST
- STEM festivals and Expo

Participating in these online and actual public events provides students with multiple opportunities to demonstrate their understanding, progress to a greater level of understanding and take ownership of their learning.

Digital Presentation Rubric - Delivery			Middle School PBL
CATEGORY	**4 - Advanced**	**3 - Proficient**	**2 - Progressing**	**1 - Beginning**

CATEGORY	**4 - Advanced**	**3 - Proficient**	**2 - Progressing**	**1 - Beginning**
Presentation	Narrative is clear, easy to understand, and well-rehearsed (without "umm", "uhhh" etc). Delivery holds audience attention.	Narrative is clear, easy to understand, and well-rehearsed (without "umm", "uhhh" etc). There are no unnecessary pauses in the narrative. Relatively interesting delivery that usually holds audience attention.	Narrative is for the most part clear and easy to understand. There may be a few "umm", "uhhh" etc. There are a few unnecessary pauses in the narrative. Delivery not smooth, but able to hold audience attention most of the time.	Narrative is hard to understand, there may be mumbling. Frequent unnecessary pauses. "umm" and "uhh" etc. Delivery not smooth and audience attention lost.
Voice	Voice quality is clear and consistently audible throughout the presentation. The pace (rhythm and punctuation) "fits" the storyline.	Voice quality is clear and consistently audible throughout the majority (85-95%) of the presentation. Occasionally speaks too fast or too slowly.	Voice quality is clear and consistently audible through some (70-84%) of the presentation. Pacing often does not fit the story line.	Voice quality needs more attention. No attempt to match the pace of the storytelling to the story line.
Video/Sound Quality	Overall, the video resolution and sound quality is exceptionally good. The video or sound does not distract form the story	Overall, the video resolution and sound quality is good. The video or sound somewhat distracts from story	Overall, the video resolution and sound quality are low but within acceptable limits. The video or sound distracts from the story	Overall, the video resolution and sound quality is too low to understand the content. The video or sound greatly distract from the story
Images	The pictures chosen or images drawn are exceptional and appropriate and support the content well	The pictures chosen or images drawn are appropriate and somewhat support the content	The pictures chosen or images drawn are acceptable. An attempt was made but it needed more work. Image choice is logical.	The pictures chosen or images drawn are limited and may not support the content. Little or no attempt to use images to communicate ideas.
Creativity & Copyright	Product shows a lot of original thought. Ideas are creative and inventive. Any outside sources used have been cited (images, quotes, facts, data, etc.).	Product shows some original thought. Work shows new ideas and insights. Effort to cite outside sources (images, quotes, facts, data, etc.) is evident.	Uses other people's ideas (giving them credit), but there is little evidence of original thinking.	None of the work seems original. Uses other people's ideas, but does not give them credit.

Figure 5. Sample rubric.

CONCLUSION

According to Popham (2001), "If we want to find out if students are capable of using a skill in a variety of settings, we must measure mastery of the skill in a variety of ways and teach students to demonstrate mastery in those various ways" (p. 115). Harmony pushes far beyond measuring student mastery of a skill in various settings, seeking to develop students' 21st century skills through the STEM project and attempting to measure the growth of these skills while still remaining grounded in its educational philosophy and mandated curriculum. Disseminating physical aspects of the curriculum is easier than propagating the fundamental philosophy on which a school designs its program. Harmony has made a significant move in this direction. Through the STEM program, Harmony has demonstrated its commitment to its fundamental educational principles of student inquiry and student success. While the Harmony STEM program in its various facets of design, implementation, and assessment is still a work in progress, it has made a significant impact on students. Students enjoy working on the projects without being aware that they are thinking critically and creatively while learning 21st century skills. The STEM SOS project is a powerful tool to promote autonomous, meaningful learning and understanding and mastery of content.

REFERENCES

Bauer, C. F., & Cole, R. (2012). Validation of an assessment rubric via controlled modification of a classroom activity. *Journal of Chemical Education, 89*(9), 1104–1108.

Britton, T. (2011). Using formative and alternative assessments to support instruction and measure student learning. *Science Scope, 34*(5), 16–21.

Demers, C. (2000). Beyond paper-and-pencil assessments. Science and Children, 38(2), 24–29.

Doran, R., Chan, F., & Tamir, P. (1998). Science educator's guide to assessment. Arlington, VA: National Science Teachers Association.

Grant, M. (2002). *Getting a grip on project-based learning: Theory, cases and recommendations.* Retrieved from http://www.ncsu.edu/meridian/win2002/514

Larmer, J., & Mergendoller, J. (2010). *8 essentials for project-based learning.* Retrieved from http://www.bie.org/tools/freebies/Project-based Learning for the 21st Century

McMillan, S. R., & Lawson, V. (2001). *Secondary science teachers' classroom assessment and grading practices.* Richmond, VA: Metropolitan Educational Research Consortium.

Miedijensky, S., & Tal, T. (2009). Embedded assessment in project-based science courses for the gifted: Insights to inform teaching all students. *International Journal of Science Education, 31*(18), 2411–2435.

Popham, W. J. (2001). *The truth about testing: An educator's call to action.* Alexandria, VA: ASCD.

Rivet, A. E., & Kastens, K. A. (2012). Developing a construct-based assessment to examine students' analogical reasoning around physical models in Earth Science. *Journal of Research in Science Teaching, 49*(6), 713–743.

Sahin, A., & Top, N. (in press). Make it happen: A study of a novel teaching style, STEM Students on the Stage (SOS)™, for increasing students' STEM knowledge and interest. *The Journal of STEM Education: Innovations and Research.*

Sahin, A., Top, N., & Vanegas, S. (2014). *Harmony STEM SOS model increases college readiness and develops 21st century skills* (Whitepaper). Retrieved from http://harmonytx.org/Portals/0/HPS_Issue-1.pdf

Solomon, G. (2003). *Project-based learning: A primer.* Retrieved from http://www.techlearning.com/db_area/archives/TL/2003/01/project.php

Squires, D. (2012). Curriculum alignment research suggests that alignment can improve student achievement. *The Clearing House: A Journal of Educational Strategies, Issues and Ideas, 85*(4), 129–135.

FARJANA YASMIN AND LEVENT SAKAR

9. TRACKING OF STUDENTS AND TEACHERS AND INCENTIVES

INTRODUCTION[1]

In 2013, Harmony Public School (HPS) started a program called STEM (Science, Technology, Engineering and Math) Student on the Stage (STEM SOS) with the help of a Race to the Top District grant (RTT-D). Instead of traditional, long-term in-class PBL projects, Harmony Public School's STEM SOS model incorporates three different levels of STEM SOS projects. As students complete these projects, they develop college readiness and 21st century abilities such as collaboration, presentation skills, technology skills and problem-solving skills (Sahin & Top, in press; Sahin, Top, & Vanegas, 2014). This chapter describes the characteristics of the three different levels of STEM SOS projects, the tracking system used to monitor progress of these projects and incentives provided to both teachers and students.

STEM SOS LEVEL I, II AND III PROJECTS

The STEM SOS Level I project lays the foundation for the STEM SOS Level II and Level III projects. Level I projects are completed in class, normally within a week. In contrast, Level II and III projects are yearlong and are primarily completed outside of class as individual projects. Level I and Level II projects are directly aligned with the state's standards and local curriculum. Students work in collaborative groups for Level I projects. Teachers are required to do at least one Level I projects in class per nine weeks. During this time, teachers do direct instruction with students, lay the foundation for the projects and teach science process and technology skills that are further required for the STEM SOS Level II and III projects (Sahin et al., 2014).

According to Harmony Public School's Race to the Top Grant STEM SOS initiative handbook (2013), STEM SOS Level I, Level II and Level III have the following characteristics.

Level I STEM SOS project

- Aligned to Texas Essential Knowledge and Skills (TEKS) for each grade level and/or subject
- Aligned to Harmony Public School's curriculum
- One Level I project is completed each quarter (total of four, in a year).

A. Sahin (Ed.), A Practice-based Model of STEM Teaching, 121–129.

- Each core subject (Mathematics, Science, English Language Arts and Social Studies) requires Level I projects.
- Project is completed in class.
- Completion takes approximately one week.
- Group of 3-4 students work in collaboration
- Teacher provides direct instruction, demonstration and guided lab to help students develop necessary skills to design an inquiry lab.
- Students design and carry out their own inquiry lab.
- Students produce a digital presentation about their inquiry lab.
- Students present their digital presentation in class to peers.

Level II STEM SOS Project

- Aligned to Texas Essential Knowledge and Skills (TEKS) for each grade level and/or subject
- Aligned to Harmony Public School's curriculum
- One Level II project is completed in a year.
- Interdisciplinary project (English and Social Studies components are embedded in the project.)
- Completed outside of class
- Yearlong projects
- Project completed individually (in some cases, teachers may allow group of two or three students to work together.)
- Teacher provides a list of topics for the students to select projects based on student's interest.
- Students design their own inquiry question and carry out the project.
- Students produce a video presentation, Google Site and an information booklet as final products.
- Students present STEM SOS project to peers and others during various competitions (STEM Festival, local, state and international STEM competitions).

Level III STEM SOS project

- Advanced projects (may not be aligned to State TEKS or HPS's Curriculum)
- Interdisciplinary project
- One Level III project is completed in a year.
- Yearlong projects
- Project is completed individually.
- Student select their topics, develop inquiry question and design their projects.
- Completed outside of class (some projects may be conducted at research facilities or at university labs.)
- Mentors from research facilities or universities may facilitate the project.

- Students produce a video presentation, Google Site and an information booklet as final products.
- Students present STEM SOS projects to their peers and others during various competitions such as the STEM Festival, and local, state and international STEM competitions.

TASK TRACKING SYSTEM

At Harmony Public School (HPS), the STEM SOS model uses a Task Tracking System to monitor teacher and student progress in the STEM SOS Level II and III projects. STEM SOS Level I projects are tracked by core subjects' Curriculum Directors (ELA, Math, Science, Social Studies). Each teacher is required to submit one digital presentation per quarter of a SOS Level I project while STEM SOS Level II and III projects are tracked by several people at HPS due to the large number of individually submitted projects. The Task Tracking System provides a snapshot of where teachers and students are for a particular task at a given time. The information available through the tracking system is then used to provide feedback, support and incentives to teachers and students, as needed. Teachers, administrators, and STEM coaches are able to add information into the various Tracking System components, which are (1) the STEM SOS School Roster for Level II and Level III projects, (2) the Teachers' Task Tracker, (3) the Teachers' Gradebook STEM SOS Assignments Tracker and (4) the Quarterly Progress and Feedback Report to each individual campus.

The SOS School Roster for Level II & Level III Projects

Each campus, depending on size, has between 200 to 500 students with active STEM SOS Level II or Level III projects. The STEM SOS School rosters help keep track of students' general project information such as student's name, teacher's name, student's grade level and section, student's Gmail account, student's Google site link, course name, Level II or III project and project title. Each student's Google site link provides direct access to his/her STEM SOS project. At the beginning of the school year, a common template using a Google Docs spreadsheet is shared by the central office with each of the campuses. Department heads and teachers work together to enter student information on this spreadsheet, which is also directly linked to the Teacher's Task Checklist Tracker (discussed later in this chapter).

The advantage of the school roster is that all project information is kept in a single Google spreadsheet and shared with the school and the central office administrators. Therefore, anyone with the link to the Google spreadsheets can track students' progress on their projects. There is a disadvantage, however, in that, initially, it takes quite a bit of time and effort for teachers to update the spreadsheets with the general information for each student's project.

An example of the school roster is given in Table 1 below:

Table 1. Sample STEM SOS School Roster

Student Name	Grade/ Section	Student's Science or Math Teacher's Name	Student's Gmail account link	Student's Google site Link	Course Name	Level II or Level III Projects	Project Title
Student 1	9A	Teacher 1	Student1@gmail.com	https://Sites.google.com/Student1	Chemistry	Level II	Chromatography
Student 2	10A	Teacher 2	Student2@gmail.com	https://Sites.google.com/Student2	Biology	Level III	Enzyme
Student 3	11B	Teacher 3	Student3@gmail.com	https://Sites.google.com/Student3	Geometry	Level II	Kaleidoscope
Student 4	9C	Teacher 4	Student4@gmail.com	https://Sites.google.com/Student4	Physics	Level II	Roller Coaster

The Teacher's Task Tracker

The Teacher's Task Checklist Tracker is a system used to monitor the progress of students and teachers for STEM SOS Level II and III projects. Again, it has been created using a Google spreadsheet, so that it can be easily shared with clusters and campuses. The most attractive feature of Google documents and spreadsheets is that they are a live document; thus, any time that changes are made, the spreadsheets are instantly updated. Furthermore, a revision history is readily available, with a time-stamp and the name of the person who edited the document.

All parties who have access to the Google spreadsheet can view and/or edit the document, based on the access permission granted. The permission for the Teacher's Task Checklist Tracker is set to "can edit" for the Department Chair and the Cluster Coach. Campus teachers and administrators can "only view" the Google spreadsheet, but cannot enter or edit any data. During Science or Math department meetings, the department chair checks and collects data from the teachers and enters it into the spreadsheets. Table 2 below provides an example of the Teacher's Task

Checklist Tracker, which can include general information about campuses, tasks and assignments and a point system for tracking.

General information. All cluster and campus information is added to the same Google spreadsheets, which allows campus and district administrators easy access to the project's progress or needs for a specific campus.

Tasks and assignments. The Central Office Curriculum Directors set all tasks and assignments for teachers, department heads and cluster coaches. For example, one of the teacher's assignments may be to order materials for the STEM SOS projects or grade student projects or one of the department chair's assignment could be to add student information to the school roster spreadsheet and then share it with the clusters.

Point system. The Teacher's Task Checklist Tracker is based on a point system, which allows administrators to receive a quantitative progress measure. A certain number of points can be gained by completion of each task or assignment. A task may receive fifteen points when fully completed, but only one point for being in progress and, of course, zero points for no work done on it. Cumulative points for each campus are automatically calculated and displayed underneath the campus name as information is added to the tracker(s). Table 2 shows an example in which campus 2 is ahead of campuses 1 and 3 due to points. This point system helps administrators in the campus, district, or central office identify struggling campuses and teachers and provide support accordingly.

Teacher's Gradebook: STEM SOS Assignments Tracker

At the beginning of each quarter, teachers are required to enter the STEM SOS assignments into the gradebook with due dates. These STEM SOS assignments have a consistent title, such as STEM SOS Task 1, Task 2, or Task 3. Each quarter has on average between six and eight tasks. Tasks are defined and assignment details are given on the SOS website for students. For example, the first assignment, STEM SOS Task 1, requires students to create an e-portfolio and select the project topic.

All teachers are required to use the same consistent naming system for each task on the gradebook. Therefore, it becomes easier to keep track of the assignments. During department meetings, the department head can follow each teacher's gradebook and enter the information in the Teacher's Task Checklist Tracker (see Table 2). Also, the cluster STEM coach can check both the school STEM SOS roster (see Table 1) and the gradebook to make sure everything is done correctly. Based on this information, the department chair and the STEM cluster coach can provide support to the teacher.

The STEM SOS Tasks are entered as a major grade on the gradebook; hence, if a student decides not to complete a STEM SOS Task, it can significantly affect his or her overall quarterly grades. Teachers are required to grade these assignments in

Table 2. Sample Teacher's Task Checklist Tracker for Science SOS Level II and Level III Projects

	Directions: This Google spreadsheets is edited by only Science Department Chairs and Cluster STEM Coaches. Administrators and science teachers can only view the data. Select, "Ok" only when the task is fully completed. Select, "In Progress" for task is not fully completed. Select, "No" if the teacher has not started on the task or assignment.	STEM SOS		Houston North Cluster		
		Campus Name		Campus 1	Campus 2	Campus 3
		School Roster Link		School Roster Link	School Roster Link	School Roster Link
	Assignment or task for high school science teachers	Points	In Progress	Total Points (18)	Total Points (61)	Total Points (47)
1	HS Science and Math teachers met and decided on, how they will share the students for Level II and III projects.	(5)	(1)	Ok (5)	Ok (5)	No (5)
2	SOS after school or during school support hour has been scheduled.	(10)	(1)	Ok (10)	Ok (10)	Ok (10)
3	All student's name and their section numbers have been added to the school roster.	(5)	(1)	In progress(1)	Ok (5)	Ok (5)
4	Science Department Chair has shared the school roster with all Biology, Chemistry and Physics teachers.	(5)	(1)	No (0)	Ok (5)	Ok (5)
5	School roster has been shared with all English and Social Studies teachers for interdisciplinary SOS connections.	(5)	(1)	No (0)	Ok (5)	Ok (5)
6	SOS project topics list has been prepared	(15)	(1)	In progress(1)	Ok (15)	Ok (15)
7	SOS project materials have been ordered for Level I, II and III	(15)	(1)	No (0)	Ok (15)	No (0)
8	Student's Task 1: Create your e-portfolio (google site) and choose your project, has been graded.	(10)	(1)	In progress(1)	In progress(1)	In progress(1)

a timely manner, provide feedback to students and offer opportunities for them to improve their grade.

In addition, if a student starts to fall behind on an assignment, the teacher is expected to notify the parents and develop an action plan. Each campus has STEM SOS project help hours scheduled, so that teachers can provide extra support to students.

Quarterly Progress Report

A Quarterly Progress Report is created, which works as a check and balance system between campuses and Central Office. The department head at the campus level is responsible for checking and updating the school STEM SOS roster and the teachers' task trackers. However, if for some reason, the department head does not provide accurate campus data, STEM coaches can check a teacher's gradebook directly and update this information.

STEM coaches monitor two items: (1) the number of tasks created and (2) the number of assignments graded in the gradebook. Gradebooks are checked twice during each quarter: mid-quarter and end-of-quarter. The report is shared with the campus administrators and central office curriculum directors and is used to track teachers' progress during that quarter. Based on the report, campus administrators, STEM coaches and curriculum directors can provide necessary support and encouragement to the teachers.

INCENTIVES

Performance-based incentive programs help increase human motivation and the quality of work (Feldman and Landsman, 2007). The STEM SOS projects are challenging and time-consuming but incentives can inspire students and teachers to prepare better quality STEM SOS products. The same types of incentives will not motivate everyone; some people are motivated by monetary incentives and others by non-monetary incentives such as awards, recognition, praise, promotion, or long-term benefits (Cherry, 2014). Therefore, HPS designed an incentives program that offers both monetary and non-monetary incentives to teachers and students that can keep everyone motivated to complete STEM SOS projects. In HPS, the Task Tracking System is used to identify teachers and students who would qualify for various incentives.

Teacher Incentives

Teachers with the most successful STEM SOS projects receive an iPad as an incentive. Other incentives for teachers include an increased salary for the following year, an added bonus and the opportunity to become a mentor, STEM coach or a trainer for others. The names of the top teachers from each content area are announced at the end of the year; they receive a special recognition title called the "STEM SOS Heroes" from the district. These top STEM teachers receive invitations to many STEM conferences as a presenter, where they are given the opportunity to share their STEM experiences and showcase students' STEM SOS projects.

Student Incentives

Student's final STEM SOS video presentations are rated and ranked by the general public. Students share their final videos on social networks such as YouTube, Google plus and Facebook and gain points based on the number of "likes" they receive. Being able to have their project shared and "liked" by the public is a huge motivation for students. In the end, both the teacher's grade and the popularity of the project on social media play a role in determining the best STEM SOS project.

Students with the best quality STEM SOS products receive an iPad, iPod, iPod-mini or gift certificate. The names of the top students are announced at the end of the year. They receive a special recognition title called the "STEM SOS Heroes" from the district. Students also get a chance to compete in various local and regional STEM competitions and to present at conferences. For example, during the STEM Education week, students are invited to the Austin capitol or

ISWEEP (International Sustainable World Energy Engineering and Environmental) for presentations. Most schools also have VIP STEM presentation team. It is a great honor for students to be part of this VIP STEM team and they receive volunteer hours counted towards their graduation plans.

Another long-term incentive of the STEM SOS project is that students can use their four years of e-portfolios as part of their college application process. Students

Figure 1. A group of students demonstrating their STEM projects at the Austin Capitol. (Please use your QR reader to scan the QR code to watch the pictures from the Capitol demo).

can write their college entrance essays about their projects and the STEM experiences they have gathered from their high school years. Students can also share their e-portfolio during college interviews, which may help them stand out among other students. Students' e-portfolios will show that they developed technology skills such as creating and editing videos, websites and presentations skills.

CONCLUSION

HPS's STEM SOS model is unique in terms of students' digital products and presentation opportunities. It incorporates college readiness skills and 21st century skills. HPS's tracking system provides a way of monitoring students' progress and need for support, as well as identifying the best teachers and students who eligible for incentives. HPS's STEM SOS projects, tracking system and incentive program can be replicated in other organizations that are looking to increase students' interest in STEM fields.

REFERENCES

Cherry, K. (2014). *The incentive theory of motivation: Are actions motivated by a desire for rewards?* Retrieved from http://psychology.about.com/od/motivation/a/incentive-theory-of-motivation.htm

Feldman, J., & Landsman, D. L. (2007). *The benefits of incentives.* Retrieved from http://www.talentmgt.com/articles/the_benefits_of_incentives

Harmony STEM Program. (2013). *Harmony Public Schools: RTT-D Grant PBL Initiative.* Retrieved from https://docs.google.com/document/d/1Iwk06YS2fXhvRwtj_LP41v4ctDRuUFyQg2BaKA6owls/pub

Sahin, A., & Top, N. (in press). Making it happen: A study of a novel teaching style, STEM Students on the Stage (SOS)™, for increasing students' STEM knowledge and interest. *Journal of STEM Education: Innovation and Research.*

Sahin, A., Top, N., & Vanegas, S. (2014). *Harmony STEM SOS™ model increases students' college readiness and develops 21st century skills.* Retrieved from http://www.harmonytx.org/Portals/0/HPS_Issue-1.pdf

Farjana Yasmin
Harmony Public Schools

Levent Sakar
Harmony Public Schools

CYNTHIA SARGENT AND FREDA HUSIC

10. AN OVERVIEW OF PROFESSIONAL DEVELOPMENT AT HARMONY PUBLIC SCHOOLS

Integral to the STEM Students on the Stage (SOS)™ model for instruction at Harmony Public Schools (HPS) is Project-based Learning (PBL). This learning model requires a significant shift in the roles of teachers and students, away from the direct instruction pedagogy of traditional teaching toward one that supports and facilitates student-centered and self-regulated learning. The PBL environment calls for a special skill set from teachers, including the application of effective classroom practices that support students' use of technology and guides students through inquiry-based activities. The success of the STEM SOS model is directly related to the development of this skill set in HPS teachers. Through research-based principles of professional development – including duration, active learning, and support for implementation – HPS provides the necessary support for its teachers to implement PBL curriculum. HPS Teacher Educators lead workshops, coach teachers in the classroom, model best practices and help facilitate teacher reflection that leads to pedagogical transformation. The HPS teacher support program and the work of the Teacher Educators clearly align with the essentials of effective professional development and have been instrumental in facilitating the high level of achievement attained by students, as evidenced by their PBL projects.

INTRODUCTION

At its inception in 2000, Harmony Public Schools (HPS) in Texas adopted a STEM (Science, Technology, Engineering and Mathematics) program with the intent to increase students' interest in STEM subjects and encourage their pursuit of STEM-based careers such as in mechanical engineering, medicine, biomedical engineering, geoscience, and hydrology. The foundation of many STEM programs is project-based learning (PBL), a pedagogical approach shown to improve students' understanding of science, in addition to supporting the development of creative problem-solving and communication skills (Diaz & King, 2007; Gordon, Rogers, Comfort, Gavula, & McGee, 2001; Kolodner et al., 2003; Liu, Hsieh, Cho, & Schallert, 2006; Novak & Gleason, 2001; Schneider, Krajcik, Marx, & Soloway, 2001). In response to the need for a STEM education program, HPS devised the STEM SOS™ (Students on the Stage) instruction model.

A. Sahin (Ed.), A Practice-based Model of STEM Teaching, 131–145.

The STEM SOS program places a significant responsibility for learning on students, incorporating project-based and inquiry-based learning with the goal of increasing students' STEM knowledge and interest, as well as producing self-motivated and self-regulated learners (Sahin, Top, & Vanegas, 2014; Sahin & Top, in press). Just as students embark on a different and non-traditional way of learning content, so must the teachers be able to support students in their quest for knowledge. To meet the challenges teachers face in facilitating learning in a project-based environment, HPS paired the implementation of their STEM SOS program with the execution of a comprehensive professional development and teacher support program for the 2013-2014 school year. The goal of the program was to help teachers build their knowledge and practices in subject content, technology and pedagogical approaches, all of which are areas critical to supporting students in the STEM SOS program. This chapter describes the various forms of professional development offered to teachers and discusses the program's alignment to essential forms of effective professional development.

THE STEM SOS TEACHING MODEL

Project-Based Learning

In addition to focusing on standards-based and student-centered teaching, the STEM SOS program enriches and extends the knowledge and problem-solving skills of students through Project-based Learning (Harmony STEM Program, 2013). Typical PBL projects engage students in problems that are curriculum-based, interdisciplinary and connected to real-life. In the process of constructing a solution for a problem, students decide how to approach that problem, what activities they will undertake and what processes they will follow. Although PBL implementations have distinctive features, there is a common set of attributes that characterizes all of them (Grant, 2002):

- An introduction to anchor the activity
- A task, guiding question or driving question
- An investigation resulting in the creation of one or more sharable artifacts
- Resources for subject expertise
- Scaffolding to help learners assess their progress
- Collaborations with peers and teams
- Opportunities for reflection, transfer and communication

The PBLs in the STEM SOS program directly align with these features. Requisites for mastery of the curriculum require students to complete a Level I PBL followed by either a Level II or advanced Level III PBL. (See Chapter 4 of Sahin & Top, in press, for a detailed description of the STEM SOS model and its impact on student learning.)

To help students work through the features described above, the teacher's function in the classroom goes far beyond the traditional role.

Teachers' Roles in STEM SOS

To align pedagogy with the use of PBL curriculum and other inquiry-based learning activities in the classroom, the teacher's role shifts from the conventional, stand-up-and-deliver scenario of teaching to a role that facilitates and enables learning. When introducing a new topic, teachers at HPS provide a short lecture on the subject to get students thinking about concepts and connections to the real world and to discuss any theoretical implications. Following these brief lectures, the teacher's role changes to one of a facilitator, helping students create their own content-related questions, promoting student discourse in small groups and classroom discussions, managing multiple student projects, providing technical assistance related to the artifacts students produce and continually assessing and responding to students' work in progress.

While a stand-up-and-deliver method of teaching relies heavily on a teacher's content knowledge, the student-centered and inquiry-focused nature of the STEM SOS PBLs require teachers to draw on varied forms of knowledge. A framework for understanding this complex knowledge system used by teachers was identified by Mishra and Koehler (2006) as "TPACK." This holistic view of teacher knowledge defines three main knowledge domains – Technological Knowledge, Pedagogical Knowledge, and Content Knowledge – and recognizes that there is a complex interplay between these domains that influences a teacher's practice in the classroom (Mishra & Kohler, 2006).

For example, in project-based learning, teachers should be able to construct effective questioning sequences, intervene to address misconceptions and help to develop students' understanding of content (Towns & Sweetland, 2008; Warner & Myers, 2008). This requires not just content knowledge on the part of the teacher, but specifically pedagogical content knowledge. If the teacher then utilizes technology such as probeware and data logging in science experiments or shared Google Docs™ documents for student collaboration, that teacher uses technological pedagogical content knowledge to facilitate a meaningful learning experience.

Developing the TPACK knowledge needed to support PBLs is a daunting and, for many teachers, unrealizable task without intensive professional development. So to support teachers in their role as facilitators of a project-based and inquiry-based teaching approach, the administration at HPS devised a comprehensive professional development program that ensures teachers receive training in all three of the TPACK knowledge domains, as well as training that addresses the complexity of the interconnectedness of these domains. The many facets of the program are tied to best practices or enduring principles of effective professional development.

ESSENTIALS OF EFFECTIVE PROFESSIONAL DEVELOPMENT

Research on teacher professional development is vast and has elucidated the attributes of professional development programs that make a difference. The following principles of professional development have been repeatedly shown to have a positive impact on teacher performance and student learning gains (Gulamhussein, 2013).

Duration

While at most schools, one-time workshops are the norm for teacher professional development, these workshops are ineffective in producing actual change in teachers' practices. In fact, some studies have suggested that fifty to eighty hours are needed to affect teacher practices in a way that improves student learning (Gulamhussein, 2013). This is not surprising if one views teacher learning in the context of "knowledge integration" in which teachers not only need to be exposed to new knowledge or ideas, but also need to have time to practice and deal with implementation implications or curriculum customization, use evidence to distinguish between their current ideas and new concepts and engage in continual reflection and integration of new and current practices to formulate a pedagogical framework. A review of literature found that professional development was effective in improving inquiry learning if the program was sustained beyond one year (Gerard, Varma, Corliss, & Linn, 2011).

In an analysis of factors that make professional development effective, two aspects of duration were considered important: time span and contact hours. The study found a positive correlation between these attributes and other essential features of professional development, such as active learning and coherence (Garet, Porter, Desimone, Birman, & Yoon, 2001). Sustained professional development over a lengthy time span involving a significant investment in contact hours is likely to increase the effectiveness of that development. With an increase in contact hours, teachers have adequate time to observe others and be observed in the classroom, discuss and practice with new content, pedagogy and technologies, and be engaged in other activities that make their professional development an integral part of their work.

Support for Implementation

The positive impact of duration is only realized if the time teachers spend in professional development activities supports them during the implementation stage. Coaching is often used to provide this support and studies have shown that coached teachers are more likely to actually integrate new teaching practices into their pedagogical repertoire (Gulamhussein, 2013). Coaching may be an effective attribute of professional development since it correlates with one of the challenges of knowledge integration, i.e., new ideas do not easily replace existing views (Gerard, Varma, Corliss, & Linn, 2011).

Professional learning communities have been shown to be effective in supporting teachers in working through implementation challenges. These learning communities carry out collaborative activities such as learning inquiry cycles and analysis of student work. In many cases, coaches or lead teachers facilitate the communities of practice (Darling-Hammond & Richardson, 2009). The collaborative participation of teachers guides teachers in transitioning to new pedagogical methods, such as project-based learning.

Active Learning

Teachers, like their students, need to actively participate in making sense of new knowledge and teaching practices. The varied, active ways in which teachers can be engaged during professional development workshops include role-playing, open-ended discussion and observing experts modelling new practices (Gulamhussein, 2013). In ongoing professional development, active learning can include opportunities to observe and be observed teaching, develop lesson plans and plan for implementation, review student work, or present, lead or write (Birman, Desimone, Porter, & Garet, 2000).

Some successful professional development programs that improved teachers' use of inquiry learning engaged them in active learning in the following ways: using technologies like a student would, experiencing or observing models of teaching practices by experts or mentor teachers, meeting on a weekly or monthly basis to reflect on implementation of new pedagogy, promoting the exchange of and customization of lesson plans and collaboratively developing solutions to address implementation challenges or student performance that fell short of expectations (Gerard, Varma, Corliss, & Linn, 2011).

Coherence and Emphasis on Content-Specific Contexts

Just as flawed as the one-shot workshop is the all too common practice of providing generic professional development to teachers. In reality, teachers can best understand and apply new practices when they are presented within the content the teacher teaches and are explicitly tied to discipline-specific concepts and skills

Figure 1. A student demonstrating his Level II project. (Please use your QR reader to scan the QR code to watch the video).

(Gulamhussein, 2013). Garet et al. (2001) found a strong correlation between an emphasis on content and a positive effect on teachers' enhanced knowledge and skills. Coherence – a clear alignment between the varied professional development activities as well as the standards and assessments to which teachers are accountable and that are consistent with teachers' goals – was also identified as an important factor in positively influencing teachers' knowledge and skills and subsequent changes in teaching practices (Garet et al., 2001; Birman et al., 2000).

TEACHER EDUCATORS AT HPS

Related to the research findings described above is the following guidance for a professional development program to be successful.

> The professional development should focus on deepening teachers' content knowledge and knowledge of how students learn particular content, on providing opportunities for active learning and on encouraging coherence in teachers' professional development experiences. Schools and districts should pursue these goals by using activities that have greater duration and involve collective participation. (Birman et al., 2000)

Harmony Public Schools has taken these goals for professional development and created and implemented a support program for their teachers that is both relevant and comprehensive. The administration identified Teacher Educators (TE) who had the content, technological and pedagogical knowledge to instruct other teachers. The Teacher Educators form several groupings: Curriculum Writers, Lead Teachers, Cluster Subject Coaches, and Cluster STEM coaches. The subject matter expertise of the Teacher Educator group includes: Biology, Chemistry, Physics, Mathematics, Social Studies, and English Language Arts.

The combined and collaborative efforts of the Teacher Educators ensure that professional development related to the PBL initiative is sustained, coherent and that teacher integration of new pedagogical practices is supported. Table 1 briefly describes the responsibilities of the Teacher Educators.

Harmony Public Schools (HPS) currently has 39 campuses across the state of Texas that participate in the PBL professional development program. A total of 99 Teacher Educators make up the pool of individuals who support HPS teachers. Curriculum writers, comprised of 43 teachers from the various campuses, provide curriculum support for several weeks at the end of the school year. There are also 10 curriculum writers in the central office who provide curriculum support throughout the year. Sixteen lead teachers were selected from a subset of the 39 schools to provide direct teacher support. There are six cluster STEM coaches and 24 cluster subject coaches who work all year round with teachers on content, technology, and pedagogy. In addition, HPS collaborated with consultants from a university, a state regional education center and a science education technology company to write the rigorous and comprehensive PBL curriculum and to provide professional development to

Table 1. Teacher Educator Responsibilities

Teacher Educators	Description of Role
Curriculum Writers	Write curriculum and assessments; provide resources that support the curriculum; train teachers in the curriculum.
Lead Teachers	Support teachers in curriculum; train teachers in the implementation of PBLs.
Cluster Subject Coaches	Observe teachers and provide feedback to improve their instruction; model lessons in the classroom; help with lesson planning; provide targeted supports when requested; provide professional development on best teaching practices.
Cluster STEM Coaches	Collaborate with teachers to organize and promote interdisciplinary activities; integrate multiple technologies to support inquiry-based learning (through PBLs).

support implementation of the curriculum.[1] A total of 13 HPS Teacher Educators and one consultant were surveyed to garner information on responsibilities, types of trainings, goals for professional development and effectiveness of the trainings. All forms of the TEs described in the table above were represented in the pool of survey participants. The TEs varied in experience from 1-5 years in their current position, and the four core subject areas were represented: Social Science, ELA, Mathematics, and Science (Physics, Chemistry, and Biology).

Forms of Professional Development

Workshops or trainings for groups of teachers were conducted by all of the Teacher Educators. Observing teachers in the classroom and providing feedback on their teaching was also identified as a prevalent form of professional development, with 67 percent of the TEs engaging in this form. Sixty percent of the TEs met with teachers to provide one-on-one private coaching. Additionally, choosing from a list of effective forms of professional development, 40 percent of TEs noted that they use in-classroom modeling of lessons or technology as a form of professional development. Although only 27 percent of the TEs established and maintained professional learning communities (PLC) within a subject area, it is important to note that this is the first year for the program and that there is potential for PLCs to grow in the coming years. PLCs are a viable option for sustaining professional development past the initial implementation period of the STEM SOS program; the HPS teachers can easily transition to this form since they are already accustomed to meeting regularly to discuss their teaching practices and collaborate with other teachers.

Also included in the professional development program is the HPS PBL Resource Website, which provides live and recorded webinars as well as video tutorials and written tutorials for the software technologies used in the PBL investigations. Both teachers and students access this resource for training on applications for the creation of digital media. Deliverables for the PBL projects, focusing on explanations of concepts learned, include: a project brochure, video presentations, digital gallery presentations, and a "My PBL Project" webpage. Although teachers can turn to TEs for help in producing these deliverables, the webinars and video tutorials serve as a thorough and comprehensive source of support materials.

The diversity in the types of support teachers receive offers them several ways to improve without having to rely on only one method.

Goals for Professional Development

Teacher Educators were asked to identify the goals for professional development that are most important for them in their work with teachers. Helping teachers gauge student understanding through informal formative assessment was ranked as most relevant by 80 per cent of the TEs. Seventy-three percent of the TEs ranked four additional goals as most relevant: improve teachers' ability to lead students through PBLs; improve teachers' daily teaching practices; improve teachers' content knowledge; and help teachers to properly assess student work. Two-thirds of the TEs indicated that helping teachers implement inquiry in the classroom was most important for them. These top six goals for professional development that TEs have for the teachers with whom they work align unmistakably to the essentials and principles of effective professional development outlined by researchers (Birman et al., 2000; Garet et al., 2001; Gulamhussein, 2013).

Evaluation of Professional Development Effectiveness

In addition to delivering the training, the Teacher Educators also took steps to evaluate the effectiveness of professional development. The most common forms of evaluation include (in order of use):

- Conducting classroom observations to identify improvements in teaching practices
- Gathering data to monitor changes in student learning outcomes
- Surveying teachers to measure instructor confidence in the classroom
- Assessing whether teachers show deeper knowledge of subject area content
- Using student evaluations of teachers

By performing these evaluations of the effectiveness of their professional development, the Teacher Educators identified the teachers who were making progress in improving their content knowledge, integrating an inquiry-based approach in their teaching and ultimately improving student learning outcomes. At the same time, they also identified teachers that were not making progress in content knowledge or pedagogy, and were able to offer these teachers more support.

Figure 2. A student demonstrating how infinity images occur in his Level II project.
(Please use your QR reader to scan the QR codes to watch the video and/or see his
e-portfolio website).

Improving Content Knowledge and Teaching Strategies

Improving teachers' content knowledge was an important goal for Teacher Educators even though their assessment of teacher knowledge was fairly high. Eighty percent of TEs evaluated teachers' content knowledge as either strong or very strong. Given this evaluation, one might assume that content knowledge was not addressed in professional development sessions to any significant extent. On the contrary, over 90 percent of the TEs reported that they addressed content knowledge in their professional development sessions either to some degree or to a large degree.

Linked to content knowledge were the teaching strategies used by teachers to impart the information to their students. In their assessment of effective teaching strategies, 67 percent thought that teachers demonstrated a moderate level of competency in their application of effective teaching strategies, while an additional 34 percent thought teachers showed a very strong application of effective teaching practices. In response to this evaluation, all of the TEs indicated they addressed teaching strategies in their professional development, with over 80 percent indicating they covered the teaching strategies to a large degree. Clearly, the HPS professional development program places a significant emphasis on ensuring that all teachers are given the opportunity to become skilled at effective teaching practices.

ALIGNMENT TO THE ESSENTIALS OF PROFESSIONAL DEVELOPMENT

The professional development program at HPS and the work of its Teacher Educators are based on proven principles for effective professional development. Specifically, the survey administered to the HPS Teacher Educators provided the following information regarding the application of these principles to the professional development that supports the STEM SOS model of teaching.

Duration

Over the summer months, teachers participated in multi-day workshops with the intention of learning and improving their content, technological and pedagogical skills. Professional development for the teachers continued throughout the school year; over 70 percent of the Teachers Educators met with teachers several times in a semester, and some as frequently as once a week. As described by one of the TEs, these frequent meetings can take on a variety of forms.

> I observe teachers and provide supportive feedback to help them improve their instruction. I help individuals and campuses analyze data for the purposes of establishing tutorials, intervention groups, and in-class small group instruction . . . I model lessons in the classroom and help with lesson planning.

Through workshops, HPS teachers receive much more than the minimum number of contact hours suggested by research (Gulamhussein, 2013). In addition to contact hours, professional development at HPS spans the length of the school year and into the next summer, which impacts the effectiveness of professional development.

> Expert teachers . maintain communication [initiated before the start of the school year] with their small groups to provide support.

The frequency and duration of professional development activities are significant and clearly align with recommendations for effective professional development programs.

Support for Implementation

Ninety-three percent of TEs indicated that classroom observations are used to identify improvements in teaching practices and 60 percent meet with teachers for one-on-one coaching and to observe in the classroom and provide feedback. This level of support is not often integrated into school reforms, such as the adoption of a school-wide PBL program, and is surely a noteworthy contributor to the success of the STEM SOS model. TEs provided the following explanations for how they support implementation of the PBLs and other inquiry-based learning pedagogy:

> I also plan [lessons] with the teachers and then observe their classes in order to evaluate the implementation of the lesson.

> I model lessons in the classroom and help with lesson planning.

> We also have cluster training where these teachers will come together for PBL, content, and technology related support. Plus, there are STEM coaches who also support PBL training and tracking teachers [progress].

We ask for their feedback on how well they were able to implement what they learned (a new strategy, lab, technology, etc.) in their classroom. If we see that teachers are able to not only implement what they have learned in the classroom effectively, but also understand how this can impact student learning, then we know that the PD given was beneficial.

During second semester we asked teachers what their struggles were for PBL projects [and planned materials and activities for future trainings to address these struggles]. We decided to do small group training sessions where group of teachers would work with an 'expert PBL teacher'.

I have created several resources for between-campus collaboration between grade level teachers.

Successful professional development requires the support of administration – to provide the professional development and to give teachers the time to participate in professional development. Harmony Public Schools provides that kind of support.

The coaches and department chairs work closely with one another to ensure that teachers that need more support have time and availability to meet with and work with the coach.

Professional development is also customized to the needs of each of the campuses. One TE explained that the professional development is tailored to meet the needs of teachers at each campus. Classroom management may be a significant issue on one HPS campus and less significant on a different campus; by having localized support, HPS can best address the challenges different campuses experience when they implement the STEM SOS program.

Active Learning

Less than a third of TEs indicated that they host or record webinars, or use other online resources as a means of delivering professional development. Watching videos or a webinar is an example of a teacher being passive. While these resources are good for supporting teachers later in the implementation stage, HPS rightfully uses in-person workshops and trainings that explicitly model active learning strategies.

As research has shown that one-shot workshops are ineffective (Gulamhussein, 2013), HPS workshops are typically multi-day events and, during these workshops, teachers are actively engaged. Two TEs explained:

The teachers' exposure to a new concept or program is always hands-on. In the summer training for chemistry teachers, the teachers experienced sequential student activities before review and study from the teacher viewpoint . The teachers found this PD strategy very helpful and appreciated the freedom of working as students first.

> We selected 12 PBL experiments to do as a model with the teachers to provide PBL content related support to the teacher . We put experienced teachers in each table who were knowledgeable [about the PBLs] . Groups of 2–3 teachers worked on a PBL experiment. They became the expert group and then were required to create 'my PBL page' on google site [just as a student would]. Also, they had to learn to take pictures and videos of their project and upload it to the googlesite . After each team finished their projects we did a gallery walk to learn about other projects.

> We write lesson plans together or tailor the lesson plans the teacher already has to be as engaging as possible.

Teacher Educators at HPS make every effort to put teachers into active learning situations with the intent of solidifying the learning experience and ensuring that the teachers are better able to carry the content knowledge and teaching skills back to the classroom.

Coherence and Emphasis on Content-Specific Contexts

Eighty-eight percent of TEs surveyed rated improving teachers' content knowledge as "very relevant" to the work they do with those teachers, through formal professional development or through coaching. The remainder of the responses rated this objective as relevant to their work with teachers. Fifty-three percent ranked this principle to be one of the top three that align most closely with HPS professional development. By having TEs for specific subject areas (Biology, Social Science, and so forth), HPS has ensured that teachers are receiving support from an expert in their subject, rather than generic support.

All too often, schools or districts provide generic professional development to teachers at the beginning of the school year. Instead, HPS offers subject-specific training, which is a strategy that aligns well with what research indicates is needed for professional development to be effective and make a difference in both teaching and learning outcomes (Birman et al., 2000).

One person described coordinating writer's workshops as a way to specifically address the needs of English Language Arts teachers and their students. Similarly, the support for Biology, Physics, and Chemistry teachers was specific to the PBL experiments for these subjects, involving teachers in carrying out some of these experiments themselves.

> Every 'student investigation' [teachers performed in a PD workshop] was followed by a review of chemistry content, mathematical reasoning, use of scientific reasoning, and the use of scientific technology for data collection and analysis.

The HPS professional development program also maintains coherence in their various activities.

Goals [that] are set at Cluster PD are followed up [on] in start of the year meetings and first walkthroughs. Working closely with department chairs ensures that teachers who need more support are able to meet with the coach.

Another example of coherence in the HPS professional development program is a common curriculum. Teachers are provided PBL projects that are aligned to the state standards for each content area. By providing training on the PBLs, HPS teachers in turn receive training in the technological pedagogical content knowledge needed to help their students master these standards.

CONCLUSIONS

Frequently, school reform is a slow process and often not fully realized, yet just two years into the implementation of the STEM SOS model, HPS has achieved a high level of performance from both teachers and students. This is a testament to the success of the professional development model that HPS has put into place to support their teachers. The HPS professional development program appears to be on a trajectory to deliver long term, effective training to its teachers, which will sustain the project-based learning curriculum implementation and encourage continual growth in teaching practices. The HPS administration was proactive in identifying the professional development needs of their teachers, and defined appropriate goals and scope for the professional development program. They created vertical teams of Teacher Educators, all specializing in content, technological and pedagogical knowledge, and planned for and provided sufficient time for teachers and Teacher Educators to work together. As a result, collaborative participation in professional development and a continuous cycle of implementation and reflection have become integral to the work of HPS teachers. Students in the STEM SOS program, with guidance by their adept facilitators of learning, become independent learners gaining 21st century skills and mastery of subject matter content.

Responses from Teacher Educators indicated a commitment to providing a professional development experience to teachers that is founded on proven principles known to impact both content knowledge and teaching practices. The essential components of effective professional development that stood out in their responses included: duration of the professional development opportunities, support for implementing curriculum and new teaching strategies, a focus on active learning over passive assimilation of information and coherence and emphasis on content-specific contexts. These aspects of professional development continually show a positive impact on teacher performance and student learning gains (Gulamhussein, 2013).

The support provided by HPS to teachers through the professional development program surely must be affecting pedagogical practices and student outcomes. HPS students exceed state standard expectations and excel in Advanced Placement® courses. The next steps in the evaluation of the program would be to determine directly the impact on teachers' content knowledge and teaching practices and in turn, assess the effect on student learning.

NOTE

[1] The external education consultants were from North American University, Texas Region 4 Education Service Center, and PASCO scientific.

REFERENCES/BIBLIOGRAPHY

Birman, B. F., Desimone, L., Porter, A. C., & Garet, M. S. (2000). Designing professional development that works. *Educational Leadership, 57*(8), 28–37.

Diaz, D., & King, P. (2007). Adapting a post-secondary STEM instructional model to K-5 mathematics instruction. In *ASEE Annual Conference and Exposition*, Honolulu, HI.

Garet, M., Porter, A. C., Desimone, L., Birman, B., & Yoon, K. S. (2001). What makes professional development effective? Results from a national sample of teachers. *American Educational Research Journal, 38*(4), 915–945.

Gerard, L. F., Varma, K., Corliss, S. B., & Linn, M. C. (2011). Professional development for technology-enhanced inquiry science. *Review of Educational Research, 81*(3), 408–448.

Gordon, P. R., Rogers, A. M., Comfort, M., Gavula, N., & McGee, B. P. (2001). A taste of problem-based learning increases achievement of urban minority middle-school students. *Educational Horizons, 79*(4), 171–175.

Grant, M. (2002). Getting a grip on project-based learning: Theory, cases and recommendations. Retrieved from http://www.ncsu.edu/meridian/win2002/514

Gulamhussein, A. (2013). Teaching the teachers: Effective professional development in an era of high stakes accountability. Alexandria, VA: Center for Public Education.

Harmony STEM Program. (2013). Harmony Public Schools: RTT-D Grant PBL Initiative. Retrieved from https://docs.google.com/document/d/1Iwk06YS2fXhvRwtj_LP41v4ctDRuUFyQg2BaKA6owls/pub

Kolodner, J. L., Camp, P. J., Crismond, D., Fasse, B., Gray, J., Holbrook, J., & Puntambekar, S. (2003). Problem-based learning meets case-based reasoning in the middle-school science classroom: Putting learning by design into practice. *The Journal of the Learning Sciences, 12*(4), 495–547.

Liu, M., Hsieh, P., Cho, Y. J., & Schallert, D. L. (2006). Middle school students' self-efficacy, attitudes, and achievement in a computer-enhanced problem-based learning environment. *Journal of Interactive Learning Research, 17*(3), 225–242.

Mishra, P., & Koehler, M. J. (2006). Technological pedagogical content knowledge: A framework for teacher knowledge. *Teachers College Record, 108*(6), 1017–1054.

Novak, A. M., & Gleason, C. (2001). Incorporating portable technology to enhance an inquiry: Project-based middle school science classroom. In R. Tinker & J. S. Krajcik (Eds.), *Portable technologies: Science learning in context* (pp. 29–36). Dordrecht, the Netherlands: Kluwer Publishers.

Sahin, A., Top, N., & Vanegas, S. (2014). *Harmony STEM SOS model increases college readiness and develops 21st century skills* (Whitepaper). Retrieved from http://harmonytx.org/Portals/0/HPS_Issue-1.pdf

Sahin, A., & Top, N. (in press). Making it happen: A study of a novel teaching style, STEM Students on the Stage (SOS)™, for increasing students' STEM knowledge and interest. *Journal of STEM Education: Innovation and Research.*

Towns, R., & Sweetland, J. (2008). Inspired issue brief: Inquiry-based teaching. Center for Inspired Teaching. Retrieved from http://www.inspiredteaching.org/wp-content/uploads/impact-research-briefs-inquiry-based-teaching.pdf

Warner, A. J., & Myers, B. E. (2008). Implementing inquiry-based teaching methods. Retrieved from http://edis.ifas.ufl.edu/wc076

AN OVERVIEW OF PROFESSIONAL DEVELOPMENT AT HARMONY PUBLIC SCHOOLS

Cynthia Sargent
PASCO scientific
Roseville, CA

Freda Husic
PASCO scientific
Roseville, CA

BURAK YILMAZ, EUGENE KENNEDY AND TEVFIK ESKI

11. STEM STUDENTS ON THE STAGE: OUTREACH

This chapter discusses outreach events and strategies the Harmony Public School District and campus leaders developed in an effort to promote the STEM SOS model and showcase student success with authentically created student exhibits. The descriptions of these outreach efforts explain how the STEM SOS model was gradually showcased to a progressively larger audience, from small communities to nationwide and international STEM events.

INTRODUCTION

Definitions and Utilization of Outreach

In education, outreach is simply reaching out to your community, introducing your school/district and showcasing what you do well. Its purpose in education is multifaceted. First and foremost, it is a way of sharing best practices in the educational community, whether it is within the district, city, region, state, or even across the nation or on an international scale. This is identical to the show-and-tell activity we often see in early elementary classrooms; students proudly sharing what they came up with serves as evidence of learning, but at the same time encourages others to strive to do just as well as their peers and have the opportunity to go on stage. Second, outreach helps connect and engage stakeholders, both internal and external, and shows them all the good things happening around the community. Third, outreach helps attract funders, entrepreneurs, government officials and other philanthropic organizations who can help replicate promising practices at other sites and/or assist in scaling these efforts to serve larger beneficiaries.

There was a decided increase in outreach efforts at Harmony Public Schools with the inception of the STEM Students on the Stage (SOS)™ model. It started internally with the basic parental instinct to enthuse that "you have got to see what my kid is able to do!" This was also the immediate reaction of Harmony's STEM teachers when they first started seeing results in the form of authentic student work with project-based learning (PBL). These educators were so eager to share their students' successes with their administrators, fellow faculty members, and with parents of course. After reaping what they had sowed, these educators were determined to present a STEM fiesta to their school communities, with students demonstrating and presenting their projects. Hence came about the concept of the "STEM School Festival."

A. Sahin (Ed.), A Practice-based Model of STEM Teaching, 147–155.

STEM School Festival

The STEM School Festival initially started as a simple way of bringing together the entire school personnel and parents to inform them about the PBL approach and showcase the student success that came with it. When students presented their work and demonstrated what they learned, the event had a much bigger impact than anyone had anticipated. First, many teachers were pleasantly surprised to see their students engaged in such authentic work, and furthermore, they were able to articulate their work so passionately. This immediately led to teacher-initiated professional learning communities (PLCs) where same grade level teachers got together to plan to take these PBL projects to the next level by making them more interdisciplinary and multi-sensory. Second, the STEM School Festival inadvertently had an impact on enrollment activities. As many school administrators would agree, word of mouth is the most effective way to get more enrollment applications for charter schools; many parents who attended the STEM School Festival suddenly had great things to say about the school and recommended it to their friends and relatives. Needless to say, successive STEM Festivals drove prospective students and parents to Harmony Public Schools. Consequently, what started out as a showcase event for the STEM SOS model turned into an open house and a community STEM expo for the school. Today, Harmony Public Schools serve around 28,000 students in the state of Texas and approximately 40,000 more are on waiting lists. Having more students on the waiting list than are enrolled in 40+ campuses says a great deal about the quality of the education in the Harmony Public School system. This can certainly be attributed to the STEM SOS model and shows how a school-wide STEM festival had a profound effect on community outreach, which in turn resulted in an exponential increase of student applications and retention rates at Harmony Public Schools.

After recognizing the outreach potential of STEM School Festival, this event quickly spiraled into an open public event to which not only faculty and parents are invited, but also community partners, businesses, elected officials, state representatives, other local government agencies and many other VIP guests, all of whom started attending Harmony's STEM Festivals to watch those students shine. This has been the emerging point of the "Share and Shine" method, which is a vital component of the STEM SOS model. With STEM School Festivals, Harmony students literally get on stage and have their very own audiences who are willing to hear and watch what they have to share. There is no doubt that these share and shine opportunities have an enormous impact on students' communication skills. One Harmony student describes his experience as follows:

It was actually kind of intimidating at first- talking to the professors – I didn't know what to expect but now I'm able to talk to them one on one like with well understanding as well as when visitors come here we have to present projects or something like that I'm able to present it well so that they understand it. (Sahin, Top, & Vanegas, 2014b; Sahin and Top, in press)

As discussed in detail in previous chapters, students who go on stage and share their work develop public speaking skills and learn how to present themselves and their work in a business-like environment. In addition to explaining their projects, students also address common misconceptions through scientific principles as well as answer any follow-up questions from the audience. This certainly helps students in the best imaginable way to prepare themselves for job/career requirements such as interviews, presentations, creating digital portfolios and using technology, just to name a few. Beyond these critical 21st century skills, being on stage and having an audience that is willing to learn from them is such a confidence booster for any school age student. Sahin et al. (2014) and Sahin and Top (*in press*) quoted a Harmony student who expressed how their self-esteem developed through giving STEM project presentations as follows:

> You know it feels nice to know something and it gives you confidence and you feel like wow ... [I was]...able to present better, get over the fear, I didn't know how to speak in public. I have already had experiences of speaking in public and this just encourages me and improves that ability more.

All Harmony students, including students with limited English proficiency and disabilities, are observed to have increased their self-esteem during their public presentations of projects; the more they share, the more they shine. And as they repeatedly go through this process, the students are able to retain knowledge and skills they learn through their PBL projects over extended periods of time. Another Harmony student stated, "I will never forget that principle because I have learned it, I saw it, I experienced it. It will stay with me forever," thus explaining how the model helps them understand science concepts and retain learned knowledge and skills (Sahin et al., 2014b).

Active versus Passive Learning

According to the learning pyramid, long believed to have been developed by NTL Institute for Applied Behavioral Sciences (Magennis & Farrell, 2005), active learning and retention of knowledge occurs more authentically when educators spend less time on passive teaching methods (e.g. lecture, reading, audio-visual, demonstration) and more time on participatory teaching methods (e.g. group discussion, practice, teaching others). Harmony's STEM SOS model follows this research-based approach to teach STEM via project-based learning in high-need and underprivileged schools. When introducing a new concept in STEM, Harmony teachers initially spend just enough time get students interested in an entry event and present basic background information along with posing intriguing high-level questions to spark student interest in the topic (Sahin & Kulm, 2008; Sahin, 2008; Sahin, 2013). Passive teaching methods are utilized to ensure initial student engagement in the projects; teachers then gradually release control over to student groups. Students are then provided with ample time to discuss their understanding, share their theories and conjectures, build on each other's ideas, and learn to agree or respectfully disagree with one another. These discussions lead to both individual and group practices where students test their hypotheses through experiments, making observations, collecting data and recording their evidence. They then report back with their findings both within and across groups, which leads to further meaningful student discussions in which their ideas and theories are backed by scientific data and experimental observations. Sahin, Top, and Almus (2014a) quoted a Harmony science teacher explaining student gains through structured authentic lessons:

> Students get to understand that failure is OK. Students learn through their failure and implement new practices the next time they run an experiment. Students also get to evaluate themselves on how well they are able to design an experiment and follow through with their plan.

When each cycle of PBL projects is complete, students are tasked with teaching what they learned back to others in a public environment where they make immediate use of their learning. That is authentic teaching and learning at its best!

Outreach Expansion and Effects

With students presenting their projects at parent nights, open house events, and STEM school festivals, Harmony Public Schools started adding more outreach opportunities to extend the stage, so to speak, in an effort to help students continue to share and shine in other public educational events throughout the year. A few good examples are local educational public festivals and fairs with STEM themes organized by other external agencies in different communities such as Sally Ride Science Festivals, Houston Energy Day, and STEM Fiesta by Workforce Development Upper Rio Grande. In these kind of public STEM events, Harmony administrators simply request booth spaces like an exhibitor, but the difference is, Harmony brings students who run the show to share and shine and build the reputation of Harmony Public Schools in their respective communities. Needless to say, these booths run by Harmony students always outshine other booths run by for-profit or non-profit STEM organizations who also share great STEM resources and demonstrate simple experiments. The visitors are always much more interested in seeing what middle and high school students are capable of when they roll up their sleeves and put on a STEM show to showcase their success and encourage their peers to promote STEM education. Many teachers and students who visit these festivals and expos as part of a field trip end up reaching out to Harmony Public Schools officials to learn more about Harmony's STEM SOS model and look for resources to start replicating this successful model that puts students at the center-stage with tremendous levels of student engagement and ownership in such authentic work.

In the Teacher Voice study conducted by Sahin et al. (2014a), one Harmony math teacher emphasized that the STEM SOS model requires students "to take charge of their own learning, to explore a topic of interest in depth, and to communicate their findings clearly to their peers and the public" (p. 10). The study also revealed the authenticity of STEM lessons delivered to students through project-based learning. "Students don't try to find one accurate answer to questions because the main question of the projects are open-ended questions. This is another thing we expect from students, to make research about open-ended questions. This also helps them build their presentation and research skills" (Sahin et al., 2014a, p.). This type of inquiry-based learning – engaging students in deeper learning, doing research to find answers to open-ended driving questions – is a key aspect of project-based learning in Harmony's STEM SOS model. The purpose of STEM outreach, among other things, is to expose this innovative learning and teaching mentality to other students and educators outside of Harmony, to set a great example and to lead them to innovation in STEM education, thus impacting lives, workforce development and the global economy beyond the walls of our classrooms.

After participating in school-wide STEM festivals and other local STEM expo events numerous times, Harmony students were now ready for a larger challenge, to present at regional and statewide STEM arenas. With strategic public relations and outreach connections, Harmony Public Schools district administrators manage to put on a statewide show at the state capitol building in Austin every year. Students from different Harmony school campuses compete to secure a place on stage at the Texas Capitol Building and proudly present their STEM projects to politicians, policy and lawmakers, state representatives, congressmen and congresswomen, etc. Some of those students impressed their audience so much that they were offered internships in public offices. All of this offers a wonderful opportunity to build a resume and a college portfolio.

Reaching out to political leaders and public servants was wonderful, but Harmony leaders felt that they needed to continue their outreach efforts with another statewide

Figure 1. A group of students doing demonstrations at the ISWEEEP public day. (Please use your QR reader to scan the QR code to watch the movie).

event to bring teachers, counselors, and school and district leaders together. This proven model of STEM education should be utilized throughout the state to lead reform movements in STEM education and ultimately close the talent and workforce shortage in STEM areas, starting with Texas. Hence, another innovative idea was born: Celebrating STEM Education Week in Texas (CSEWT). With the help of an advisory board consisting of industry leaders and higher education partners in the Houston area, Celebration of STEM Education Week in Texas was born in 2012 and has become an annual public event as proclaimed by the then governor of Texas, Rick Perry, and almost every single mayoral city in the state each year. With Harmony's leadership, many schools around the state have become part of this phenomenon and organized public events and activities in and out of their classrooms to promote and celebrate STEM education for an entire week in early May. The week culminates with a national and international science project Olympiad, International Sustainable World Energy Engineering Environment Project (I-SWEEEP) that, every year, brings the brightest young talent from forty-three US states and over seventy countries around the globe to Houston, Texas, the energy capital of the world. It made so much sense to form this week around I-SWEEEP as the organization brings hundreds of talented students and STEM educators together in Texas, which becomes an international hub of information exchange with the common denominator of STEM. CSEWT includes panel discussions, workshops and resource fairs with the purpose of bringing industry leaders, educational leaders and practitioners together to collaborate on how to move our communities forward with STEM education, understand the needs and challenges of both industry and the education sector and share best practices and resources to promote and emphasize STEM in schools.

One day during I-SWEEEP is dedicated to public viewing at which time hundreds of Harmony students from around Houston compliment the research projects of I-SWEEEP finalists with their STEM demonstrations to offer visitors a plethora of taste in all imaginable shades of STEM. The I-SWEEEP Public Day and Celebration of STEM Education Week in TX opened another outreach door for the Harmony family to showcase amazing student artifacts in other national STEM conferences and events. Harmony Public Schools district leaders then started identifying similar STEM conferences and expo events around the nation to spotlight Harmony STEM SOS Model with the most effective marketing strategy of showing it in action, with students presenting their PBL projects. Below is a concise list of nationally recognized STEM events that Harmony students attend every year:

- National Science Teachers Association (NSTA) STEM Conference & Expo
- American Physical Society (APS) Plasma Science Expo
- USA Science and Engineering Fair (USASEF)
- South by Southwest (SXSW) Technology Conference
- Texas STEM Conference (T-STEM)

In almost all of these public STEM events at which Harmony students present, it is common to find an audience that represents all generations, from 5 year-olds to 75 year-olds, all eager to see innovative science tricks. Harmony educators have expressed the great joy of watching their students master the art of public speaking and adjusting their language to be age-appropriate for their audience one minute to the next. Sahin et al. (2014a) quoted one Harmony teacher talking about this very 21st century skill in their Teacher Voice Study:

> They are presenting and explaining everything to people. At these events, there aren't just educators and high school kids, but sometimes there are 5 year olds or 70 year old seniors asking "What is going on?" The students are talking to people who have no idea what is happening. Whenever they do this again and again, you can see and realize that they are changing the way they are explaining depending on the visitor. If it is a kid, they try simplifying it. If it is a senior or someone who knows about the subject, they try to go more in depth. For me, presenting and communicating with people of different backgrounds are very important skills they will need in both college and life.

> In terms of college readiness skills, the study also points to the fact that the share and shine approach brings out the best in each child and guides them through a self-discovery of what they can achieve in traditionally hard-to-learn STEM disciplines. In one of Harmony teachers' own words, "regular teaching is teacher centered in education, but the STEM SOS model is student centered, so students have more of a chance to shine and discover their own abilities, which will help them in college." (Sahin et al., 2014a, p. 15)

As explained throughout this chapter, Harmony's STEM SOS model has gained well-deserved attention and popularity in so many school communities, not only in Texas, but also around many different corners of the United States. Every year, HPS district leaders receive dozens of invitations from different schools (public, private, and charter) across the nation; upon request, HPS STEM curriculum directors have hosted and trained many groups of science and math teachers from California, Nevada, Arizona, New Mexico, Oklahoma, Louisiana, Arkansas, Missouri, Illinois, New Jersey and New York, to name a few.

The STEM SOS model is unique, but sustainable. The model has been replicated by a number of other charter management organizations in several of the aforementioned states; in particular, Louisiana is a great example of this replication. Several years ago, a stand-alone STEM academy in Kenilworth, LA eagerly adopted Harmony's STEM SOS model and the K-8 charter school has quickly seen tremendous results, with improved test scores and student engagement. Besides improved student outcomes, school leaders in Kenilworth strategically used the STEM SOS model to build public support and engage their community, actually taking Harmony's school-wide STEM festival idea and turning it into a state-wide celebration of STEM. By putting their middle school students on stage explaining their interesting STEM projects with such enthusiasm, the predominantly African-American student body of Kenilworth showed the entire community what they are capable of given the right

153

approach to STEM education. Now called the Louisiana STEM Expo, middle school students from this Kenilworth charter school showcase their success in this state-wide public STEM event. The event brings together professors and engineers from area universities and research centers to evaluate student projects and organizers also invite a number of other STEM professionals to throw a career fair for students. What an amazing way to celebrate success and promote STEM for young students!

CONCLUSION

This chapter described outreach initiatives specifically targeted at Harmony Public Schools to celebrate student success and build public support through STEM SOS model. The outreach strategies outlined here serve as the means for both students and educators to meet with other fellow students and educators to share a proven model of STEM education that has shown exciting results. While these outreach efforts were primarily intended to extend learning opportunities for students, they created a significant momentum within all school communities in terms of engaging various stakeholders and promoting Harmony schools in their respective communities.

REFERENCES

Magennis, S., & Farrell, A. (2005). Teaching and learning activities: Expanding the repertoire to support student learning. In G. O'Neill, S. Moore & B. McMullin (Eds.), *Emerging issues in the practice of university learning and teaching*. Dublin: All Ireland Society for Higher Education/Higher Education Authority.

Sahin, A., Top, N., & Almus, K. (2014a). *Teachers' reflections on STEM students on the stage (SOS)™ model*. Retrieved from http://www.harmonytx.org/Portals/0/HPS%20Issue-2.pdf

Sahin, A., Top, N., & Vanegas, S. (2014b). *Harmony STEM SOS model increases college readiness and develops 21st century skills*   (Whitepaper). Retrieved from http://harmonytx.org/Portals/0/HPS_Issue-1.pdf

Sahin, A., & Top, N. (in press). Make it happen: A study of a novel teaching style, *STEM Students on the Stage* (SOS)™, for increasing students' STEM knowledge and interest. *The Journal of STEM Education: Innovations and Research*.

Sahin, A. (2013). Teachers' awareness and acquisition of questioning strategies. *Sakarya University Journal of Education, 3*, 17–36.

Sahin, A., & Kulm, G. (2008). Sixth grade mathematics teachers' intentions and use of probing, guiding, and factual questions. *Journal of Mathematics Teacher Education, 11*, 221–242.

Sahin, A. (2008). The effects of teachers' types, quantity, and quality of teacher questions students achievement. In G. Kulm, (Ed.), *Teacher knowledge and practice in middle grades mathematics* (pp. 19–27). Rotterdam, The Netherlands: Sense.

Burak Yilmaz
Center for STEM Education
Harmony Public Schools

Eugene Kennedy, Ph.D.
Associate Professor
School of Education
Louisiana State University

Tevfik Eski, Ph.D
Superintendent
Kenilworth Science and Technology Charter School

12. EQUITY IN STEM & STEM FOR ALL

This chapter provides a discussion on equity in STEM education, gender and minority gaps in the STEM workforce and how the STEM SOS model helps to close these gaps and overcome the underrepresentation of women and minorities in STEM majors and the STEM workforce. "STEM for All" is one of the five core values of Harmony Public Schools and it implies that in Harmony, every student will graduate with a strong understanding and appreciation of STEM and how it connects to the real world. This chapter is intentionally titled *Equity in STEM and STEM for All* since we believe and have observed that the *"STEM for All"* approach to STEM education empirically helps in closing the gaps in equity in STEM Education.

INTRODUCTION

STEM education is very critical in growing the workforce and is needed to drive our nation's innovation and competitiveness. A presidential report (PCAST, 2010) states that STEM education is going to play the most crucial role in determining who is going to lead other nations in technological innovation and provide solutions to urgent problems in energy, health, and environment. According to a report from the U.S. Department of Commerce (ESA, 2011), the growth in STEM jobs was three times as fast as growth in non-STEM jobs during the 2000-2010 period and is projected to grow by 17% from 2008 to 2018, whereas non-STEM jobs' growth is 9.8% as shown in Figure 1.

However, the gap between STEM jobs and the percentage of students interested in STEM majors is widening. According to MyCollege (2012), there will be a demand for an 8.6 million US STEM workforce by 2018, but only 25% of students are interested in STEM majors. More importantly, there are growing concerns related to equity in STEM education especially between male and female students and among different demographic groups. The misconception that STEM education is only for high-achievers results in fewer students participating in STEM programs and choosing STEM majors. Without increasing the number of students selecting STEM major by cultivating STEM interest in students from all demographic backgrounds and genders, it is inevitable that the shortage in skilled STEM workers will have a negative impact on the U.S. position as a global leader in technological innovation.

A. Sahin (Ed.), A Practice-based Model of STEM Teaching, 157–167.

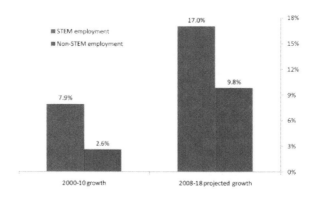

Figure 1. Growth in STEM and non-STEM employment.

STEM WORKFORCE GAP

Before we discuss the gender and minority gaps in STEM education and thus in the STEM workforce, we discuss the bigger issue that contributes greatly in widening these gaps even further: the gap between the STEM workforce needed and the number of students choosing STEM majors. As stated before, the U.S. STEM workforce is projected to grow to 8.6 million by 2018, but only a quarter of high school students are interested in STEM majors. The gap is widening because 38% of students who enters into a STEM major do not graduate with a STEM degree and 43% of STEM graduates do not work in STEM occupations (Carnevale, 2011). A recent report by My College Options and STEMConnector reports that high school seniors are about 10% less likely than high school freshmen to indicate interest in STEM majors and careers (MyCollege, 2012). These striking statistics show that in order to close the STEM workforce gap, a comprehensive approach is needed to: (1) increase the number of students interested in STEM majors, (2) engage students with STEM activities who initially plan to pursue STEM majors but change their minds by the time they are seniors, (3) make sure that students graduate college with a strong understanding and appreciation of STEM. A similar finding is voiced in the presidential report (PCAST, 2010) that to improve STEM education, the key goals are to focus on both the preparation and inspiration of students to learn STEM and, by doing so, motivate them to pursue STEM-related college degrees and careers.

THE GENDER GAP

According to the U.S. Department of Commerce's *Women in STEM* report, even though women make up to 50% of all jobs in the U.S. economy, they hold less than 25% of STEM jobs as shown in Figure 2 and women with a STEM degree are less likely to work in a STEM job; they are more likely to work in education or healthcare (USDC, 2011).

A survey of 5.5 million high school students, which covers 95% of U.S. high schools reports that male students are more than three times likely to be interested in STEM majors and careers, compared to female students. Figure 3 illustrates the gender gap in STEM interest over the last 20 years. While the gender gap had remained relatively steady over a long period of time in the past, it is now increasing at a significant and alarming rate (MyCollege, 2012). Considering the fact that women with STEM jobs earn 33% more than women in non-STEM jobs, closing the gender gap in STEM workforce will also help in reducing the gender pay gap between college-educated men and women in U.S.

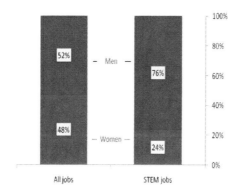

Figure 2. Gender shares of total and STEM jobs, 2009.

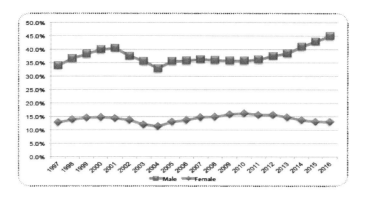

Figure 3. National 20-Year trends in STEM interest by gender.

159

Women in STEM. A Gender Gap to Innovation report (USDC, 2011) that aggregates the research to understand the underrepresentation of women in STEM fields reveals three main reasons: 1) negative stereotypes about women's abilities in math and science (gender stereotyping), 2) female students' lack of interest in STEM and issues related with STEM degree programs, and 3) STEM workplace including less family-friendly environments and bias toward women. Historically, boys have outperformed girls in math; however, in last decade girls have been doing as well as boys in math on average (Hyde et al., 2008). Also as shown in Figures 4 and 5, girls

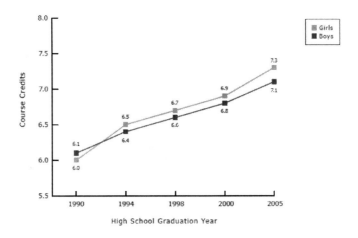

Figure 4. High school credits earned in math and science, by gender, 1990–2005.

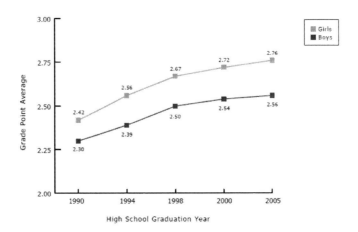

Figure 5. GPA in high school math and science (combined) by gender, 1990–2005.

are earning high school math and science credits at the same rate as boys and are earning slightly higher grades in those classes (NCES, 2007).

With the elimination of gender stereotyping in math and science achievement for women, the key issue to closing the gender gap in STEM degree programs and STEM workforce, then becomes cultivating STEM interest in female students and graduating them college and career ready for STEM majors and STEM workforce. Throughout this book, student statements show that female and minority students who are normally reluctant to pursue STEM majors in college because of aforementioned reasons, change their mind once they participate in STEM SOS type hands-on activities and start taking AP classes in Science, Statistics, Physics or Chemistry to prepare for college. The testimonials and the survey results of the female students confirm that they developed STEM interest through their enjoyment of scientific experiments and became more interested in STEM subjects. One student stated: "I have never really been great in science, but I have learned that when you really focus on it, you add interest" (Sahin, Top, & Vanegas, 2014, p. 7).

STEM for All envisions closing the gender gap by engaging all students both male and female through student-driven PBL projects as part of the STEM SOS model, which is a process that leads to mastery of critical content knowledge as well as acquiring critical skills including teamwork, communication, perseverance, creativity, and problem solving.

The YouTube video of two female Harmony students who talk about how the STEM SOS project helped them to develop self-confidence in speaking in front of public and eventually winning 1st place in a debate championship is a true testament of this aspect of the STEM SOS model. The students also talk about how they were encouraged to take AP Science and AP English. http://www.youtube.com/watch?v=Fc8GgMqu-vk

Figure 6. Two female students talking about how they won 1st place in debate championship. (Please use your QR Reader to scan the QR code to watch the video).

A recent study (Sahin, Willson, & Capraro, 2013) that examined Harmony's achievement scores found that by implementing the STEM SOS model, Harmony schools do better in female and Hispanic students at grades 4-11 in math and reading and significantly better at grades 7-11 in mathematics and grades 6-11 in reading than their counterpart public schools.

DISADVANTAGED STUDENTS & MINORITY GAP

According to (Gates, 2011), STEM disciplines pose some of the highest barriers to college readiness for students from disadvantaged and underserved backgrounds. Yet, as shown in Figure 7, there is a significant gap in the level of interest in STEM among students from different demographic backgrounds (MyCollege, 2012). Up until 2001, African American students had the highest level of interest in STEM after Asian students. However, since then, African American student interest in STEM majors/careers has dropped by nearly 30% and is now lower than any other ethnicity. According to (National Science Board, 2008), African American and Hispanic students are less likely to have access to advanced courses in math and science in high school, which negatively affects their ability to enter and successfully complete STEM majors in college (Frizell & Nave, 2008; Tyson et al., 2007). For example, 25% of Asian American and 10% of white high school graduates took either the AP or IB exam in calculus, compared to just 3.2% of African American and 5.6% of Hispanic graduates.

Harmony schools serve more than 24,000 students of diverse backgrounds: 56% of Harmony students are low income and 80% of students are minorities: 45% Hispanic, 19% African American, and 16% Asian. Without a comprehensive "*STEM for All*" type of approach to STEM education that will attract students from all racial/ethical backgrounds to STEM majors, we will not be able to grow the

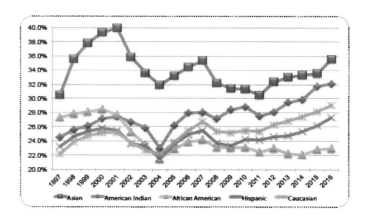

Figure 7. National 20-year trends in STEM interest by ethnicity.

Figure 8. A student presenting her project in front of a camera for her e-portfolio (Please use your QR reader to scan the QR codes to watch her presentation and/or see her e-portfolio website).

STEM workforce needed to sustain economic development and global leadership. Every school should provide the necessary tools and support to all their students in closing the minority gap with the expectation that all their minority and low-income students will be performing as well as their white peers in each school and across the state. *STEM for All* envisions closing these gaps by engaging students from all ethnic backgrounds, gender and achievement levels, through personalized, student-driven PBL projects as part of the STEM SOS model. Students design an experiment or demonstration about a STEM topic of their choice and learn to use the scientific method, work with peers, teach their classmates about their topics, and present their findings on a website, or a brochure, or a movie. This process leads to mastery of critical content knowledge as well as acquiring critical skills including teamwork, communication, perseverance, creativity, and problem solving. Moreover, since the projects are largely student-driven with respect to both the topics and the process, it has been observed that this increases the levels of motivation of students; they see the value in what they are learning because they are pursuing things based on their own interests and learning styles. An example of the video presentation of such a project is given below:

The YouTube video of a minority background Harmony student whose research question is "the principle of resonance and acoustics" The video clearly demonstrates how highly motivated and engaged the student is in articulating to investigate such an important concept in a clear way with the help of STEM SOS approach. https://www.youtube.com/watch?v=fNJQUHXsweg

CLOSING THE GENDER AND MINORITY GAPS & COLLEGE READINESS

Another reason for the underrepresentation of female students and minorities in STEM majors and STEM workforce is the problem of college readiness for STEM fields. This makes sense since student achievement in STEM disciplines in high school is among the strongest predictors of success in college and is one of the prime indicators of college readiness (Gates, 2011). In his extensive study, Conley (2007) identifies three categories of skills that are key to the college readiness: (1) cognitive skills like analysis, reasoning, and problem-solving skills, (2) behavioral skills including study skills, teamwork, time management, and persistence, and (3) contextual knowledge that students must demonstrate to be successful in college.

In Harmony, all three categories of skills are reinforced through activities in the STEM SOS model. Students take AP Science and AP Math classes, develop STEM-focused PBL projects, compete in science fairs and other competitions often judged by college professors, analyse a problem, develop a hypothesis, run experiments, propose a solution, make a logical conclusion and present the findings to an audience including judges who often are college professors or graduate students. These experiences help young students prepare for the college environment and ease the transition from high school to college avoiding a serious level of culture shock. Student statements and research presented in Chapter 4 show that STEM SOS activities positively affect student achievement and improves both cognitive and non-cognitive skills of students, which play the major role in college success.

As far as the 3rd skill set is concerned, through extensive research, it is known that PBL provides opportunities for students to acquire rigorous content knowledge and students in PBL classrooms learn more about critical subject areas through activities that stimulate critical thinking, collaboration, creativity, and communication (Boss, 2012). The students at Harmony reported that STEM SOS PBL projects help them better understand complicated subjects and appreciate the learning experience more by experimenting with the real world application of the concepts (Sahin & Top, in press; Sahin, et al., 2014). One of the biggest advantages of STEM education is that it can empower students, help them to develop natural curiosity about world affairs and technology and acquire problem-solving skills.

Table 1 shows a subset of the results of a study conducted in Harmony, as part of the application for a Race-to-Top-District grant, to measure the impact of AP-class taking and participation in STEM SOS activities on pursuing STEM majors and college readiness.

Table 1. % College-Ready Graduates for 2007-2010

% College-Ready Graduates	Harmony	State	Region
College Ready in ELA and Math Class of 2010	75	66	67
College Ready ELA and Math Class of 2009	54	62	64
College Ready in ELA and Math Class of 2008	48	59	60
College Ready in ELA and Math Class of 2007	29	49	51

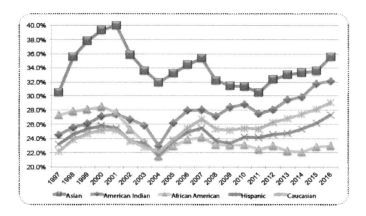

Figure 9. College readiness level in ELA and math.

The trend analysis of this data is shown in Figure 9.

As the steady progress each year compared to previous year illustrates in the figure, participation in STEM SOS activities and taking AP classes significantly impacted the college readiness level of students.

Custom Day: Closing the Achievement Level Gap

Another obstacle in attracting more students to STEM majors is the misconception that STEM education is only for certain types of high achieving students. This misconception often results in fewer students participating in STEM programs and therefore fewer students choosing STEM majors. In order to overcome this obstacle, all students are encouraged to participate in STEM SOS programs like science fair competitions, science Olympiad teams, STEM internships, university partnerships, robotics program and competitions (Harmony STEM handbook, 2013). Students are supported through a custom day schedule, which enables them to receive remediation and extra support in math and English Language Arts (ELA). As part of the Race to The Top-District (RTT-D) grant implementation, a custom day initiative is implemented in Harmony schools for math and English Language Arts. Depending on an individual student's needs, two hours a day is devoted to intervention, enrichment, or elective courses. The custom day initiative provides the time and structure within the school day for students to receive individualized support to master skills at the pace and through the modality most suited to their specific learning needs. Custom day is a great tool to help minority and female students in catching up to their male and white peers in STEM fields and receive support to achieve a high-level of STEM interest by addressing the needs of these students in an effective fashion.

CONCLUSION

STEM education and the STEM SOS model have had a positive impact on students' college readiness and a critical set of skills that are often called 21st century skills. But more importantly, through PBL projects, female and minority students can engage in complex, authentic learning activities that deepen content knowledge and develop skills key to success in the 21st century. The results and survey of students from diverse backgrounds and both genders show that the STEM SOS model cultivates STEM interest among female and minority students and encourages them to pursue STEM majors in college (Sahin & Top, in press; Sahin et al., 2014

Additionally, throughout the course of STEM SOS activities, students learn to use the scientific method, work with peers and experts, teach their classmates about their topics, and present their findings using technology. These activities not only help them master knowledge in the critical subject area, but also helps to develop students' higher-order thinking skills, as well as critical skills such as teamwork, communication, perseverance, creativity, and problem solving. The PBL projects helps students in creating a college culture, where every student has the mindset that she or he can and will go to college and makes an explicit link between a strong STEM foundation and success in career.

In conclusion, the "STEM for All" approach to STEM education seems to be helping in closing the gender and minority gaps in STEM workforce overcoming the underrepresentation of women and minorities in STEM majors and STEM workforce (Sahin, Wilson, Capraro, 2013). As a side benefit for female students, a STEM career is also a matter of pay equity considering the fact that women with STEM jobs earn 33% more than women in non-STEM jobs. Therefore, through the STEM SOS approach, closing the gender gap in STEM workforce, also helps to reduce the gender pay gap between college-educated men and women in the U.S.

REFERENCES

Boss, S. (2012). *Project-based learning: A short history.* Retrieved from http://www.edutopia.org/project-based-learning-history

Carnevale, A. P. (2011). STEM. Georgetown University Center on Education and the Workforce.

ESA, U.S. Department of Commerce, Economics and Statistics Administration. STEM: Good Jobs Now and for the Future. *ESA Issue Brief #03-11.* July 2011. Retrieved from http://esa.doc.gov/sites/default/files/reports/documents/stemfinalyjuly14_1.pdf

Conley, D. T. (2007). *Redefining College Readiness.* Educational Policy Improvement Center.

Frizell, S., & Nave, F. (2008). *A preliminary analysis of factors affecting the persistence of African-American females in engineering degree programs.* Paper presented at the American Society for Engineering Education Annual Conference, Pittsburgh, PA.

Gates. (2011). *STEM Education.* Retrieved from http://www.gatesfoundation.org/college-ready-education/Pages/stem-education.aspx

Harmony STEM Program. (2013). *Part II: Harmony public schools (HPS) project-based learning initiative.* Retrieved from https://docs.google.com/document/d/1Iwk06YS2fXhvRwtj_LP41v4ctDRuUFyQg2BaKA6owls/pub

Hyde, J. S., Lindberg, S. M., Linn, M. C., Ellis, A., & Williams, C. (2008, July 25). Gender similarities characterize math performance. *Science, 321,* 494–495.

My College Options® & STEMConnector.org®. (2012). *Executive summary: Where are the STEM students?* Retrieved from http://www.stemconnector.org/sites/default/files/store/STEM-Students-STEM-Jobs-Executive-Summary.pdf

National Science Board. (2008). *Science and engineering indicators 2008* (Volume 1, NSB08-01; Volume 2, NSB 08-01A). Arlington, VA:

NCES, U.S. Department of Education, National Center for Education Statistics, 2007, The Nation's Report Card: America's high school graduates:

PCAST, T. P. (2010). K-12 Education in Science, Technology, Engineering, And Math (STEM) For America's Future. *President's Council of Advisors on on Science and Technology.* Retrieved from http://www.whitehouse.gov/sites/default/files/microsites/ostp/pcast-stem-ed-final.pdf

Sahin, A., Willson, V., & Capraro, R. M. (2013). *Can charter schools be silver bullets to the American educational system?* Proceedings of American Educational Research Association (AERA), San Francisco, CA.

Sahin, A., & Top, N. (In press). Make it happen: A study of a novel teaching style, STEM Students on the Stage (SOS)™, for increasing students' STEM knowledge and interest. *The Journal of STEM Education: Innovations and Research.*

Sahin, A., Top, N., & Vanegas, S. (2014). *Harmony STEM SOS model increases college readiness and develops 21st century skills* (Whitepaper). Retrieved from http://harmonytx.org/Portals/0/HPS_Issue-1.pdf

Tyson, W., Lee, R., Borman, K. M., & Hanson, M. A. (2007). Science, technology, engineering, and mathematics (STEM) pathways: High school science and math coursework and postsecondary degree attainment. *Journal of Education for Students Placed at Risk, 12*, 243–70.

USDC, U.S. Department of Commerce, Economics and Statistics Administration. Women in STEM: A Gender Gap to Innovation *ESA Issue Brief #04-11*. July 2011. Retrieved from http://esa.doc.gov/sites/default/files/reports/documents/stemfinaljuly14_1.pdf

Oner Ulvi Celepcikay
University of Houston-Downtown

Soner Tarim
CEO, Harmony Public Schools

SECTION 4
MODEL OUTCOMES

As the model emerges and its tenets are clarified, the chapters in this section highlight the benefits of the model at both the student and school levels. The first chapter investigates the critical 21st century skills students developed through participation in the STEM SOS model. The following chapter discusses how the STEM SOS model contributes to an effective school culture and high-quality school climate as well as establishing and sustaining a school environment free of harassment, bullying and discrimination.

ALPASLAN SAHIN

13. HOW DOES THE STEM SOS MODEL HELP STUDENTS ACQUIRE AND DEVELOP 21ST CENTURY SKILLS?

The skills necessary for the 21st century workforce have evolved as the world has transformed from an industrial society to a knowledge-based society; therefore, today's employers are often looking for employees equipped with a new set of skills that are more sophisticated than typical qualifications. This case study examines how students attending a Harmony Public school (HPS) that implements the Science, Technology, Engineering and mathematics (STEM) SOS model in their mathematics and science courses develop 21st century skills. The STEM SOS model was developed by HPS and incorporates project-based learning activities by using ready-to-teach projects developed by the HPS science department. The sample was comprised of 120 11th grade students. The data were analysed by grouping students' responses according to common themes. Results revealed that students developed oral communication and teamwork/collaboration skills, persistence and a strong work ethic, critical thinking/problem solving, leadership, creativity and innovation, information technology, ethics/social responsibility and mathematics and science skills through the STEM SOS model. This chapter will discuss how the STEM SOS model helps students develop the skills necessary to be successful in the 21st century workforce.

INTRODUCTION

21st Century Skills Literature

The 21st century has brought many changes to our lives, from manufacturing to broader dissemination of information and technology. Today's students know that the future holds jobs that require more advanced skills (Roblin, 2012; Sahin, Ayar, & Adiguzel, 2014) because many traditional jobs have been outsourced or replaced with high-tech tools. Because of rapidly changing technology, students must also be prepared for jobs that do not yet exist (Dede, 2010). Research on the skills that today's workforce needs has yielded important findings about what skills employers are looking for. In this regard, Deloitt Development (2005) surveyed manufacturers to find out what types of skills they look for in employees. The manufacturers reported that they look for basic employability skills such as attendance, timeliness,

A. Sahin (Ed.), A Practice-based Model of STEM Teaching, 171–186.

and a strong work ethic in addition to problem-solving, collaboration, and reading, writing and communication skills. Casner-Lotto and Barrington (2006) conducted a similar study with 400 business executives and managers, asking them to rank the relative importance of 20 skills and fields of knowledge. Respondents ranked professionalism/work ethic, teamwork/collaboration and oral communication as the top three skills that they desire in employees. Science knowledge was ranked 17th in importance in the list of 20 skills expected from high school graduates and critical thinking/problem solving, information technology application, teamwork/ collaboration, and creativity/innovation were ranked as the skills that would become the most important in the next five years. These skills are quite similar to the 21st century skills defined by the Partnership for 21st Century Skills, 2011, Educational Testing Services, 2007, and The North Central Regional Education Laboratory, 2008. In addition to the above skills, this group of researchers also included traditional subjects as well as civic literacy, global awareness, financial, health and environmental literacy (Pacific Policy Research Center, 2010).

Therefore, contemporary schooling should provide students with a more comprehensive education that prepares them for the 21st century workforce (Pacific Policy Research Center, 2010). More specifically, students should acquire 21st century skills that will enable them to a) collect and/or retrieve information, b) organize and manage information, c) evaluate the quality, relevance, and usefulness of information and d) generate accurate information through the use of existing resources (Educational Testing Service, 2007). A body of research also encourages educators to focus on real-world problems and processes, support inquiry-based learning experiences, provide opportunities for collaborative project approaches to learning and focus on teaching students how to learn (Pacific Policy Research Center, 2010). Active learning methods in which students take responsibility for their own learning and participate in inquiry- and project-based learning are seen as pivotal to fulfilling these goals.

Role of PBLs in Cultivating 21st Century Skills

Project-based learning (PBL) is an innovative educational approach in which students work collaboratively on ill-defined tasks that have multiple solutions and real-world connections. This approach has substantial benefits for students' preparation for the future workforce. In this regard, students who participate in PBL lessons have greater autonomy in the classroom and more opportunities to acquire 21st century skills such as collaboration, oral communication and critical thinking (e.g., Mergendoller, Markham, Ravitz, & Larmer, 2006). The completion of collaborative projects and presentations makes PBL a very appropriate teaching and learning method for students to develop 21st century skills. PBL also benefits students who struggle with traditional lecture learning, as it is highly engaging and may be a better fit for students' learning style and preference (Darling-Hammond et al., 2008).

In a recent study, researchers found that PBL creates opportunities for students to learn rigorous content knowledge and 21st century skills (Ravitz, Hixson, English, & Mergendoller, 2012). According to this study, teachers who use PBL and attend extended professional development do more teaching and assessment of 21st century skills compared with a closely matched comparison group. That is, students in PBL classrooms spend more time learning about important content through activities that emphasize critical thinking, collaboration, creativity and communication (Boss, 2012).

Brief Summary of the STEM SOS Model

Research on active learning methods has shown that PBL projects can increase students' interest in STEM and students' engagement with the material being taught by solving authentic problems, collaborating with others and building products that have real-life connections and applications (Fortus, Krajcikb, Dershimerb, Marx, & Mamlok-Naamand, 2005). Recently, Harmony Public Schools (HPS) developed their own STEM curriculum that incorporates project-based and inquiry-based learning. This curriculum was codified and named "STEM Students on the Stage (SOS)™" (Sahin & Top, in press; Sahin, Top, & Vanessa, 2014) (read Chapter 3 for an explanation of the full model). The development of the STEM SOS model was funded by a Race to the Top grant through the U.S. Department of Education with the goal of increasing students' STEM knowledge and interest and also producing self-motivated and self-regulated learners (Harmony STEM Program, 2013).

The primary purpose of the STEM SOS model is "to maintain the focus on standards-based and student-centered teaching while enriching and extending the learning of students through PBL projects. The goal is to promote collaborative skills, student ownership of learning and student success in meeting state and national standards" (p.x) through student projects on Levels I, II, and III. All students must complete a Level I project followed by either a regular Level II or advanced Level III project (read Chapter 3 for more details on Level I, II, and III projects/assessments).

The purpose of the study was to investigate students' development of 21st century skills at a school where the STEM SOS model was implemented. An additional aim of the study was to understand the lived experiences of students participating in the STEM SOS model in order to determine which activities helped them acquire those skills. At that stage in the research, the STEM SOS model was generally defined as the desirable model for students to acquire 21st century skills.

The specific research questions were:

1. What types of 21st century skills did students develop at a school where the STEM SOS model was implemented?
2. What types of STEM SOS activities were associated with the development of specific 21st century skills if students believed they developed those skills?

METHOD

Sample

Convenience sampling was used for this study. One of the Harmony high schools was selected due to its close proximity to the researcher. The sample was comprised of 120 11th grade students, with female students comprising 51% of the sample. 78% of the students received either a free or reduced lunch. Students' demographics were 45% Hispanic, 27% African American, 16% white, and 13% Asian. The 11th grade students were selected for the study sample because they had participated in three mathematics courses (Algebra I, Geometry, and Algebra II) and three science courses (Biology, Chemistry, and Physics) in which the STEM SOS curriculum was implemented.

Instrument

We developed a 30-item online survey including both Likert-type and open-ended questions to gather information about students' perception of their level of specific 21st century skills and how they developed those skills. If students responded "somewhat agree" or higher to items asking whether they developed the 11 specific 21st century skills, they were then asked to describe how they developed those skills. The survey measured students' perception of their level of 21st century skills using a Likert-type scale ranging from 1 to 7 with 7 being "strongly agree." The Likert-type items about 21st century skills were adapted from research by Casner-Lotto & Benner (2006). High instrument reliability for the 14 items was estimated using a calculation of Cronbach's alpha (a = 0.942).

Survey Administration

First, survey questions were entered into Survey Monkey. Next, we contacted the STEM coordinator at the school, who emailed the survey link to the 11th grade students' homeroom teachers. The homeroom teachers administered the survey during one of the homeroom periods between May 12-16th of 2014. Of the 120 students that began the survey, 72 completed all the questions.

Data Analysis

First, measures of central tendency were calculated. Next, student responses explaining how they developed those skills were analyzed. After the meanings of significant statements were formulated, common themes emerged and were coded by grouping those formulated meanings.

RESULTS

Descriptive statistics were provided to show students' ratings on different skills (see Table 1).

Table 1. Student Ratings for 21ˢᵗ Century Skills

Skills	N	Mean	Mode
Oral communication skills	72	5.39	6
Teamwork/collaboration skills	72	5.56	6
Persistence and Work ethic	72	5.43	6
Critical thinking/problem solving skills	72	5.39	6
Written communication skills	72	5.24	4
Ethics/social responsibility skills	72	5.43	6
Leadership skills	72	5.38	6
Information technology skills	72	6.25	6
Creativity and innovation skills	72	5.43	6
Skills to get along with many kinds of different people	72	5.45	6
Mathematics skills	72	5.44	6
Science skills	72	5.39	6
English language skills	72	5.29	4
Self-direction and self-initiative skills	72	5.35	4

We provide results for the skills that have mode of 6 to ensure that most students believed that they developed those skills. If students reported "somewhat agree" or higher, they were asked to provide written responses explaining how they developed those skills.

Oral Communication Skills

Almost three-fourths (53) of participants reported that STEM SOS PBLs helped them master oral communication skills (N=72, M=5.39). The mode for the oral communication skills was 6, indicating that most students agreed that they developed oral communication skills through PBLs. Most of the student responses discussed the importance of preparation and presentations in STEM SOS in regards to the development of oral communication skills. Students reported that they had to give presentations on the projects they completed in their science classes and this helped them develop their public speaking skills. Two student quotes are provided below:

> During our [STEM SOS] PBL projects, we were expected to communicate with our audience and present the project we were assigned, which personally improved my communicate skills.

Figure 1. A group of students demonstrating their Level II project. (Please use your QR reader to scan the QR code to watch the video).

I had to explain how things work to other classmates in order to help them. Also, during our projects/experiment, I had to communicate with them and figure things out, which made my oral communication skills stronger.

A more specific example of how students developed their public speaking skills is seen in this quote from a student:

We were doing science demonstrations to visitors coming to our school. We had people from all walks of life like parents, children, politicians, and such. So we had to do presentations and communicate with them according to their education level and age. Most of us presented in school while some of us presented in the STEM EXPO, and ISWEEEP.

So, it is clear that the STEM SOS model provided students with many opportunities to communicate with fellow students and teachers while completing projects and give presentations to their classmates and others.

Teamwork/Collaboration Skills

The majority of participants (53) indicated that they developed teamwork and collaboration skills through the STEM SOS projects in their mathematics and science courses (N=72, M=5.56). The mode for the skills was 6, which also supported the idea that most students agreed on the importance of STEM SOS projects in developing these skills. Students reported that the lab activities they completed during their science classes also helped them develop their collaboration skills. They emphasized that PBL projects, as part of STEM SOS increased their collaboration opportunities. This is demonstrated in the following student quotes:

In school, we do a lot of group activities. This helps to bring together our teamwork skills because in order for our project to be good we have to collaborate our ideas.

As part of their assessments, students must produce a digital presentation of their projects including videos of their experiments, demos, and presentations. Collaboration is an important skill because they are expected to recruit other students to help them accomplish this task. They have to communicate, collaborate and be a leader in order to successfully produce a digital presentation.

The math PBL allowed me to assertively place myself as a leader and follower multiple times to complete various projects before a very close deadline. My science teacher also assigned various group projects in previous years, which allowed me to strengthen my ability to work in a group to complete the quarterly and yearlong projects.

The PBL projects that we did were individual projects, but it indirectly required working with my classmates to complete them.

As seen in the student responses, STEM SOS projects are an important component of the science and mathematics curriculum and consist of both individual and group projects. In level II projects, students present their findings and projects through a video presentation, which requires advanced movie editing skills and Microsoft Office knowledge.

Persistence and Work Ethic

More than two thirds (50) of students reported that they developed persistence and a stronger work ethic through their mathematics and science courses and the STEM PBL projects they completed (N=72, M=5.43). Most students responded "agree" to the question asking how well they felt they had mastered persistence and work ethic skills relative to other students of their age (Mode = 6).

Students indicated that the rigor of their mathematics and science classes helped them to develop their work ethic and persistence because they had to keep up with challenging coursework and rigorous projects.

The science and math classes I took were extremely rigorous and, in order to do well, you always had to keep up with everything.

STEM SOS projects also helped students learn how to manage deadlines and fulfill their academic responsibilities. This is illustrated in the following student quotes:

The PBL project definitely developed my work ethic. There were times during the project that I didn't want to work on my PBL; however, due to the fact that it was due – I had to.

177

> I used to do things inefficiently, but then in my classes, I learned that in life, you have to do things when they need to be done. This project helped me develop my time management skills and work ethic. This will be good as time goes on and I get older and move on to larger projects.

Overall, results showed that students were very aware of the benefits of STEM SOS projects and the importance of responsibility toward their schoolwork. As one student very succinctly stated: "Work is what defines our characteristics for the future."

Critical thinking/Problem Solving Skills

Almost two thirds (47) of students agreed that the science and mathematics courses they took at their Harmony school helped them develop their critical thinking skills (N=72, M=5.39). The majority of students reported that they mastered critical thinking/problem-solving skills relative to other students of their age (Mode=6).

Students' responses provided insight into their perceptions of how they mastered their critical thinking and problem-solving skills. Some students reported that thinking outside of the box is the first step to critical thinking. In this regard, one student stated, "There are always problems that demand us to think outside of the box so [we can] think critically and use reasoning skills." They also indicated that their mathematics (Algebra I, II, and Geometry) and science courses (Biology, Chemistry, Physics, and AP Physics) were especially helpful in mastering critical thinking and problem solving skills.

> AP Chemistry and Physics require . a number of ways, and being able to figure out a number of ways to the solution was a skill learned in these classes.

The PBL projects they completed as part of STEM SOS also played an important role in helping students boost their critical thinking and problem-solving skills. For example, one student wrote:

> PBL and science project helped me develop my critical thinking and problem-solving skills.

One of the requirements of their Level I task is to prepare a project that is different from previous ones in terms of presentation and how it is done, although the task is about the same law/content. One student described the Level I task, stating: "For the critical thinking skill, students are given a project and they have to figure out a new way to present it and incorporate English and Social Studies relevancy." Some students reported that critical thinking is involved "during the construction of the project." Because students are given STEM projects in their mathematics and science courses, they have an opportunity to complete those projects in an authentic way within a given period of time. This also facilitates their critical thinking/problem solving skills development. One of the students explained this clearly, stating: "As my teachers (both science and math) gave us Level I projects and told us to work by ourselves, it helped me and my classmates improve our problem solving skills and critical thinking."

Leadership skills

More than half of the participants (43) reported that taking mathematics and science courses and participating in PBLs provided extensive opportunities for them to develop their leadership skills (N=72, M=5.38). Most students indicated that they developed their leadership skills (Mode=6).

Students' responses revealed that they primarily found opportunities to develop their leadership skills during collaborative group projects. This was especially true when they had to complete STEM SOS PBLs for mathematics and science classes. Relevant quotes from students are provided below:

> Leadership skills were seen in every assignment that consisted of group work since not everyone would step up to do work right away.

> My leadership skills grew because a lot of the time someone has to step up in the group and get things started.

> My science class pushed me to take initiative to get the job done, no matter how uncooperative circumstances and peers may be. The math PBL also pushed me to use this initiative and bring others to reach their goal as well.

> The PBL taught me leadership skills because I had to help others in their projects, from the building to the scientific principles.

To sum up, student responses highlighted the critical role of the STEM SOS model in developing their leadership skills.

Creativity and Innovation skills

Almost seventy percent of students reported that taking mathematics and science classes and completing STEM PBLs helped them develop their creativity skills (N=72, M=5.43). Most students chose "agree" when asked whether they developed creativity and innovation skills while they were at their Harmony school (Mode=6).

Students emphasized the importance of their mathematics and science classes, and PBL projects in providing opportunities for them to develop their creativity. This is illustrated in the following student quotes:

> The classes demand a certain think outside the box method that improves creativity.

> I have always been creative and somehow Algebra II had made me feel closer to that.

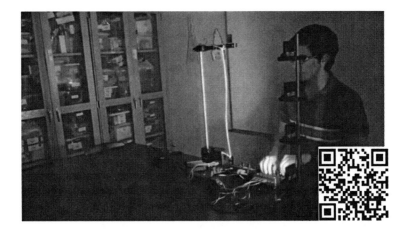

Figure 2. A student demonstrating his Level II project. (Please use your QR reader to scan the QR code to watch the video).

> My creativity comes out in my science classes through the process of problem solving.

PBL activities are something in which students continuously participate in their mathematics and science courses as part of the STEM SOS curriculum. Because they have to design and produce a product that has real-life connections, they must be creative and innovative. A number of students discussed how important the STEM SOS PBL projects were in developing their skills. This is illustrated in the following student quotes:

> Many projects and the science fair competitions along with daily classroom activities showed me how to come up with various ideas.

> Creativity was definitely involved with the PBL program. I needed creativity to design my website, as well as other aspects of the project like the brochure.

> Students had to be creative to make their project interesting.

> PBL opened up my imagination and helped me put it to the test.

Overall, it appears that putting *students on the stage* and encouraging their creativity and innovation through real-world, open-ended projects is one of the best things that educators can do.

Information Technology Skills

More than half of the students (45) reported that they developed their information technology skills by taking mathematics and science courses relative to other students of the same age (N=72, M=6.25. Mode=6).

Students at Harmony had many opportunities to develop their information technology skills through their computer classes, Chromebook integration and STEM SOS Level I, II and III assessments. Participants discussed how the STEM SOS model helped them develop their technology skills as they were required to design their own websites for projects, make videos of their experiments, create a YouTube account and upload their videos to their YouTube account. This is illustrated in the following student quotes:

Making your web sites, you need to learn how to go and link things. [For instance], I learned from someone how to link a picture. So I didn't know how to do that.

I made a video and uploaded it to the website I've created for the project I chose.

I learned to make a web page, videos for my PBL and upload them on my YouTube channel.

Accordingly, it is clear that students benefited from STEM SOS assessments. Participants also pointed out how the Chromebook laptops extended their learning in terms of information technology skills. One student stated, "When I go home, I am usually working on editing videos and putting them together." Other opportunities were also mentioned in student responses, including lab software, engineering and computer classes, use of Chromebooks in all core courses and doing research for classes:

The labs and experiments needed students to use different software and technology to perform the tasks.

Figure 3. The video providing a tutorial for students to learn how to create a Google site where students gather all their products. (Please use your QR reader to scan the QR code to watch the tutorial.).

Researching and examining data greatly increased my ability to work.

Strong engineering courses along with computer technology classes.

We have Chromebook and computer classes, which helped to improve our technology skills.

Overall, students reported that they had significant opportunities to develop their information technology skills in mathematics and science courses.

Ethics/Social Responsibility Skills

Two thirds (48) of students reported that they developed their ethical understanding and social responsibility through PBL projects in their mathematics and science classes (N=72, M=5.43). The mode of students' answers was 6, indicating that most students believed that they developed these skills.

Participants' responses revealed that PBL group projects and school assignments were primary factors in helping them to develop their ethical understanding and social responsibility skills. Quotes from participants showed how they developed these skills:

Science classes helped me a lot because of certain labs we had to do, which is good, because we have to be on point on things and be responsible on certain things.

Both [mathematics and science] classes have provided me with various opportunities to connect big ideas to the real world as well as push me to socialize and work together in a group. However these abilities stemmed more from student-teacher-student interaction, and not necessarily from the activities, though the academic portion of the classroom certainly gave me the basis to express and refine these skills.

I learned to be responsible with my work and with my team's PBL work so all members finish their portion on time.

School has taught me to be responsible for my own actions and assignments.

The emphasis on collaboration in the STEM SOS model appears to be an important avenue for students to develop their ethical understanding and social responsibility skills.

Skills to Get Along with Many Kinds of Different People

Almost two thirds (44) of students reported that they learned to get along with students of diverse backgrounds through the group work in their mathematics and science courses (N=72, M=5.43). Participants indicated that they had to develop the skills to get along with others because their courses required many group projects, including quarterly and yearlong STEM SOS PBL projects (Sahin, Top, & Vanegas, 2014).

In order to work together and understand concepts, you were placed in groups where you did not necessarily know the person, so you had to be able to communicate well with them.

We worked with different people and did many different projects for both science and math classes; these helped me a lot to learn how to get along with others.

Students also developed the "life skills" that are necessary for being a member of society through group projects. This is illustrated in the following quotes from students:

With groups sometimes being chosen for us, it showed me how to compromise and work with others.

You have to be able to handle being with people you don't like or people you are not normally with because when you have a project, you cannot always choose your groups.

Another major theme that emerged from student responses was the diversity of their school. Many students emphasized how the diversity of their school helped them learn how to get along and work with others. To this end, students stated:

Since my school is extremely diverse and you're expected to interact with everyone, I believe my skills have improved.

Our classes are very diverse, which allows us to interact with people from different backgrounds and opinions.

Diversity in the school teaches you to get along with everybody.

Students taught with the STEM SOS model usually participate in several science fairs, science Olympiads, and STEM DEMOs including the International Sustainable Energy, Engineering, and Environment Project Olympiads (ISWEEEP). This provides them with the opportunity to interact with other students and individuals from all over the world. The importance of these opportunities is illustrated in the following student quotes:

When we go to the ISWEEEP either as a contestant or a group to do science demos, we meet with lots of new students coming from different states and countries. You experience the challenges of meeting with new people who have different backgrounds and perspectives on things. So you have to respect and get along with them.

> Our school provides classes, which take us on field trips like I-SWEEEP in which all Harmony [campuses] meet in one place and people come visit to view our projects. We also get to know them and their culture.

Overall, it appears that the STEM SOS model's emphasis on collaboration among students and opportunities to meet students from diverse backgrounds through science fairs and science Olympiads supports students' development of skills to get along with others and respect of diversity.

Mathematics Skills

Almost two thirds (46) of participants indicated that the Harmony STEM SOS model helped them master their mathematics skills relative to their peers (N=72, M=5.44). Students' most frequent response for mathematics skills was "agree/6", showing how confident they were in terms of developing their mathematics skills.

Students described how the STEM SOS PBLs and projects played important roles in cultivating their mathematics skills. One student stated, "Through STEM [SOS] PBL and experiments, I have learned many new mathematics skills." Furthermore, one student described how mathematics content and skills are intermingled among subjects, stating, "I developed my mathematics skills not only through mathematics classes and [STEM SOS PBL] projects, but through other science subjects. [For example] Physics was based mostly on math." Another student gave a similar explanation of his development of mathematics skills, stating, "In my chemistry course, math was highly involved so of course it helped improve my math skills." Another group of students highlighted the daily connections of their lessons and projects in terms of mastering their mathematics skills:

> My Algebra II class has taught me a lot of math that I can use in daily life.

> Learning about the concepts of geometry in real life scenarios through PBL projects developed my math skills.

It is clear that students had many opportunities to develop their mathematics skills. Overall, STEM SOS PBLs provide authentic learning environments where students thrive and grow academically.

Science Skills

Two thirds of participants (48) reported that they mastered their science skills at their school (N=72, M=5.39). The most frequent rating for the science skills was 6, indicating that the "*agree*" rating was the most popular response among participants.

Participants described the importance of their science STEM SOS PBLs for enhancing their understanding of the relationship between what is happening in daily life and its scientific explanation.

Knowing why things occur in our world is very important and it taught us that physics is the main reason. So I have learned many new and fascinating facts about science through PBL projects.

I enjoy science. I do many scientific experiments or projects and it tells you everything that's going on around you.

You learn what happens. You never realize it; you know when the car moves, there is something you are learning, what is happening beneath the wheels, and it is interesting to learn that.

Participants also described how lab activities help them develop their science skills.

I am able to develop my science skills with labs that let me apply what I am learning with not just written examples.

The labs and experiments I did in science classes helped me master my science skills. I feel more confident in science content and how it is relevant to my life.

Overall, students reported that the STEM SOS projects and labs they did in their science classes were crucial for their development of science skills.

CONCLUSION

The purpose of the present study was to examine students' development of critical 21st century skills in the context of the STEM SOS model implemented in Harmony Public Schools. Findings revealed that students developed many of the skills important in the 21st century job market through the mathematics and science courses they took at Harmony School, including critical thinking/problem solving, creativity and innovation, oral communication, teamwork/collaboration, work ethics and persistence and leadership. Students also reported that the emphasis on collaborative real-world projects in the STEM SOS model and opportunities to present their projects at local and international science competitions helped them to develop these skills.

REFERENCES

Boss, S. (2012). *How project-based learning builds 21st century skills.* Retrieved from http://www. edutopia.org/blog/21st-century-skills-pbl-suzie-boss

Casner-Lotto, J., & Benner, M. (2006). *Are they really ready for work? Employers' perspectives on the basic knowledge and applied skills of new entrants into the 21st century workforce.* New York, NY: The Conference Board, Inc., the Partnership for 21st Century Skills, Corporate Voices for Working Families, & the Society for Human Resource Management.

Darling-Hammond, L., Barron, B., Pearson, P. D., Schoenfeld, A. H., Stage, E. K., Zimmerman, T. D., Cervetti, G. N., & Tilson, J. L. (2008). *Powerful learning: What we know about teaching for understanding.* San Francisco, CA: Wiley.

Dede, C. (2010). Comparing frameworks for 21st century skills. In J. Bellanca & R. Brandt (Eds.), *21st century skills: Rethinking how students learn* (pp. 221–240). Bloomington, IN: Solution Tree Press.

Educational Testing Service. (2007). *Digital transformation: A framework for ICT literacy.* Retrieved from http://www.ets.org/Media/Tests/Information_and_Communication_Technology_Literacy/ictreport.pdf

Harmony STEM Program. (2013). *Part II: Harmony public schools (HPS) project-based learning initiative.* Retrieved from https://docs.google.com/document/d/1lwk06YS2fXhvRwtj_LP41 v4ctD RuUFyQg2BaKA 6owls/pub

Mergendoller, J. R., Markham, T., Ravitz, J, & Larmer, J. (2006). *Pervasive management of project-based learning: Teachers as guides and facilitators.* In C. M. Evertson & C. S. Weinstein (Eds.), *Handbook of Classroom Management: Research, Practice, and Contemporary Issues.* Mahwah, NJ: Lawrence Erlbaum, Inc.

Pacific Policy Research Center. (2010). *21st Century skills for students and teachers.* Honolulu, HI: Kamehameha Schools, Research & Evaluation Division.

Partnership for 21st Century Skills. (2011). *21st century skills, education and competitiveness: A resource and policy guide.* Retrieved from: www.21stcenturyskills.org

Ravitz, J., Hixson, N., English, M., & Mergendoller, J. (2012). *Using project-based learning to teach 21st century skills: Findings from a statewide initative.* Retrieved from http://bie.org/images/uploads/gene ral/21c5f7ef7e7ee3b98172602b29d8cb6a.pdf

Roblin, N. P. (2012, November*). 21st century competences: A new challenge for Higher Education institutions?* Retrieved from http://www.fue.es/HTML/PDFS/01%20EUGRAD%20 DISSEMINATION/%20SEMINA R_21st%20CENTURY%20SKILLS.pdf

Sahin, A., Ayar, M. C., & Adiguzel, T. (2014). STEM-related after-school program activities and associated outcomes on student learning. *Educational Sciences: Theory & Practice, 14*(1), 309–322.

Sahin, A., & Top, T. (in press). Make it happen: A study of a novel teaching style, STEM Students on the Stage (SOS)™, for increasing students' STEM knowledge and interest. *Journal of STEM Education: Innovations and Research.*

Sahin, A., Top, N., & Vanegas, S. (2014). *Harmony STEM SOS™ Model increases students' college readiness and develops 21st century skills* [White paper]. Retrieved from http://www.harmonytx.org/NewsRoom/ResearchPolicy.aspx.

Waxman, H. C., Connell, M. L., & Gray, J. (2002). *A quantitative synthesis of recent research on the effects of teaching and learning with technology on student outcomes.* Naperville, IL: North Central Regional Educational Laboratory. Retrieved from http://www.ncrel.org/tech/effects/effects.pdf

Alpaslan Sahin
Harmony Public Schools

KADIR ALMUS, STEVEN BUSCH AND ANGUS J. MACNEIL

14. THE IMPACT OF THE STEM SOS MODEL IN INFLUENCING A CULTURE AND CLIMATE IN HARMONY PUBLIC SCHOOLS THAT SUPPORTS INSTRUCTION IN SCIENCE, TECHNOLOGY, ENGINEERING, AND MATHEMATICS (STEM)

A significant body of research from both the fields of business and education suggest that the culture and climate of an organization can support productivity, and in the case of schools, student success. The cultural values and beliefs within schools create the environment that promotes student achievement. Harmony Public Schools (HPS) has implemented deliberate systems within its schools to encourage student success in STEM content. HPS leaders and teachers have developed systems within the culture of schools that increase collaboration and friendship among students and teachers and provide a warm and supportive instructional environment within which students excel. The Harmony STEM SOS model serves as the cultural platform for this increased student engagement and learning.

INTRODUCTION

Harmony Public Schools (HPS) has achieved the status of the largest and one of the most successful charter schools systems in the United States. This level of success and growth has been accomplished to a large degree by the core beliefs within Harmony Public Schools that recognize the importance of school culture and climate. The mission, as stated in Harmony 2020, Taking Action: Shaping the Future, is:

> Harmony's mission is to prepare each student for higher education by providing a safe, caring, and collaborative atmosphere featuring a quality, student centered educational program with a strong emphasis on Science, Technology, Engineering, and Math (STEM).

The mission of HPS focuses on providing a culture and climate that is conducive to learning for both teachers and students. The core values and beliefs of Harmony 2020 encourage the development of a learning culture and environment that support STEM instruction:

- High Expectations
- Dedicated Staff

A. Sahin (Ed.), A Practice-based Model of STEM Teaching, 187–200.

- Working Together
- Character Matters
- STEM for All

The purpose of this chapter is to describe the manner in which the STEM SOS model influences the culture and climate in Harmony Public Schools and how that supports instruction in STEM areas.

Importance of Culture and Climate

Edgar Schein (1985), an organizational psychologist, stated that, "there is a possibility underemphasized in leadership research, that the only thing of real importance that leaders do is to create and manage culture and the unique talent of leaders is their ability to work with culture" (p. 2). Roland Barth (2001) suggested that a school's culture has far more influence on the life and learning in schools than the state department of education, superintendent, school board or principal and that the major purpose of a school is to create and sustain an environment that supports learning.

School cultures are often described as being comprised of the values, symbols, beliefs and shared community that drive the school. Culture defines what is valued in the school and informs the way teachers, staff and students think, feel and behave. Culture is also described as the customs, traditions, habits, norms, expectations and shared assumptions regarding the purpose of the school (Deal & Peterson, 1999; Sergiovanni, 2001). That which is valued in a school is what gets done and those values and beliefs are modeled and reinforced in the following ways:

- **Heroes:** Persons who perpetuate the organization's values, serve as role models, symbolize the organization to others and set standards that motivate participant achievement. Who are some good examples of heroes in school cultures?
- **Rites and Rituals**: Everyday activities and celebrations that characterize the organization. Rites and rituals illustrate what is valued by the organization.
- **Communication Networks:** Values are transmitted to the organization through dialogue in the school. Communication in strong cultures surrounds positive values and a shared mission. In the healthiest school cultures, leadership comes from many people, not just the principal.

The climate of the school represents the atmosphere and environment of that school that results from the implementation of the values and beliefs within the culture. Lunenburg and Ornstein (2010) suggested that climate represents the total environmental quality of the school. Schein (1985, 1996) believed that climate manifests from the values, norms, and rituals within the culture.

Importance of Leadership

In schools where achievement was high and where there was a clear sense of community, we invariably find that the principal made the difference (Boyer, 1983). Researchers have found that the manner in which principals most effectively influence the achievement of students within a school is through their interaction with the culture and climate of that school (Hallinger & Heck, 1998; Maslowski, 2001; Witziers, Bosker, and Kruger, 2003).

Student achievement is impacted when principals influence stakeholders and processes within the school (Davis, Darling-Hammond, Lapointe, & Meyerson, 2005). These sentiments are further supported by Leithwood (2004), who reported that the most important thing that good leaders do is set the direction for the school. Research supported by Cotton (2003) and Marzanno, Waters, and McNulty (2005) suggests that the behaviors and responsibilities of school leaders that relate to student achievement include providing safe and orderly schools, high expectations, visibility, clear focus, supportive culture, communication and positive relationships, accessibility, emphasis on community and parents, shared leadership and decision making, supporting teachers, collaboration, intellectual stimulation, instructional leadership, monitoring and feedback, professional development and role modeling the values of the school. Much of what is written on effective leadership and good schools references stable environments and the collaborative attitudes of the adults in the school (Hoy, Tarter & Hoy, 2006; Hudson, 2009; Meier, 2002; Sergiovanni, 2001).

Needless to say, it is reasonable to suggest that the academic and instructional mission of HPS, supported by principals and implemented by caring and talented teachers, will influence the learning culture and student achievement in STEM in a positive manner. The remaining portions of this chapter will address the manner in which this influence occurs.

The Impact of STEM Students on the Stage (SOS)™ Model on School Culture and Climate

In recent years, a series of studies were conducted to explore the components of the Harmony STEM SOS model. Researchers studied the Harmony STEM model and conducted interviews with a sample of students, teachers and parents from the Harmony schools in which this model is implemented (e.g., Sahin et al., 2012; Sahin & Top, 2014, Sahin, Top, & Vanegas, 2014). Findings from those studies showed that the STEM SOS model has positive influence on school culture and climate by providing the following impacts. The model:

1. Positively influences students' school and personal lives by

   a. Increasing collaboration and friendship among students
   b. Improving the classroom climate and teacher-student communication
   c. Improving classroom management

2. Increases student engagement and motivation by

   a. Creating authentic learning experiences
   b. Promoting scientific thinking
   c. Increasing deeper understanding of content

3. Makes students more college-ready and helps them plan their future college and career lives by

   a. Creating learning experiences that support successful academic pursuits
   b. Helping students realize their abilities
   c. Encouraging students to apply their knowledge and skills to improve the lives of others or to pursue personally meaningful careers
   d. Helping students acquire 21st century skills, which are beneficial across disciplines

4. Provides positive reinforcement from adults in school community by

   a. Publicly recognizing and celebrating students' accomplishments and achievements
   b. Guiding families to services within school

5. Offers professional growth opportunities for the teachers by

   a. Helping them improve their content knowledge and develop their teaching skills
   b. Helping beginner teachers overcome first-year challenges
   c. Fostering a culture of collaboration

Positive Influences on Students' School and Personal Lives

Increased Collaboration And Friendship Among Students. In the STEM SOS model, students work together, learn from each other and get help from upper-grade level students to complete their projects. Collaboration is encouraged in this process. In Sahin and Top's (in press) study, one of the students described the relationship among students who are involved in this process as follows:

> I guess because you are not doing it by yourself only, you have other people doing it and it's a good club to meet other people other grades like friends like all the people in here, well most of them, are seniors and they all know me and we all speak even though I'm a 10th grader, you know? It's just really nice.

Students who work together are able to develop a level of friendship that is not confined to schoolwork. They spend time with each other in their out-of-school lives and seek each other's help when they are in need. An increase in collaboration opportunities for participating students not only results in development of their collaboration skills, but also helps to develop friendships that go beyond the school borders. This is an

Figure 1. A group of students working on their project.

important outcome that positively influences the school climate. Research indicates that cooperative student activities increase group cohesiveness, diversify friendship patterns and increase concerns for peers (Schmuck & Schmuck, 2001).

The following statement from another student revealed this point more explicitly:

> Like we're nice to each other and we help each other out and if a person needs help, like if their partner is sick like if they have a cold and they need somebody to fill in for them, then definitely you can find anybody who would be willing to just like help you out. (Sahin & Top, in press)

Improved Classroom Climate and Teacher-Student Communication

Control over their learning. A recent study conducted with Harmony teachers investigating their reflections and experiences with STEM SOS model reported that the model positively affected their classroom climates (Sahin, Top, & Almus, 2014). It was also reported that this is due to the presence of positive relationships between teachers and their students. One of the main factors contributing to positive relationships is the active participation of students in their own learning in this model; students have the freedom to choose their projects, design the process and present the findings/outcomes to their friends in the classroom and to the public outside of the school.

The following statement from a teacher in a Teacher Voice Study reveals this fact:

I do not want my students be passive knowledge receivers. I want them to be active and involved in my teaching. So basically "I Do It, You Do It, We Do It." Method is [a] simple, yet effective way to teach new concepts to my students. (p. 10)

Another teacher adds:

With those projects, I am trying to get their attention and to engage them. After that point, students do the work. And this is the difference of that project. There are a lot of teachers out there that do a lot of demonstrations and explain them but students are kind of passive there. In this model, I only give the initiative; this project allows students to work on the project more in detail and explain it with their own words. (p.10)

Current literature and research support this finding that students perform more productively when they experience a sense of control or power over their learning (Glasser, 1986; Jones & Jones, 2013). Being allowed to choose a topic of special interest to study is one of the ways to experience a sense of power (Coopersmith, 1967).

The following statement from a student underlines this point from a student's perspective:

. . . I was like ooo this is fun. It is like you know cute and can come up with ideas even think I can bring someone and change the color and … it when with the carbon dioxide [hand in the air] it fades away so it was really cool. (Sahin & Top, in press).

Another student said:

I always like I said science was not always my biggest thing, but being in demos (student projects) let you know that it is just not listening and drawing or writing down your equations or writing down the words that the teacher said you can get hands on you can figure out something and you can learn about it and apply it to everyday. (Sahin & Top, in press)

Teacher-student Communication. Another important factor contributing to positive relationships between teachers and students is that this model provides opportunities for students to work and spend time with their teachers in informal learning settings, such as after-school hours and trips to science fairs, contests and exhibitions. The following statement from a teacher from the Teachers' Voice Study (Sahin et al., 2014) study reveals this fact:

I have a very good communication with my students thanks to the STEM SOS Model. When I assign them projects, I meet with my students several times a week to answer their questions and clarify some points in completion of the

Figure 2. A student demonstrating how a resonance ball works. (Please use your QR reader to scan the QR code to watch the video).

projects. Most of these meeting are not scheduled and students feel they need to see me and ask questions. We also go to different competitions together to do STEM demonstrations. These are all important means and locations to make positive contributions to our communications. (p. 13)

Another teacher illustrates this in the following quote:

It affected [student-teacher communication] well because you don't only see them in classroom, they stay after school to work on their projects. So you are becoming more than a teacher for them. Plus, during STEM expos, you are having trips with them and you build up a friendship and they become more engaged to classes and they are more comfortable to ask you question and learn better. (p. 13)

Positive Classroom Climate. The teachers who participated in the Teachers' Voice Study also reported that the STEM SOS model positively affected their classroom climate. Since students get to know each other well and have a good level of interaction with their teachers, the classroom atmosphere is relaxed. It was reported that students could ask questions comfortably without fear of embarrassment or of making mistakes. Teachers also indicated that students found classroom activities engaging and fun. This finding is congruent with existing literature that indicates that teachers who do not know their students well are more likely to misunderstand and fear them. Students know when the teacher enjoys being with them and is comfortable and eventually react positively (Jones & Jones, 2013, p. 66). The following statement from another teacher articulates this fact:

The classroom is always fun and they will always ask questions. Whenever I ask a student a question and he or she can't explain it very well, the other kids will comment, saying: "That's not how it works. Remember when he showed us the other demonstration?" They are always acting like really close friends and constantly trying to fix their mistakes; and also, trying to teach each other. They talk freely and are not scared . everyone is asking questions, commenting on the demonstrations and are generally really comfortable. Everyone is laughing, but that does not mean that we are not doing anything. Of course, we are learning, but it is a really comforting environment to learn in. Hopefully, at the end of the year, we can see how well we did in class. (p.13)

Improved Classroom Management.   The positive relationship between students and teachers, positive climate, and engaging and student-centered classroom activities result in better classroom management. A meta-analysis conducted by Marzano, Marzano, and Pickering (2003) of more than 100 studies reported that a positive teacher-student relationship was an important element of effective classroom management and could reduce behavior problems by 31% (as cited in Jones & Jones, 2013, p. 56). The following teacher quote from the Teachers' Voice Study is aligned with this finding.

I do not have any classroom management issues but if I taught with regular system not using STEM SOS method I would have classroom management issues I guess. It would be difficult to engage students in class. With the model, they are always on task and they know what to do. They have [always] something to do and keep busy with something. So it helps me manage my classroom. (p. 13)

Another statement provided below talks about how the model effectively increases students' intrinsic motivation, which is much more effective than the extrinsic motivation tools that the teacher implemented prior to this model. It also emphasizes the importance of involving students in rules and the policy setting process, which gives them power and control over their learning so that they feel greater ownership.

Without the STEM SOS PBL model, my rules to maintain classroom management based on rewards and punishments were not effective enough. Students sometimes were so quiet but not ready to learn or other times they were so active but again not on task. It was really challenging and difficult the first 2 years of my teaching. I was seeking new approaches to classroom management so I would solve my classroom management issues and teach better. When my principal suggested me to attend STEM SOS workshop in Houston, I didn't know that was going to change everything about my teaching philosophy. After the workshop, I realized that STEM SOS model not only helps students develop self-discipline and responsibility to create their own projects but also it increases students' self-esteem as well. We built new rules with my students with PBL Project. When my students helped me determine classroom rules and consequences, they took the ownership of those as many experts state. (p. 13)

The STEM SOS Model Increases Student Engagement and Motivation by Creating Authentic Learning Experiences, Promoting Scientific Thinking and Increasing a Deeper Understanding of Content.

The role of the teacher in STEM SOS model is that of a facilitator (Sahin et al., 2014). The model actively involves students by giving them power and control over their own learning and therefore results in higher degree of intrinsic motivation (Moore, 2012, p. 347). Sahin and Top's (in press) study reported that students are able to deeply understand the content and make connections between this knowledge and real-life applications due to their active participation in their learning, freedom to choose their project and design the process and execute it in their own way. One student in that study said that, "Yes, I will never forget that principle because I have learned it, I saw it, I experienced it. It will stay with me forever" while another expressed how the model promotes scientific thinking by stating that "I think I developed how to study the right way. Like how to learn, how to approach the problem and then how to apply it in real life."

The model not only promotes scientific thinking and increases deep understanding of the content, but increases STEM interest as well. Students who think of themselves as not being good at science started to develop interest and enjoy it after they got involved. One of the students in the Sahin & Top (in press) study epitomized this phenomenon, stating, "I have never really been great in science, but I have learned that when you really focus on it, you add interest." Another student added, "Science demo are like one of those, it is fun, you learned it and it is not so hard that you know you stressing about it."

The STEM SOS Model Makes Students More College-Ready and Helps Them Plan their Future College and Career Lives.

The STEM SOS model makes students more college-ready and helps them plan their future college and career lives by creating learning experiences that will support successful academic pursuits, helping students realize their abilities, encouraging them to apply their knowledge and skills to improving the lives of others or pursuing personally meaningful careers and helping them acquire 21st century skills, which are beneficial across disciplines.

As one of the teachers in Teachers' Voice Study expressed, "students have more chances to shine and discover their own abilities" in this model. Students control the process and make and execute the plans. This student-centered approach helps students improve their self-study and self-planning skills, which are vital for college success. The following teacher statement from the Teachers' Voice study emphasized this:

> Students are required to understand the assignments on their own; pace themselves so they finish the assignment on time, and implement experiments that they have designed themselves. I have even taken the 'designing your

own experiments' to the next level this year and given my students access to the basic lab equipment under their lab tables so they have to decide what materials to use and when to use (Sahin et al., 2014, p. 15).

The model helps students acquire 21st century skills that are beneficial to them in their college and career lives (Sahin & Top, in press). These skills include self- confidence, technology skills, life and career skills, collaboration skills and communication skills. As part of the process, students are required to create videos and prepare a webpage about their projects. They develop a variety of advanced technological skills throughout this process such as advanced video editing techniques and then present their projects in different settings: to their peers in the classroom, visitors and parents in school-wide events and the general public in city and statewide events. These opportunities increase their self-confidence and improve their presentation and public speaking skills, which are needed for college and career success. Other important 21st century abilities that students acquire in this process are life and career skills. Sahin and Top's study reported that the skills students acquire when working together in this process, such as sharing and helping each other, continues in their out-of-school life too. Student statements in this study revealed that they not only help their friends whom they know from school, but their awareness of helping those who are in need in the general public also increased.

Another important gain for students is the increase in research interest in higher education in STEM fields. Students expressed their desire to continue to do research after they graduate from high school, with one student from Sahin and Top's (in press) study saying that "hopefully, I can carry all those skills over not only to higher education, but also to college, graduate school and my career." Another student

Figure 3. A student demonstrating his project. (Please use your QR reader to scan the QR code to watch the video).

expressed this as follows: "I feel more comfortable like I can already do [research] by myself with other students, I can create study groups and always feel like teacher kind I like having back and forth communication like really helps you."

The STEM SOS Model Provides Positive Reinforcement From Adults in School Community.

Student works are recognized and accomplishments are celebrated in the school system. Parents, the general public and officials are invited to schools for special events so that students can present their projects. Schools attend all the project competitions/fairs/contests so that students present their work to different audiences. The school system arranges big events at central places for students to present their work; for example, students from Harmony Houston High School went to the state capitol building and demonstrated their work to state senators and representatives in 2011. In this atmosphere, students feel that their efforts are valuable and that they are supported. As one of the founders stated, "At Harmony Schools, the joke is that the annual science fair is prom" (Addressing the Needs of Our Nation, Building STEM Talent and Work Force for the Next Generation, 2014).

Parents also play an important role. They are given guidance on how to help their children with their projects. and also assist in organizing the events and helping teachers during trips. This increases their involvement and support and high levels of parent involvement positively affect the school culture and climate.

Figure 4. A Harmony student presenting her project to Houston Representative Alma Allen in the Austin Capitol.

The STEM SOS Model Offers Professional Growth Opportunities for the Teachers.

The STEM SOS model helps teachers grow professionally, largely in the areas of teaching, content knowledge and development of some skills such as technology skills (Sahin et al., 2014). One of the teachers who participated in that study expressed this by saying "STEM SOS model helped me grow professionally. I learn 21st century skills with my students. Before the STEM SOS model, I did not know how to create a website, upload a movie on YouTube, make a poster and handout that require technology use." Another teacher explained that the program is a good tool for new teachers to overcome the challenges of their first year in teaching as follows:

> This is my first actual job after college. And in my first year, I've realized that I don't really know anything. Equations didn't mean anything; I didn't know how to make equations meaningful to my students. But the demonstrations came with the model helped me a lot and I remembered all the things about physics I learned in college. The difference was the content I learned in college starting make sense when I started teaching with the STEM SOS because I clearly saw how the theory and formulas were connected to the things happening around me. And then, you learn how to teach. (p. 16)

The program also fosters a culture of collaboration by creating opportunities for teachers to work together. They not only share their expertise and coordinate opportunities for their students to work with their colleagues in the same field, but also work with other STEM area teachers. As a program requirement, Level II and III projects have an interdisciplinary component in which STEM area teachers collaborate with English and Social Studies teachers. At higher levels (Level II and III projects), students are required to prepare a website, a brochure introducing their website and project and a video demonstrating and explaining their projects. In addition, there is an ELA and SS connections component where students explain how the project affects students' daily lives and how they use it in real life (Sahin et al., 2014). English and Social Studies teachers grade students for their parts in the project.

CONCLUSION

Harmony Public Schools (HPS) has grown to be the largest and one of the top performing school systems in the state of Texas and across the nation. HPS has distinguished itself with its rigorous STEM curriculum and has the honor of being the pioneer Texas Science, Technology, Engineering and Mathematics (T-STEM) schools in the state (About Harmony Public Schools, 2014). There are currently only 91 schools statewide for the 2014-15 school year that are designated as T-STEM academies, and 25 of them are Harmony campuses (T-STEM at Harmony, 2014). HPS has created an environment that promotes student success, especially in STEM education, for a diverse student population of 28,500 students located in different regions across the state. Educators in the HPS system have fulfilled the vision of the founders, who were passionate about creating a unique approach to mathematics and science education by developing a system with a culture promoting collaboration among students, teachers, school administrators, and parents that provides a warm and supportive school environment where students can excel and reach their fullest potential.

The Harmony STEM SOS model serves as the cultural platform for this success by influencing the learning culture, school climate, and student achievement in a positive manner with a range of positive impacts for students. These impacts include: (1) positive influences on students' school and personal lives, (2) increases in student engagement and motivation, (3) preparing students for college and helping them plan their future college and career lives, (4) providing positive reinforcement from adults in the school community and (5) offering professional growth opportunities for teachers.

REFERENCES

About Harmony Public Schools. (2014). *Harmony public schools*. Houston, TX. Retrieved from http://harmonytx.org/AboutUs.aspx

Addressing the needs of our nation, building STEM talent and work force for the next generation. (2014). *STEM Focus, 8, Harmony Public Schools. Houston, TX*. Retrieved from https://www.harmonytx.org/webshare/b.yilmaz/STEM-Newsletter-Issue-8.pdf

Barth, R. S. (2001) *Learning by heart*. San Francisco, CA: Jossey-Bass.

Boyer, E. (1983). *High school: A report on secondary education in America*. NY: Harper and Row.

Cotton, K. (2003). *Principals and student achievement: What the research says*.Alexandria, VA: Association for Supervision and Curriculum Development.

Davis, S., Darling-Hammond, L., LaPointe, M., & Meyerson, D. (2005). *School leadership study: Developing successful principals (Review of Research)*.Stanford, CA: Stanford University, Stanford Educational Leadership Institute.

Deal, T. E., & Peterson, K. D. (1999). *Shaping school culture: The heart of leadership*. San Francisco, CA: Jossey-Bass.

Emmer, E. T., & Evertson, C. M. (2013). *Classroom management for middle and high school teachers*. New York, NY: Pearson.

Glasser, W. (1986). *Control theory in the classroom*. New York, NY: Harper and Row.

Hallinger, P., & Heck, R. H. (1998). Exploring the principal's contribution to school effectiveness: 1980-1995. *School Effectiveness and School Improvement, 9*(2), 157–191.

Hoy, W., Tarter, C., & Hoy, A. (2006). Academic optimism of schools: A force for student achievement. *American Educational Research Journal, 43*(3), 425–446.

Johnstone, W. (1988). *Organization health instrument*. Technical manual.

Hudson, D. (2009). *Good teachers, good schools*. New York, NY: Routledge.

Jones, V., & Jones, L. (2013). *Comprehensive classroom Management: Creating Communities of Support and Solving Problems*: Pearson.

Leithwood, K., Louis, K., Anderson, S., & Wahlstrom, K. (2004). *How leadership influences student learning*. New York, NY: The Wallace Foundation.

Lunenburg, F. C., & Ornstein, A. C. (2004). *Educational administration: Concepts and practices, 4th ed.* Belmont, CA: Wadsworth/Thomson Learning.

Marzano, R., Waters, T., & McNulty, B. (2005).*School leadership that works: From research to results*. Alexandria, VA: ASCD.

Maslowski, R. (2001). *School culture and school performance: An explorative study into the organizational culture of secondary schools and their effects.* Endschede, The Netherlands: Twente University Press.

Meier, D. (2002). *In schools we trust.* Boston, MA: Beacon Press.

Moore, K. D. (2012). *Effective instructional strategies: From theory to practice* (3rd ed.). Los Angeles, CA: Sage Publications, Inc.

Sahin, A., Akgun, O. A., Erdogan, N., Cavlazoglu, B., Cetin, C. S., Capraro, R. M., & Capraro, M. M. (2012, November). *Effects of STEM-Related activities on high school students' motivation, learning strategy use, and self-regulation.* Paper presented at the annual convention of School Science and Mathematics Association (SSMA), Birmingham, AL.

Sahin, A., Top, N., & Vanegas, S. (2014). *Harmony STEM SOS model increases college readiness and develops 21st century skills.* Retrieved from http://harmonytx.org/Portals/0/HPS_Issue-1.pdf

Sahin, A., Top, N., & Almus, K. (2014). Teachers' reflections on STEM students on the stage (SOS)™ model. Retrieved from http://www.harmonytx.org/Portals/0/HPS%20Issue-2.pdf

Sahin, A., & Top, N. (in press). Making it happen: A study of a novel teaching style, *STEM Students on the Stage* (SOS)™, for increasing students' STEM knowledge and interest. *The Journal of STEM Education: Innovations and Research.*

Schein, E. H. (1985). *Organizational culture and leadership.* San Francisco, CA: Jossey-Bass.

Schein, E. H. (1996). Culture: The missing concept in organization studies. *Administrative Science Quarterly, 41*(2), 229–240.

Sergiovanni, T. J. (2001). *The principalship: A reflective practice perspective* (4th ed.). Needham Heights, MD: Allyn and Bacon.

Schmuck, R., & Schmuck, P. (2001). *Group processes in the classroom* (8th ed.). Boston, MA: McGraw-Hill.

T-STEM at Harmony. (2014). *Harmony Public Schools. Houston, TX.* Retrieved from http://harmonytx.org/AboutUs/TSTEMatHarmony.aspx

Witziers, B., Bosker, R., & Kruger, M. (2003) Educational leadership and student achievement: The elusive search for an association. *Educational Administration Quarterly, 39*(3), 398–423

Kadir Almus
Department of Education
North American University

Steven Busch
Department of Educational Leadership and Policy Studies
University of Houston

Angus MacNeil
Department of Educational Leadership and Policy Studies
University of Houston.

SECTION 5
TEACHERS' VOICE

This section presents an analysis of interviews carried out with teachers who have been teaching with the STEM SOS model. This book would be incomplete without hearing the voices from STEM Heroes who are in the field and have firsthand experience with the Model. This chapter revisits the STEM SOS Model from teachers' perspectives.

ALPASLAN SAHIN AND NAMIK TOP

15. TEACHERS' REFLECTIONS ON STEM STUDENTS ON THE STAGE (SOS)™ MODEL

This chapter examines a novel teaching method, the STEM Students on the Stage (SOS)™ model, in which teachers receive regular training and implement a well-developed project-based learning curriculum. Specifically, we investigated the STEM SOS model teachers' reflections and experiences with the model. Seven teachers volunteered to participate in the study. The subjects taught by teachers included physics, mathematics, chemistry, and biology. The methodology used in this study was consistent with the principles of the phenomenological approach in which each participant experienced the same phenomenon (Creswell, 2007). The common phenomenon in this study was that all teachers taught with STEM SOS model. Within the analysis, emerging significant statements formulated the participants' feelings. After grouping those formulated statements, common themes and sub-themes were identified. We found that teachers focused on two fundamental themes: how the STEM SOS model works and benefits gained from implementing the STEM SOS model. Teachers described their teaching in two groups, as the things happening within and after school. The within group had two sub-themes: teacher and student. The after-school group also had two sub-themes: talking about chapter projects and rigorous Level II and III projects. Benefits of the STEM SOS model were grouped under benefits for teachers and students, with a total of 7 sub-themes. Themes and implications are discussed in this chapter.

INTRODUCTION

STEM education has become critical to the professional success of our children and the economic well-being of our nation. Research has estimated that nearly 80% of future careers will require STEM knowledge and awareness (Afterschool Alliance, 2011). Thus, it is necessary to provide rigorous and stimulating STEM education to our children in order for them to develop the basic analytical, problem-solving, and critical thinking skills that are central to academic achievement and workforce readiness in an innovation-driven 21st century (Afterschool Alliance, 2011).

Project-based learning (PBL) has been seen as a way to provide a high-quality STEM education (e.g., Markham, 2014; Wayne RESA, 2014). Current research on project-based learning shows that PBL projects can increase student interest in STEM subjects because they engage students in solving real-life problems, working with

A. Sahin (Ed.), A Practice-based Model of STEM Teaching, 203–222.

others and coming up with products that have real-world connections (Fortus, Krajcikb, Dershimerb, Marx, & Mamlok-Naamand, 2005, as cited by Laboy-Rush, 2011). Other research has found that PBL instruction helps close the achievement gap by engaging lower-achieving students (e.g., Penuel & Means, 2000). Although there has been a myriad of positive news supporting project-based learning, there are some limitations of the model in terms of research and application. David (2008) pointed out that because project-based learning doesn't have one standardized definition, it is difficult to research its effectiveness; that is why there have been few studies on the effect of project-based learning on student achievement. Another limitation of the model is that it has no commonly shared norms for what constitutes an acceptable project (David, 2008). Moreover, many teachers find it difficult to implement because of limited school support and a lack of ready-to-teach materials. In this study, we investigated another STEM education model, STEM SOS, and examined what teachers who have been using the model think about it in terms of teaching and its benefits and challenges.

CONCEPTUAL FRAMEWORK AND REVIEW OF RELEVANT LITERATURE

This section provides a literature review on the history of project-based learning, research on project-based learning, and the STEM SOS model to develop the "skeletal structure of justification" (Eisenhart, 1991) that will serve as a guide for data collection, analysis and interpretation of the results.

The History of Project-Based Learning

It is believed that Confucius and Aristotle were early advocates of learning by doing (Boss, 2014). Socrates was another pioneer in the use of different learning methods with his students, such as questioning and inquiry (Boss, 2014), which are considered components of critical thinking (Wagner, 2012). The role of John Dewey, an American educational theorist and philosopher, cannot be underestimated because he believed and showed that students should be active participants in their learning endeavor; i.e., project-based learning goes back to the time of experiential education and the philosophy of John Dewey (Coffey, 2010).

In the mid-twentieth century, problem-based learning was introduced as a practical teaching strategy in medicine, engineering, economics and other subjects. Problems were complex and had more than one right answer. Problem-based learning helped medical students learn to diagnose and treat actual patients. They also had opportunities to ask questions and discover answers (Boss, 2014). This was considered a precursor to project-based learning (Coffey, 2010).

More recently, K-12 education adopted a new teaching and learning strategy, project-based learning, which is more open-ended than the problem-based approach and gives students greater freedom to come up with their own solutions and products. Projects that are assigned to students have to be solved within a given time frame and with a limited budget (Sahin, 2012). For example, problems might include, "How can we reduce our school's carbon print?" or "How do we measure the impact of disasters?" (Boss, 2014).

A number of factors have contributed to the popularity of project-based learning in the 21st century. These factors include developments in cognitive research, which have advanced our understanding of how we learn and develop interests in the subjects we study (Boss, 2014; Coffey, 2010), and the change in the educational environment (especially with the advent of the Internet and mobile technology).

Research on Project-Based Learning

Project-based learning is an instructional approach whereby students are challenged with real-world problems that capture their interest and engage them by giving them responsibility for their own learning in a problem-solving context. The role of teachers is facilitating students' learning. Students work in groups and try to solve an open-ended real-world problem (David, 2008; Sahin, 2012).

Although research on project-based learning has yielded a number of benefits for students ranging from deeper learning of academic content to stronger motivation to learn (Buck Institute for Education, 2013), there has been limited research measuring its effectiveness due to the lack of a unified definition (David, 2008). For instance, Boaler (2002) studied students' mathematics achievement in two similar British secondary schools where one used traditional instruction and the other used project-based learning instruction. Three years of data showed that students who were taught with project-based learning outperformed the students taught with traditional instruction in mathematics skills and conceptual and applied knowledge (cited in David, 2008). In another study, Fortus et al. (2005) (as cited by Laoy-Bush, 2011) found that students taught with the project-based approach developed greater interest in STEM subjects because they were involved in solving authentic problems, working with others and building artifacts. Overall, it appears that just a handful of studies have examined the effectiveness of project-based learning.

These research studies imply that project-based learning works when it is fully implemented (David, 2008). However, implementation of project-based learning is not easy because it requires school support and access to ready-to-teach full curriculum including assessment materials, and continuous teacher training (David, 2008).

STEM SOS Model

Research on active learning methods has shown that PBL projects can increase students' interest in STEM and content matter by engaging them in solving authentic problems, collaborating with others and building products that have real-life connections and applications (Fortus, Krajcikb, Dershimerb, Marx, & Mamlok- Naamand, 2005, as cited by Laboy-Bush, 2011). With those findings in mind, Harmony Public Schools (HPS) developed their own STEM curriculum that incorporates project-based and inquiry-based learning. This curriculum was codified and named "STEM Students on the Stage (SOS)™" (Sahin & Top, 2014) (read Chapter 3 for an explanation of the full model). The development of the STEM SOS model was funded by a Race to the Top grant through the U.S. Department of Education with the goal of increasing students' STEM knowledge and interest and also producing self-motivated and self-regulated learners (Harmony STEM Program, 2013).

The primary purpose of the STEM SOS model is "to maintain the focus on standards-based and student-centered teaching while enriching and extending the learning of students through PBL projects. The goal is to promote collaborative skills, student ownership of learning and student success in meeting state and national standards" (Harmony STEM Program, 2013, p.x) through student projects: Levels I, II, and III. All students must complete a Level I project followed by either a regular Level II or advanced Level III project (Sahin & Top, in press; Sahin, Top, & Vanessa, 2014)

This study examines a novel teaching method, STEM Students on the Stage (SOS)™, in which teachers receive regular training and utilize a full and well-developed project-based learning curriculum. Specifically, we investigated STEM SOS model teachers' reflections and experience with the model.

METHOD

Participants

11 teachers were invited to be interviewed for the study. Seven teachers volunteered to participate in the study. The seven teachers represented a range of STEM subjects, including: two physics, two mathematics and two chemistry teachers and one biology teacher. There was only one female teacher in the study.

Selection Criteria

All participants were selected from a group of teachers who have a minimum of two years experience using the STEM SOS model. They all have experience teaching with STEM SOS model in Harmony schools. We used criterion sampling based on the belief that "when all individuals studied represents people who have experienced the phenomenon" (Creswell, 2007, p. 128).

Research Design

The methodology used in this study was consistent with the principles of the phenomenological approach in which each participant experienced the same phenomenon (Creswell, 2007), that being that all teachers used the STEM SOS model in their teaching. The Advocacy/Participatory orientation was the paradigm in the study. Participatory research should provide an agenda for altering the lives of participants (Kemmis & Wilkinson, 1998). This study could yield a better understanding of the experiences of teachers using the STEM SOS model, which may provide benefits for teachers and students.

Data Collection

The first author conducted face-to-face, semi-structured interviews with five teachers. Interviews were conducted between September 2-21, 2014 and each face-to-face interview lasted approximately 50 minutes. Two teachers returned their responses to the first author via e-mail.

Data Analysis

Participants' transcripts were analyzed using the phenomenological method developed by Colaizzi (1978). This method helped us "obtain an overall feeling for them" (Creswell, 2007; p. 270) by reading the transcripts several times. Through the analysis, emerging significant statements formulated the participants' feelings. After grouping those formulated statements, common themes and sub-themes emerged. An in-depth description of the phenomenon will be available with the outcomes of the process.

RESULTS

From the six verbatim transcripts of teachers, 70 significant statements were obtained. After the formulated meanings were arranged into clusters, two fundamental themes and multiple sub-themes emerged. The two fundamental themes on which the teachers generally focused were how STEM SOS model works and benefits from STEM SOS model (see Figure 1).

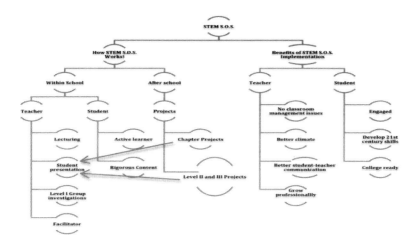

Figure 1. STEM SOS Model from teachers' perspectives.

How the STEM SOS Model Works

One of the chief categories concentrated on during interviews was comprised of the components of the STEM SOS model by which it contributes to the process of education. Teachers described their teaching in two groups: as the things happening within and after school. The within group had two sub-themes: teacher and student. The after-school group had two sub-themes: talking about chapter projects and rigorous Level II and III projects (see Figure 1).

Within School. Teachers described the initial step in teaching with the STEM SOS model as lecturing. This is where they lay the framework for the class, model how and what to teach and provide students with expectations for when they prepare their chapter and Level I projects. All of this happens within the classroom.

Lecturing. Lecturing or teacher-directed teaching is the start of any STEM SOS instruction. Although the term "lecturing" does not generally have positive connotations, lecturing in the STEM SOS model is intended to be vivid and engaging. For example, one teacher stated, "It is not just lecturing on the board. I try to have a demonstration for each class, but of course it is not easy to have a demo for every single class. I also use videos, but interesting videos that are related to the topic and pictures sometimes. We don't just watch and say, "Oh it is cool." I ask questions from those videos and pictures so it is not just lecturing on the board."

Another teacher described how his lecture style utilizes different hands-on and multimedia tools to engage students: "I try to have a video, picture, demo and an activity. And kids wonder what they are going to learn. It is not like, 'It is another boring physics class!' They always ask questions and they are engaged by the demonstrations."

Another physics teacher emphasized the importance of lecturing, stating, "But of course, I also have lecturing time because physics is not an easy subject that students can read from the book and understand." One of the mathematics teachers who uses the STEM SOS model also reported that he starts lessons with a short lecture that includes engaging material with real-life connections and addresses the objective of the lesson.

> Every day, I try to bring new projects to class that catch their interest and make connections between real life and math. If I would do the lecture in 90 minutes, students would get bored and ignore. To learn math objectives, I prepared a new way to teach math. I've started with a lecture for 10-15 minutes at the beginning of the class. Without real-life connections or STEM SOS PBLs, my students had a hard time solving questions from ALEKS and Odyssey [mathematics learning software] but when they see that math is in their real lives, they had impressive progress on these online resources. It depends on the objective, but after my lecture, the remaining time they start to do their self-assessment or group work activities.

The content of lectures varies by teacher. All teachers reported that they began their instruction with a short lecture. One physics teacher indicated that he starts his teaching with a bell-work assignment and then starts lecturing. He stated, "I do start with a bell-work assignment and then lecture around 15-20 minutes associated with demonstrations."

A chemistry teacher described her lecturing as being somewhat different; instead of spending 20 minutes of class time lecturing, she has students watch a movie of a lecture she made as homework. She spends the first part of class answering students' questions about the lecture. Then they continue with students' demonstrations and experiments.

> I have "flipped" my PAP Chemistry classes, meaning students get their first introduction [lecturing] to new material at home at their own pace and at their own place. I have my students take notes on my Prezi website, which I check the next time I see the students in class. With note taking out of the classroom and assigned as homework, my class time is spent doing hands-on activities, labs and practice problems. I find the "flipped" classroom works extremely well. It helps students understand topics faster and more in-depth and it results in less confusion with the math in chemistry, since I am there to answer any questions they may have.

Student presentations. This is one of the central parts of the STEM SOS model because the name of the model, Students on the Stage (SOS) comes from the fact that students come on the "stage" and act like a teacher. Teachers reported that their students do two types of presentations: chapter projects and/or Level II and III yearlong projects during class. It seems that the teacher decides to whom and which projects he/she needs for the class ahead. This might be a simple chapter demo or a more advanced yearlong project, as one teacher explained:

> Along with our teaching [lecturing], we include student presentations that are related to the content I am teaching. Students either do demonstrations as part of simple chapter projects or Level II or III yearlong projects. Teachers decide how many students he or she will use for the class.

Another important feature of the student presentations is that students not only do presentations and teaching during classes in which new content is being taught, but also during the review process, either for the end of course (EOC) or for the Advanced Placement (AP) exams.

> They present their projects twice throughout the year. The first one they do is when they work on it. In the first one, they might not be fully ready to present their projects, but their teachers help them understand the concept and show how they will complete their project. But the interesting thing is that although they may not be fully ready to teach in the first one because chapter projects are usually assigned not a very long time ago, they learn a lot because they are on the stage and teach (try to teach it [teacher laughs]) it. The second one is that they present their projects during the review time once they complete everything.

Teachers reported that student presentations help them in multiple ways. First, students develop important workforce skills they need for the 21st century. Second, it positively changes the classroom climate. Third, they develop leadership skills by doing presentations before classmates and teachers.

> I believe that students improve their 21st century workplace skills when they prepare projects and do presentations in class. After presentations, I see a major change in my classroom climate. They gain a positive attitude to be a leader in the classroom activities.

From teacher statements, it seems that some teachers are still trying to adjust to the curriculum because they are new to the model; as one of the physics teacher stated: "One hands-on activity that kids do. And I try to do it for every single class but I am not there yet."

Another thing we found was the order of student presentations. Teachers utilize student presentations or demonstrations when they are teaching the related content. This might be at the beginning of the class or after teacher lecturing. Instead of doing the activity himself/herself, they let students do it, as was described by an algebra teacher. This teacher stated, "They have the chance to do presentations before my lecture starts as long as their projects are related to the content I am teaching."

Student presentations are usually done within a given time frame and depend on the teachers and subjects. For instance, one of the algebra teachers said, "I usually give 20-25 minutes for student STEM SOS PBL presentations for each class."

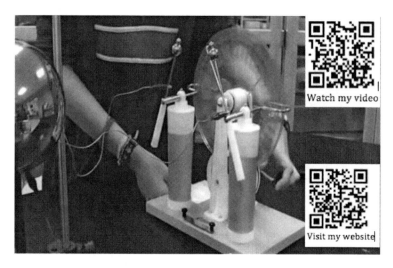

Figure 2. A female student demonstrating her Level II projects. (Please use your QR reader to scan the QR codes to watch the student video and/or her e-portfolio website).

Level I. After student presentations, students mostly work on their Level I group investigation. This is a group project in which students work on a given experiment on the related topic. Students are given the freedom to design their own experiments and choose materials to carry out their investigations. The scope and types of experiments change from subject to subject, but it is one of the routines done in each STEM SOS classroom. One physics teacher described the Level I group investigation as follows:

> The Level I investigation is a group or team project that provides an opportunity for students to work together. It is a part of the model [STEM SOS] and they complete four investigations a year. Each semester, they do two Level I investigations. As a product, they do an investigation report and photo gallery presentation to complete their assignments.

One chemistry teacher described how she implements the Level I investigation in her classroom. She stated, "I have even taken the designing your own experiments to the next level this year and given my students access to the basic lab equipment under their lab tables so they have to decide what materials to use and when (previously I have always given them the equipment they needed . now they must figure it out on their own)." One of the mathematics teachers described the purpose of these experiments as being "to take charge of their own learning, to explore a topic of interest in depth, and to communicate their findings clearly to peers."

The Level I experiment enables students to test the design of their experiment as a group. If they fail during their first attempts, they learn that initial failure is just part of the learning process that will take them to success. This was reiterated by one of the chemistry teachers:

> Students get to understand that failure is OK. Students learn through their failure and implement new practices the next time they run an experiment. Students also get to evaluate themselves on how well they are able to design an experiment and follow through with their plan.

One of the teachers described the Level I projects as follows: "Level I part is the part that you do in class and in short time, you don't have time make a research and explain the concepts in detail, you briefly explain the project with pictures and captions."

The Level I project from a chemistry teacher's perspective was defined in the following quote with an example:

> When we do a PBL Level I activity, we only provide a list of materials and the title of that experiment. Then students work as a group to come up with a design to perform that experiment. Let me give an example, when we do the Empirical formula of Magnesium Oxide investigation, we only provide materials such as magnesium ribbon, crucible, burner, etc. We also provide students with the title, which, in this case, is the Empirical formula of Magnesium Oxide. By

looking at the materials, students need to come up with an idea to find the empirical formula of Magnesium Oxide. Before starting the experiment we all discuss each design and then choose the best design to achieve our goal.

The facilitator. All seven teachers we interviewed described their role in the STEM SOS model as a facilitator. They do not teach the entire time and are not an information transmitter as in the traditional teaching model, as was emphasized by one of the physics teachers: "I think that my role is being an effective teacher and a facilitator for my students."

Another physics teacher described himself as a role model in terms of showing students how to implement the projects written in the curriculum as well as facilitating their learning: "My role is applying the project basically. This is just a project written on a paper, but how do you do this? So I am making it real by showing an example."

One of the mathematics teachers we interviewed explained his way of facilitating students' learning by attracting student interests and motivating them. He emphasized the importance of student involvement and engagement in order to teach them and facilitate their learning journey. That is, "Spark student interest, motivate them to ask their own questions, and guide them through the process."

The scope of the teachers' role as facilitator was described in detail by one of the chemistry teachers as follows: "I think my role is a facilitator in STEM SOS The teacher facilitates everything in this model. However, it is not the most important role in this model because the student is in the center in this model and the student does everything. As a teacher, our job is to check if everything is going smoothly."

Active learner. Another sub-category operating within the school that demonstrates how STEM SOS PBL works was student engagement. In the model, students are not passive learners, but instead are active learners and designers. They actively participate in the learning process and actually "own their learning when we give them more freedom and responsibility for choosing and presenting their outcomes." As one mathematics teacher emphasized, students are required "to take charge of their own learning, to explore a topic of interest in depth, and to communicate their findings clearly to peers and the public." One of the physics teachers stated the following:

> I do not want my students be passive knowledge receivers. I want them to be active and involved in my teaching. So basically 'I Do It, We Do It, You Do It.' This method is a simple, yet effective way to teach new concepts to my students.

Another physics teacher spoke about the importance of real-life demonstrations and being active as follows:

> With those projects, I am trying to get their attention and engage them. After that point, students do the work. And this is the difference of that project. There

are a lot of teachers out there that do a lot of demonstrations and explain them, but students are kind of passive there. In this model, I only give the initiative; this project allows students to work on the project more in detail and explain it with their own words. Besides, they are finding real-life applications through SS and ELA connections and they explain it in their website.

It was stated that one of the best things about the STEM SOS model is: "Students don't try to find one accurate answer to questions because the main question of the projects are open-ended questions. This is another thing we expect from students, to make research about open-ended questions. This also helps them build their presentation and research skills."

In the model, students direct projects by themselves and present their projects in front of their peers and public in the STEM festivals. One of the teachers mentioned this and explained why the model's name, Students on the Stage (SOS), makes sense:

They are not simple projects. First, they have to do good background research for their projects and learn what's going on. Then, they can complete their projects. They are not done. They need to become experts in what they study. They participate in different STEM festivals including ISWEEEP, Texas STEM festivals and their own school festivals to explain their projects according to audiences coming from different levels and ages. Therefore, they never forget what they do. These are all in addition to their presentations within their classroom. Those students become experts on the topic they complete their project on. That's why it is called "student on stage."

Rigorous content.   Teachers all reported that the STEM SOS model helped them teach rigorous content. One teacher explained this key component of the STEM SOS model as follows:

I think the STEM SOS model provides rigorous content to my students. They took regular physics last year and we did STEM SOS PBL in regular physics and then this year most of my students are taking AP Physics. I think they learned well and they believed that they are going to make it. That is why so many students are taking AP Physics. I think that the STEM SOS model made them love physics.

Students not only learn the content, but also combine the knowledge they already had with the new information they learn. This process explained by a teacher as follows: "Students are not only learning the content I bring to the classroom, but they also have to use their previous knowledge as well in order to complete their projects."

The project completion requires them to explain everything they do in their projects. For instance, students learn and use different technological tools and Internet sources to show and tell how and what they do during completion of the projects. They are required to use video presentations where students have to take pictures of each and every step of their projects, make movies, websites, and upload them to their websites and YouTube channel. So I believe the definition of "rigorous" should be something like what we do in our STEM SOS PBLs.

After School

This is the second and last theme of how the STEM SOS model works and a central part of the STEM SOS model in which most of the learning happens and student responsibilities develop. All the chapter and Level II and III projects are completed during afterschool hours. Students stay after school, come in on weekends and/or continue working at home to complete their projects. It seems that a great deal of dedication, effort and time are put into this process.

Chapter projects. As explained previously, chapter projects are simple demonstrations that teachers assign students to perform during classes as part of their lecturing. One of the physics teachers described the purpose and scope of the chapter projects as follows:

> I assign simple physics demos to my students during class time. So they can get ready after school hours and present during classes on that topic. They do the hands-on part so they take ownership of their learning.

Level II and III projects. Teachers stated that Level II and III projects are a central component of the model. These are yearlong projects that require students to complete a number of steps, which are described in the curriculum. One chemistry teacher explained the Level II and III projects as follows:

> Levels II and III are yearlong projects. We assign those projects at the beginning of the year. Students may choose projects depending on their own interest. Let's say a student is interested in acids and bases; then the student can choose a project related to acids and bases. If a student has his or her own project idea, then I review that idea and approve or deny that project. Students may also work together on the same project.

Unlike Level I projects, Level II and III projects have an interdisciplinary component through which teachers collaborate with English and social studies classes. In addition, we learned what students' products are like:

> Level II and Level III projects also have a cross-curricular component, which extends their knowledge to a higher level. In the end, a final product each student creates is a website that has a brochure introducing their website, a video demonstrating and explaining their projects ELA and SS connections, how the project affects students' daily lives and how we use it in the real world.

Figure 3. A student demonstrating how fireworks get their color. (Please use your QR reader to scan the QR code to watch the video)

The three levels are supplementary to each other to improve students' learning process. Teachers try to "bring new projects to class that would catch their interest and to make connection with real life." A math teacher explained this as follows:

When they see that mathematics is in their real lives, they have impressive progress on these online resources. It depends on the objective, but after my lecturing, with the remaining time they start to do their self-assessment or group work activities.

Benefits of STEM-SOS Model Implementation

As a second fundamental theme, teachers focused on how the STEM SOS model benefits the process of education through the key components mentioned under the first main category, how the STEM SOS model works. Within this theme, there are two sub-groups: teachers and students who benefit from the model. The teacher sub-theme has four sub-groups which include: classroom management, classroom climate, student-teacher communication and professional growth. The student sub-theme has three sub-groups of benefits, including: engagement, 21st century skills, and college readiness described from the perspective of teachers who teach using the STEM SOS model.

Teacher. Teacher interviews revealed benefits for two important stakeholders of education: teachers and students. We found that the benefits for teachers were in classroom management, classroom climate, professional student-teacher communication and growth.

Classroom management. The teachers we interviewed reported that they have no classroom management issues when they use the STEM SOS model. Teachers emphasized that the way they teach is engaging, fun and puts students on the stage; therefore, students love their classes and don't have time to do other things. For example, one chemistry teacher said, "students behave better in labs because they are responsible for designing their own experiment. This takes the "boring" aspect of the lab away and gives the students ownership of their lab experience." A physics teacher confessed that it would be very difficult if he were not using STEM SOS model:

> I do not have any classroom management issues, but if I taught with a regular system not using STEM SOS method, I would have classroom management issues I guess. It would be difficult to engage students in class. With the model, they are always on task and they know what to do. They [always] have something to do and keep busy with something. So it helps me manage my classroom.

An algebra/mathematics teacher explained the change in his classroom after he started teaching with STEM SOS model as follows:

> Without the STEM SOS model, my rules to maintain classroom management based on rewards and punishments were not effective enough. Students sometimes were so quiet, but not ready to learn or other times they were so active, but again not on task. It was really challenging and difficult the first 2 years of my teaching. I was seeking new approaches to classroom management so I would solve my classroom management issues and teach better. When my principal suggested that I attend the STEM SOS workshop in Houston, I didn't know that was going to change everything about my teaching philosophy. After the workshop, I realized that STEM SOS model not only helps students develop self-discipline and responsibility to create their own projects, but also increases students' self-esteem as well. We built new rules with my students with PBL projects. When my students helped me determine classroom rules and consequences, they took the ownership of those as many experts state.

Another physics teacher pointed out that because the things they do in STEM SOS classrooms are engaging, inspiring and different, students wonder what is happening. Thus, they remain actively engaged as described below:

> To be honest, in a few cases, I have seen classroom management issues. Because of the [positive] student-teacher communication, sometimes the students will talk about other teachers' classes (and I don't allow them to use the teacher's names) and what is happening in their classes and what makes

them bored . When the students see that they are not learning anything, it results in classroom misbehavior. I may say that because of STEM SOS there will never be issues. They are always going to wonder what is happening and what is this crazy guy going to do. Because they are always wondering, they will always see a misconception in the class. That keeps the kids quiet because they are actively learning and trying to understand.

Climate. Participants also felt that the STEM SOS model positively affected the classroom climate. Teachers reported that they have a positive classroom climate where everybody can ask questions without fear of embarrassment. Everyone treats others nicely and there is a lot of fun going on in each and every class. As one of the physics teachers elaborated:

The classroom is always fun and they always ask questions. Whenever I ask a student a question and he or she can't explain it very well, the other kids will comment saying: "That's not how it works. Remember when he showed us the other demonstration?" They are always acting like really close friends and constantly trying to fix their mistakes and also trying to teach each other. They talk freely and are not scared, everyone is asking questions, commenting on the demonstrations, and are generally really comfortable. Everyone is laughing, but that does not mean that we are not doing anything. Of course we are learning, but it is a really comforting environment to learn in. Hopefully, at the end of the year, we can see how well we did in class.

An algebra teacher reiterated what the physics teacher described above:

My classroom climate definitely changed positively; there was an Algebra I Spirit among the STEM SOS students. I didn't have any major problems last year.

Another physics teacher made a similar statement about how the positive climate in his classroom enables students to feel comfortable with peer teaching and asking questions: "Students actively engage in my class and do group work. They do peer teaching; they explain their projects to each other and ask and answer questions comfortably."

Student-teacher communication. Teachers also reported that their communication with their students improved through the STEM SOS model because they meet with their students to complete student projects as well as travel and spend time together for competition and demonstration purposes:

I have very good communication with my students thanks to the STEM SOS model. When I assign them projects, I meet with my students several times a week to answer their questions and clarify some points in completion of the projects. Most of these meeting are not scheduled and students feel they need to see me and ask questions. We also go to different competitions together to do STEM demonstrations. These are all important means to positively develop our communication.

In the following quote, another teacher explained how their communication develops through participation in the STEM SOS model:
It affected [student-teacher communication] well because you don't only see them in classroom, they stay afterschool to work on their projects. So you become more than a teacher for them. Plus during STEM expos, you are going on trips with them and you build up a frienuship and they become more engaged in classes and they are more comfortable asking you questions and learn better.

Professional growth.   Participants emphasized the importance of the model for their professional growth. This growth seemed to happen mostly in teaching, content knowledge and development of some of the critical skills that are needed in the 21st century. For instance, several teachers reported that they improved their technology skills as follows:

> The STEM SOS model helped me grow professionally. I learned 21st century skills with my students. Before the STEM SOS model, I did not know how to create a website, upload a movie on YouTube or make a poster and handout that require technology use. I now know how to create a website, make a movie, and use different video editing programs thanks to the STEM SOS model. Frankly, the STEM SOS model is not only good for students, but it is also beneficial for teachers too.

Because the assigned projects are all student-directed and centered, teachers are facilitating their learning. Teachers have to communicate with students regularly. Their communication skills are pivotal in providing timely and clear feedback in order for students to progress in their completion of projects. One of the mathematics teachers described how the STEM SOS model helped them develop important skills, including communication and collaboration:

> Yes, I am 100% sure the STEM SOS model helps me grow professionally because after integrating the STEM SOS model to my teaching, not only did I start to become a better teacher because the model helped me improve and develop my communication, collaboration, information, and technology literacy skills. So I was able to make real-world connections and better reach my students.

It seems that teaching with the STEM SOS model helped teachers become better teachers in terms of content and teaching. One of the physics teachers described this process:

> This is my first actual job after college. And in my first year, I've realized that I don't really know anything. Equations didn't mean anything; I didn't know

how to make equations meaningful to my students. But the demonstrations that came with the model helped me a lot and I remembered all the things about physics I learned in college. The difference was the content I learned in college starting making more sense when I started teaching with the STEM SOS model because I clearly saw how the theory and formulas were connected to the things happening around me. And then you learn how to teach.

Students

The second group of benefits that teacher interviews revealed was for students. Teachers believed that students benefited from the STEM SOS model in engagement, developing 21st century skills and college readiness.

Engaged. Because the STEM SOS model was designed to "spark student interest, and motivate them to ask their own questions," they were more inclined to learn with love, thus they became intrinsically motivated. Teachers noticed that students became more willing participants in the learning process because the model provided them with more exciting activities and engaged them during class. One of the physics teachers stated:

Well, of course, not all of my classes are like that, but in most of them, I try to have a video, picture, demo and an activity. And kids wonder what they are going to learn it is not like 'It is another boring physics class!' They always ask questions and they are engaged by the demonstrations.

A mathematics teacher emphasized how students' motivation and expectations also inspired them come up with more interesting projects:

Every day, I try to bring new projects to class that would catch their interest and to make connection with real life and Mathematics. I prepared a new way to teach mathematics. I've started with lecture 10-15 minutes from beginning of the class. Without real life connections or STEM SOS PBLs, my students had a hard time solving [mathematics] questions, but when they see that mathematics is in their real lives they are more engaged and involved with their learning process.

STEM demonstrations, during which students travel away from the school and perform, are another dimension of the STEM SOS model that helps increase student engagement. One of the physics teachers explained:

We don't only see our students in classroom; they stay after school to work on their projects. So you are becoming more than a teacher for them. Plus during STEM expos you are having a trip there and you build up a friendship and they become more engaged in classes and they are more comfortable asking you questions and learn better.

21st Century skills students develop. One of the benefits of the STEM SOS model for students was the development of 21st century skills. For example, one teacher stated that the model provided opportunities for students to develop some important 21st century skills, including presentation and communication skills. One of the physics teachers gave an example showing how students develop their presentation and communication skills:

> They are presenting and explaining everything to people. At these events, there aren't just educators and high school kids, but sometimes there are 5 year olds or 70 year old seniors asking "What is going on?" The students are talking to people who have no idea what is happening. Whenever they do this again and again, you can see and realize that they are changing the way they are explaining depending on the visitor. If it is a kid, they try simplifying it. If it is a senior or someone who knows about the subject, they try to go more in depth. For me, presenting and communicating with people of different backgrounds are very important skills they will need in both college and life.

Another skill group that one of the STEM teachers highlighted was collaboration and getting along with others. One of the teachers explained the development of these skills in the following quote:

> When they complete their Level I projects, they have to collaborate with other [group members]. These are group projects. They learn how to get along with each other and negotiate their ideas. If there is a conflict they have to compromise. So they learn how to get along with different ideas and people.

Another area emphasized was the technology and information skills students use during project completion. One of the chemistry teachers described how students learn technology and information skills during project completion, stating, "When they complete their projects, they are supposed to create a website to show and explain their projects in detail. They also prepare a video presentation that requires lots of advanced video editing techniques. They also have to learn how to upload a video on YouTube."

College readiness. Another sub-theme in this main category was college preparation. A mathematics teacher noted that "regular teaching is teacher- centered in education, but the STEM SOS model is student-centered, so students have more of a chance to shine and discover their own abilities, which will help them in college." As underscored, student-centered and directed teaching might be beneficial for preparing students for college life and courses where they have to determine almost everything they do, from course selection to how to complete assignments. A physics teacher also explained this as follows:

> Students are required to understand the assignments on their own, pace themselves so they finish the assignment on time, and implement experiments

that they have designed themselves. I have even taken the designing your own experiments to the next level this year and given my students access to the basic lab equipment under their lab tables so they have to decide what materials to use and when to use.

Teachers felt that this was also related to 21ˢᵗ century skills because to them, developing 21ˢᵗ century skills contributes to college preparation, as described in the following quote:

It helps them for college. I give them projects and they are responsible for completing these projects by the due date so when they go to college, they will do the same thing. With the STEM SOS model, students learn how to use technology for their projects so that they will use those abilities in college too. Such as doing a website, uploading a movie on YouTube, create an account and those thing will be easy for them to adjust college.

A physics teacher approached the topic in the same way and underscored the importance of the problem-solving skills students gained through STEM SOS model:

Well, first of all, they learn the subject and I think this is the most important part. Because they didn't just play with the 'toys', they also solved problems about projects and they've learned the subjects. In college, that's what is going to help them the most. Besides that, with the "if…what" types of questions, they are learning how to solve the problem. If the problem is that, what I should do to solve the problem?

CONCLUSION

The purpose of this study was to hear the experiences of teachers who utilize the STEM SOS model in their teaching. We specifically wanted to examine teachers' experiences and thoughts about the model. Seven teachers were interviewed and their interview transcripts were analyzed using the phenomenological approach. Analyses revealed that all the findings could be grouped under two main themes: how the STEM SOS model works and benefits of the model for teachers and students. We found that the STEM SOS model takes place both within school and after school hours. Teachers described their ways of teaching in three sub-groups: lecturing, student presentation and Level I group investigation. We also found that the role of teachers was as a facilitator whereby the students were active learners and the model provided them with rigorous content. The after school sub-theme had two categories of projects: chapter and Level II and III. The second main theme, the benefits of the STEM SOS model, benefited teachers in the areas of classroom management, classroom climate, student-teacher communication and professional growth. Students' benefits were in engagement, 21ˢᵗ century skills development and college readiness. It seems that students experience a full PBL experience by completing all level I and II and/or Level III projects.

REFERENCES

Afterschool Alliance. (2011). *After school and summer programs: Committed partners in STEM education.* Retrieved from http://www.afterschoolalliance.org/STEM_JointPositionPaper.pdf

Eisenhart, M. A. (1991). *Ideas from a cultural anthropologist: Implications for mathematics education researcher.* In Thirteen Annual Meeting of the North American Chapter of the International Group for the Psychology of Mathematics Education, Blacksburg, VA.

Coffey, H. (2010). *Project-based learning. K-12 Teaching and Learning.* Retrieved from http://scholar.google.com/scholar?q=Project-based+learning%2C+Heather+Coffey&btnG=&hl=en&as_sdt=0%2C44

Colaizzi, P. F. (1978). Psychological research as the phenomenologist views it. In R. Valle & M. King (Eds.), *Existential phenomenological alternatives in psychology* (pp. 48–71). New York, NY: Oxford University Press.

Creswell, J. W. (2007) *Qualitative inquiry and research design: Choosing among five traditions.* Thousand Oaks, CA: Sage.

David, J. L. (2008). What research says about project-based learning. *Educational Leadership, 65*(5), 80–82.

Kemmis, S., & Wilkinson, M. (1998). Participatory action research and the study of practice. In B. Atweh, S. Kemmis & P. Weeks (Eds.), *Action research in practice: Partnerships for social justice in education* (pp. 21–36). New York, NY: Routledge.

Laboy-Rush, D. (2011). *Integrated STEM Education through Project-Based Learning. Learning. com,* Retrieved from http://www. rondout. k12. ny. us/common/pages/DisplayFile. aspx.

Markham, T. (2014). *Strategies for embedding project-based learning into STEM education.* Retrieved from http://www.edutopia.org/blog/strategies-pbl-stem-thom-markham-buck-institute

Penuel, W. R., & Means, B. (2000). *Designing a performance assessment to measure students' communication skills in multi-media supported, project-based learning.* Paper presented at the Annual Meeting of the American Educational Research Association, New Orleans, LA.

Sahin, A. (2012). *STEM project-based learning: Specialized form of inquiry-based learning.* In R. M. Capraro, M. M. Capraro & J. Morgan (Eds.), Project-based learning: An integrated science, technology, engineering, and mathematics (STEM) approach (2nd ed., pp. 59–64). Rotterdam, The Netherlands: Sense.

Sahin, A., Top, N., & Vanegas, S. (2014). Harmony STEM SOS model increases college readiness and develops 21st century skills (Whitepaper). Retrieved from http://harmonytx.org/Portals/0/HPS_Issue-1.pdf

Sahin, A., & Top, N. (In press). Make it happen: A study of a novel teaching style, STEM Students on the Stage (SOS)™, for increasing students' STEM knowledge and interest. *Journal of STEM Education: Innovations and Research.*

Wagner, T. (2012). *Creating innovators: The making of young people who will change the world.* New York, NY: Simon and Schuster.

Wayne RESA. (2014). Integrating STEM and project-based learning. Retrieved from http://www.resa.net/curriculum/curriculum/science/technology/integrating-stem-and-project-based-learning.

Alpaslan Sahin
Harmony Public Schools

Namik Top
Texas A&M University

SECTION 6
RESOURCES FOR TEACHERS AND STUDENTS

This section provides resources for teachers and students, including sample projects for Mathematics and Physics.

APPENDICES

1. STEM SOS Model Student Tasks (These are required for all lessons and subjects).

    a. Level I
    b. Level II and III

3. Mathematics-Level I

    a. Twisted Square-Student Handout-Level I
    b. Twisted Square-Teacher Guide-Level I
    c. Rubric Level I

4. Mathematics-Level II

    a. Making Beehives-Student Handout-Level II
    b. Making Beehives-Teacher Guide-Level II
    c. Rubric-Level II

4. Physics-Level-II

    a. Balancing Demonstrations Student Handout-Level II
    b. Balancing Demonstrations Teacher Guide-Level II
    c. Summative Assessment

5. ELA and Social Studies

    a. Level II and III Options (These are given in Chapter 8 appendices).

1.A. LEVEL I STUDENT TASKS

STUDENT PRODUCT 1: Investigation report

1. Upon the completion of Level I projects, your product (investigation report, journal, etc.) will be graded with a specific rubric. Each subject will have a different rubric.
2. Please consider using Google docs and Google Drive when you are writing and sharing your investigation reports. This will make sharing your files with your teachers easier.

STUDENT PRODUCT 2: Producing Digital Photo Gallery Presentations

1. Math, English and Social Studies' students for each semester you will have one project from Level I. There will be one Digital Photo Gallery Presentation for each semester.

2. Science Students for each semester you will have two projects from Level I. Digital Photo Gallery Presentation will be prepared for only one of the two projects.
3. There will be one Digital Photo Gallery Presentation for each semester.
4. Each team will have one Digital Photo Gallery Presentation.
5. Preparing Digital Photo Gallery Presentation is optional for Social Science and English courses.

1.B. LEVEL II AND III STUDENT TASKS

FIRST GRADING PERIOD (1st Quarter):

TASK 1: Create your e-portfolio (Google Site) and choose your Project (Graded by Science or Math Teacher)
TASK 2: Present Background research and maintain your project materials (Graded by Science or Math Teacher)
TASK 3: Creating "About My School" page (Graded by Science or Math Teacher)
TASK 4 & TASK 5: Creating "My PBL Project" page (Graded by Science or Math Teacher)
TASK 6: Post "investigation part" to your PBL Page (Graded by Science or Math Teacher)

SECOND GRADING PERIOD (2nd Quarter):

TASK 7: Choosing the ELA and SS (Social Studies) components of your project (Graded by ELA and SS Teacher)
TASK 8: Posting the ELA component and SS connection. (Graded by ELA and SS Teacher)
TASK 9 & TASK 10: PBL Video Presentation (Digital Story) (Graded by Science or Math Teacher)
TASK 11: Designing and Publishing Project Brochure (Graded by Science or Math Teacher)
TASK 12: Video Presentation - ELA component and SS Connection (Graded by ELA and Social Studies Teacher)

THIRD GRADING PERIOD (3rd Quarter):

This quarter will be a make-up period, teachers will grade previous tasks from 1st and 2nd quarter again, so that the students will have chance to update their projects.

The students who are behind may continue doing the missing previous tasks

TASK 13: "My School" Page (Graded by Science or Math Teacher)
This task is make -up for **TASK 3**
(the students will be graded again from the same task 3)

TASK 14: **"My PBL Project" Page** (Graded by Science or Math Teacher)
    This task is making -up for **TASK 4 and TASK 5.**
    (the students will be graded again from the same task 4&5)

TASK 15: Video Presentation (Graded by Science or Math Teacher)
    This task is make-up for TASK 9 and TASK 10.
    (the students will be graded again from the same task 9&10)

TASK 16: Homepage and Brochure (Graded by Science or Math Teacher)
    This task is make-up for **TASK 11**
    (the students will be graded again from the same task 11)

TASK 17: **"ELA component" and "SS connection" Page** (Graded by ELA and Social Studies Teachers)
    This task is make-up for **TASK 8**
    (the students will be graded again from the same task 8)

TASK 18: Movie Presentation – ELA component and SS connection (Graded by ELA and Social Studies Teachers)
    This task is make-up for **TASK 12**
        (the students will be graded again from the same task 12)

2.A. MATHEMATICS-TWISTED SQUARE-STUDENT HANDOUT-*LEVEL I*

TWISTED SQUARE

Driving Question

How can congruence, similarity, and other rules of geometry be used to determine—without measurement—the area of a square constructed using four segments within a larger square?

Background

Before computers or other types of technology made it easy to produce exact copies of images, people made use of clever mechanical devices such as the pantograph to copy or rescale drawings or images. A pen used for drawing or tracing over the original drawing is linked to a second pen by an arrangement of hinged parallelograms. Depending on the arrangement of the hinged parallelograms, the original drawing may be copied at the same scale, producing a second, congruent image. Or, the original can be copied at a smaller or larger scale and thus resized so that the second image is similar to the original but not congruent.

A Hoberman Sphere, with mechanical hinges similar to the pantograph, is a special type of 3-dimensional structure that can expand or contract while retaining its spherical shape. Some Hoberman Spheres are displayed as exhibits in museums and science centers, and use motorized mechanisms to expand and contract their hinges, increasing or decreasing their diameter while they maintain similarity. Smaller, plastic Hoberman Spheres are made as toys.

The pantograph and Hoberman Sphere illustrate how similarity is related to scale and congruence. In this project you will produce a scaled and transformed square and investigate the properties of congruence and similarity that give rise to this smaller, "twisted" square.

Project Objectives

In this project you will work with the members of your group to:

- construct a series of larger squares with smaller, twisted squares inscribed in them according to a sequence of instructions.
- experiment with geometric transformations of triangles, squares, and other polygons in the plane.
- describe the rotations and reflections that carry a triangle or square onto itself.
- given a geometric figure and a rotation, reflection, or translation, draw the transformed figure using graph paper, tracing paper, or geometry software.
- determine the area of composite two-dimensional figures comprised of a combination of triangles, trapezoids, and other regular polygons.
- prove the congruence of two or more polygons visually.
- use trigonometric ratios and the Pythagorean equation to solve right triangles.

- make connections between the mathematical concepts in this project and real life applications.
- present your results and conclusions to your class.

Materials and Equipment

Mandatory Equipment

- Graph paper, several sheets
- Construction paper, several sheets
- Colored pencils
- Ruler or straightedge
- Scissors
- Tape

Optional Equipment

- Dynamic geometry software
- Drawing compass

Key Concepts for Background Research

Research your project topic based on the driving question above. Use any resources available to research background information that will help you to complete your project.

Below is a list of key concepts that may be helpful when doing your background research.

- Transformation (rotation, translation, reflection)
- Slope of parallel lines
- Slope of perpendicular lines
- Midpoint of a segment
- Opposite side (of an angle)
- Adjacent side (of an angle)
- Pythagorean equation for right triangles
- Similarity
- Scale factor
- Angle-Angle Theorem for proving similarity

- Ratio of similarity
- Congruence
- Sine of an acute angle (in a right triangle)
- Cosine of an acute angle (in a right triangle)
- Vertex (plural – vertices)
- Inscribed
- Tessellation
- Quadratic equation
- Roots or solutions of a quadratic equation

Safety and Maintenance

Add this important safety precaution to your normal classroom procedures:

– Handle all sharp objects carefully, including drawing compasses, scissors or craft/ hobby knives.

Investigation

Use these guiding questions to help answer the driving question:

1. Use graph paper to draw and cut out four right triangles whose perpendicular sides are 15 units and 20 units respectively. You may find it helpful to draw the 15-unit sides in one color, the 20-unit sides in a second color, and the hypotenuse in a third color:

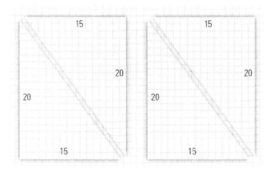

2. Arrange the four right triangles to form a square with sides each 35 units in length. Without measuring, how can you determine the length of one side of the inner square? What is its length?
3. In the previous step you used four right triangles to form the largest square possible. Rearrange the four right triangles to form a smaller square whose sides are less than 35 units in length, without overlapping the triangles. What is the length of a side of the twisted inner square? How can you determine this without measuring the side?
4. Form an even smaller twisted square by rearranging the triangles again. This time overlap the four right triangles to form a square whose sides are 20 units in length. Can the length of the inner square's side be found using the same method as for the two previous inner squares? Justify your answer.
5. Draw and cut out a square that is 20 units on each side. This square is congruent to the square in the previous step.
6. Use one of the right triangles to divide each side of the 20 x 20 square into two segments – one segment of 15 units, one segment of 5 units. Mark a point on each side to indicate this division:

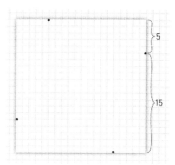

7. Connect each vertex of the square to the point on the opposite side by drawing a segment along the hypotenuse of the right triangle:

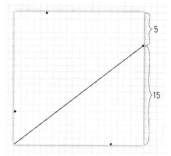

8. Cut out one or more of the small triangles. Later in this activity you will derive the area of the "twisted square" formed in a construction similar to this. Part of the derivation requires you to apply the following skills: calculating acute angles in triangles, and solving for unknown side lengths in right triangles. Practice these skills within this construction.

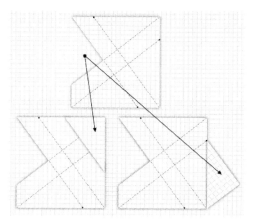

a. Using colored pencils identify the opposite and adjacent sides of one of the acute angles in the 15 unit x 20 unit right triangles.

b. To find the acute angles of the right triangle, which of the following trigonometric relationships do you need to apply: sine, cosine, or tangent?

_____

_____

_____

c. Calculate the acute angles and show your steps.

d. How many degrees are in the measure of the third angle of the right triangle? Show the steps of your calculation.

e. Use the grid squares to verify your calculations.

9. Use the small triangle(s) to prove visually that the inner twisted square is actually a square. Describe or draw your method.

_____

_____

_____

10. Define a square ABCD, with side length of 10 units. Name the midpoints M, N, P, R, of sides AB, BC, CD, and DA, respectively. Draw the segment that joins vertex A to midpoint N. Do this for the remaining vertices and midpoints. Use the grid provided.

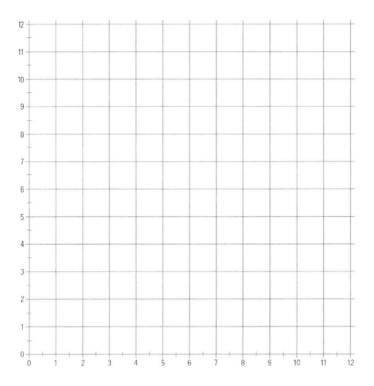

11. What other types of polygons have been formed inside the square ABCD as a result of constructing the smaller square?

12. What is the length, in units, of the segment that connects the larger square's vertex to the midpoint on the opposite side? Show your method and calculations for determining the length.

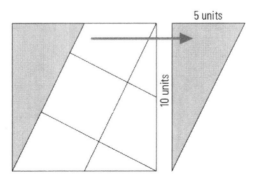

13. Describe at least one way in which one of these polygons can be transformed to create a new square congruent to the "twisted" square. Use additional paper to trace images if necessary.

    _____

    _____

    _____

14. Use transformations to construct additional squares congruent to the smaller square, to form a 5-square cross that is similar to a "plus sign" or the symbol on the flag of Switzerland. Use additional paper to trace images if necessary.

15. Using additional graph paper onto which you trace the original square ABCD and any transformations, prove visually that all of the triangles created by transformations are congruent both to one another and to the small triangles within the large square ABCD.

16. Using additional graph paper as needed, prove visually that all of the smaller squares are congruent.

17. The segment length calculated in Question 12 forms the hypotenuse of a right triangle. What is the number in degrees in the acute angles of this triangle? How can you determine the angle without measuring the angle directly?

18. What theorem can you apply to prove that two triangles are similar? Apply this theorem to prove that any one of the larger triangles in square ABCD is similar to any of the smallest triangles you constructed within square ABCD.

19. Show two different ways to find the area of the smaller twisted square. Verify your results by shading in the grid squares to sum the total area.

Synthesis Questions

The answers to the following questions will guide you to further critical thinking about your project topic, and will build knowledge to help answer questions that your classmates may ask when you present.

1. **How does the definition of congruent polygons allow you to prove congruence visually? What are some possible shortcomings of this kind of proof?**

   _____

   _____

   _____

2. **If a classmate unfamiliar with your work on this project saw the diagram below and stated that one of the angles formed by the segments appeared to be obtuse (for example ∠BGA'), how could you verify without using a protractor to measure that the apparent obtuse angle contains more than 90°?**

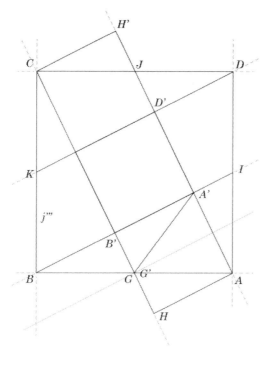

   _____

   _____

   _____

3. Integers that satisfy the Pythagorean equation for right triangles are called "Pythagorean triples." There are infinitely many such sets of integers, but the 3-4-5 right triangle is the smallest Pythagorean triple. The triangles you drew and used in the first part of this project were multiples of the 3-4-5 right triangle. How can you confirm this?

_____

_____

_____

4. How can you prove algebraically that pairs of adjacent segments that form the smaller square are, in fact, perpendicular and that opposite pairs of segments are, in fact, parallel? Use additional graph paper as needed.

_____

_____

_____

Extension and Real Life Application

The answers to the following questions will help you make connections between the concepts relevant to your project topic and their applications to real world problems, and will further add to your knowledge to help answer questions that your classmates may ask when you present.

1. Discuss at least one real life application (and extension) of concepts relevant to this entire project.

_____

_____

_____

2. Create a set of four congruent right triangles that satisfy the Pythagorean triple of 5-12-13, and use these triangles to construct a small inner square as you did in investigation Questions 1 – 10. What is the area, in square units, of the inner square?

_____

_____

_____

3. Suppose a right triangle has its shortest side 8 units in length. If the dimensions of the perpendicular side and the hypotenuse complete a Pythagorean triple, what would be the area, in square units, of an inner square constructed as in the previous question?

_____

_____

_____

4. If you constructed the square from the right triangles in the previous question, what percent of the area of the largest possible square is the area of the smallest possible square you can make using the methods followed in this project?

_____

_____

_____

5. The ancient Egyptians used ropes knotted at regular intervals to measure right angles. Three ropes were connected and each rope had a different number of knots tied at regular intervals. When pulled taut, a right triangle was formed which could be used to ensure that a stone block had each face perpendicular to the faces adjoining it. How many knots would have been tied in each rope? Explain your thinking.

_____

_____

_____

6. Suppose you have eight congruent right, scalene triangles with sides of length a, b, and c. Show how you can use four of the triangles to create two congruent rectangles of length a and width b, and another four of the triangles to create a square with sides length c. How can these figures be used to demonstrate the Pythagorean Theorem?

_____

_____

_____

7. Suppose you can construct a point anywhere on the side of the larger square and connect that point to the opposite vertex. This point divides the side into segments of length a and b. Create the smaller, inner square in this manner by constructing congruent points and segments on each side of the larger square. What must be the ratio of the lengths a and b such that the area of the smaller square is one-half that of the larger square?

_____

_____

_____

8. An artist wants to create a sculpture based on multiple rotations of a square tile, stacked one on top of the other. She plans to make a series of squares that are successively smaller, and rotate them by some fixed amount as she stacks each new layer. She has seen a 2-dimensional design on a Cartesian coordinate system with the vertices of a square at points (0, 0), (100, 0), (100, 100), and (0, 100) respectively. She observes that a rotated inner square was

formed by plotting the vertex of an inscribed square at points $(0, a)$, which is some distance above the origin. Another vertex of this inscribed square has been plotted at $(a, 100)$. This defines a right triangle whose short leg has length a, whose long leg has length b, and whose hypotenuse is one side of the inscribed square. What must be the ratio of a to b so that each new square can be rotated by a fixed amount when she stacks it on top of the one below it? What is the ratio of similarity for the squares?

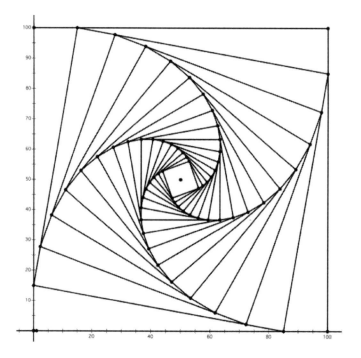

2.B. MATHEMATICS-TWISTED SQUARE-TEACHER GUIDE-*LEVEL I*

TWISTED SQUARE

Student Objectives

Students answer their driving question and investigation questions through collaborative research, and then deliver their results to their classmates in a concise. The student will:

Mandatory

- Construct a series of larger squares with smaller, twisted squares inscribed in them according to a sequence of instructions.
- Experiment with geometric transformations of triangles, squares, and other polygons in the plane.
- Describe the rotations and reflections that carry a triangle or square onto itself.
- Given a geometric figure and a rotation, reflection, or translation, draw the transformed figure using graph paper, tracing paper, or geometry software.
- Determine the area of composite two-dimensional figures comprised of a combination of triangles, trapezoids, and other regular polygons.
- Prove the congruence of two or more polygons visually.
- Use trigonometric ratios and the Pythagorean equation to solve right triangles.
- Make connections between the mathematical concepts in this project and real life applications.
- Present results and conclusions to the class.

TEKS Objectives

This project correlates to the following TEKS objectives:

(c)1   The student uses mathematical processes to acquire and demonstrate mathematical understanding. The student is expected to:

B. Use a problem-solving model that incorporates analyzing given information, formulating a plan or strategy, determining a solution, justifying the solution, and evaluating the problem-solving process and reasonableness of the solution;

C. Select tools, including real objects, manipulatives, paper and pencil, and technology as appropriate, and techniques, including mental math, estimation, and number sense as appropriate, to solve problems;

D. Communicate mathematical ideas, reasoning, and their implications using multiple representations, including symbols, diagrams, graphs, and language as appropriate;

(c)11   Two-dimensional and three-dimensional figures. The student uses the process skills in the application of formulas to determine measures of two- and three-dimensional figures. The student is expected to:

     B.   Determine the area of composite two-dimensional figures comprised of a combination of triangles, parallelograms, trapezoids, kites, regular polygons, or sectors of circles to solve problems using appropriate units of measure;

     C.   Apply the formulas for the total and lateral surface area of three-dimensional figures, including prisms, pyramids, cones, cylinders, spheres, and composite figures, to solve problems using appropriate units of measure; and

     D.   Apply the formulas for the volume of three-dimensional figures, including prisms, pyramids, cones, cylinders, spheres, and composite figures, to solve problems using appropriate units of measure.

This project correlates to the following Common Core State Standards:

HSG.GMD.A   Explain volume formulas and use them to solve problems:

     1   Give an informal argument for the formulas for the circumference of a circle, area of a circle, volume of a cylinder, pyramid, and cone.

     3   Use volume formulas for cylinders, pyramids, cones, and spheres to solve problems.

HSG.GMD.B   Visualize relationships between two-dimensional and three-dimensional objects:

     4   Identify the shapes of two-dimensional cross-sections of three-dimensional objects, and identify three-dimensional objects generated by rotations of two-dimensional objects.

HSG.MG.A   Apply geometric concepts in modeling situations:

     1   Use geometric shapes, their measures, and their properties to describe objects (e.g., modeling a tree trunk or a human torso as a cylinder).

     2   Apply concepts of density based on area and volume in modeling situations (e.g., persons per square mile, BTUs per cubic foot).

     3   Apply geometric methods to solve design problems (e.g., designing an object or structure to satisfy physical constraints or minimize cost; working with typographic grid systems based on ratios).

HSG.SRT.C   Define trigonometric ratios and solve problems involving right triangles:

> 6   Understand that by similarity, side ratios in right triangles are properties of the angles in the triangle, leading to definitions of trigonometric ratios for acute angles.

> 8   Use trigonometric ratios and the Pythagorean Theorem to solve right triangles in applied problems.

Project Background

Given a unit square, a second—smaller—"twisted" square can be created by connecting each of the four vertices of the unit square to a point on the opposite (nonadjacent) side. The initial choice of a vertex and corresponding point on the nonadjacent side is arbitrary; for example it can be made to divide the opposite side into two segments that are one-third and two-thirds of a unit respectively, or one-fourth and three-fourths of a unit respectively, or any proportional length a to $1 - a$. Once the point has been chosen on one side of the unit square, congruent lines should be constructed from each of the remaining vertices The result is a smaller square that is rotated some number of degrees off the axis of the original square.

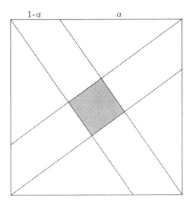

The original square is similar to the smaller, rotated square. By definition, all squares are similar to each other because their corresponding angles are congruent—that is, all angles are 90°, and their corresponding side lengths are proportional. A less formal expression of this concept is that all squares are similar to each other because they have the same shape but are not necessarily the same size.

In this project students will first draw and cut out triangles and these use these to form three squares of 35 units in length, 25 units in length, and 20 units in length, respectively. They will use these constructions to review and apply the skills necessary before introducing a more complex problem. Students next construct a square that is 10 units on a side, and then connect the midpoint of each side to the vertices to construct the smaller, rotated square within it. They will use their construction to investigate the properties of congruence and similarity, and will experiment with transformations that enable them to demonstrate congruence visually by superimposing a polygon on one it is identical to.

Students will apply the Pythagorean equation, the sine and cosine relationships for right triangles, and the Angle-Angle Theorem for proving similarity of triangles to solve for missing measures of a variety of polygons. They will apply prior knowledge of algebra to prove lines either parallel or perpendicular based on their slopes being the same or having a product of −1. Students will be asked in the Extension and Real Life Applications questions to solve a quadratic equation and choose the most logical solution to determine the point that makes the ratio of the sides of the larger square such that the inner square's area will be half that of the larger square.

Materials and Special Preparation

Mandatory Equipment

□ Graph paper, several sheets
□ Construction paper, several sheets
□ Colored pencils
□ Ruler or straightedge
□ Scissors
□ Tape

Optional Equipment

□ Dynamic geometry software
□ Drawing compass

The student handout for this activity lists the mandatory and optional equipment shown above that can be used as part of the student's project. Please review these items prior to providing them to the student.

Safety and Maintenance

Be certain that students add this important safety precaution to their normal classroom procedures:

• Handle all sharp objects carefully, including drawing compasses, scissors or craft/hobby knives.

Time Guidelines

Students working together in a group should be able to complete Investigation Questions 1 – 16 (Easy to Moderate degree of difficulty) within one 50-minute class period. A second class period will be necessary to complete the remaining Investigation Questions.

Presentation Guidelines

Use the following guidelines to assess the student's preparation, content knowledge, and presentation delivery.

Investigation Guidelines

Follow these guidelines to assess each of the investigation questions from three parts of the student project handout. The third column indicates the difficulty level of the concept addressed in the investigation question.

Investigation Questions	Suitable Response	Difficulty
1. Use graph paper to draw and cut out four right triangles whose perpendicular sides are 15 units and 20 units respectively.		Easy
2. Arrange the four right triangles to form a square with sides each 35 units in length. Without measuring, how can you determine the length of one side of the inner square? What is its length?	 Find the length of inner square's side using the Pythagorean equation: $$c^2 = a^2 + b^2$$ $$c^2 = 15^2 + 20^2$$ $$c^2 = 625$$ $$c = \sqrt{625}$$ $$c = 25$$	Easy

Investigation Questions	Suitable Response	Difficulty
3. In the previous step you used four right triangles to form the largest square possible. Rearrange the four right triangles to form a smaller square whose sides are less than 35 units in length, without overlapping the triangles. What is the length of a side of the twisted inner square? How can you determine this without measuring the side?	The length of the square's side is 5 units. This determined by subtracting the shorter side of the right triangle from the longer side: 20 units − 15 units = 5 units.	Moderate
4. Form an even smaller twisted square by rearranging the triangles again. This time overlap the four right triangles to form a square whose sides are 20 units in length. Can the length of the inner square's side be found using the same method as for the two previous inner squares? Justify your answer.	The same method cannot be used to find the length of the square's side because addition or subtraction of sides of the larger right triangles does not yield the length of a segment congruent to the square's side.	Moderate

244

Investigation Questions	Suitable Response	Difficulty
5. Draw and cut out a square that is 20 units on each side.		Easy
6. Use one of the right triangles to divide each side of the 20 × 20 square into two segments – one segment of 15 units, one segment of 5 units. Mark a point at each side to indicate this division.		Moderate
7. Connect each vertex of the square to the point on the opposite side by drawing a segment along the hypotenuse of the right triangle.		Moderate

Investigation Questions	Suitable Response	Difficulty
8. Cut out one or more of the small triangles. Later in this activity you will derive the area of the "twisted square" formed in a construction similar to this. Part of the derivation requires you to apply the following skills: calculating acute angles in triangles, and solving for unknown side lengths in right triangles. Practice these skills with this construction. a. Using colored pencils identify the opposite and adjacent sides of one of the acute angles in the right triangles. b. To find the acute angles of the right triangle, which of the following trigonometric relationships do you need to apply: sine, cosine, or tangent? c. Calculate the acute angles and show your steps.	 b. The trigonometric relationship that relates the opposite and adjacent sides of an acute angle is the tangent. $$\tan \theta = \frac{opp}{adj}$$ c. $$\tan \theta = \frac{15}{20}$$ $$\tan \theta = 0.75$$ $$\tan^{-1} \theta = 36.9° \approx 37°$$ d. Use the sum of the interior angles of a triangle: $$m\angle 1 + m\angle 2 + m\angle 3 = 180°$$ $$180° - m\angle 1 - m\angle 2 = m\angle 3$$ $$m\angle 3 = 180° - 90° - 37°$$ $$m\angle = 53°$$	Moderate

Investigation Questions	Suitable Response	Difficulty
9. Use the right triangles to prove visually that the inner twisted square is actually a square.		Easy
10. Define a square ABCD, with side length of 10 units. Name the midpoints M, N, P, R, of sides AB, BC, CD, and DA, respectively. Draw the segment that joins vertex A to midpoint N. Do this for the remaining vertices and midpoints. Use the grid provided.		Easy
11. What other types of polygons have been formed inside the 10 unit² square as a result of constructing the smaller square?	Right scalene triangles and trapezoids have been formed in addition to the smaller square.	Easy

Investigation Questions	Suitable Response	Difficulty
12. What is the length, in units, of the segment that connects the larger square's vertex to the midpoint on the opposite side? Show your method and calculations for determining the length.	Use the Pythagorean equation for right triangles, with sides 10 and 5 units, to solve for the hypotenuse: $$a^2 + b^2 = c^2$$ $$c = \sqrt{a^2 + b^2}$$ $$c = \sqrt{10^2 + 5^2}$$ $$c = \sqrt{125}$$ $$c = 11.180$$ $$c \approx 11.2$$	Moderate
13. Describe at least one way in which one of these polygons can be transformed to create a new square congruent to the "twisted" square.		Moderate

Investigation Questions	Suitable Response	Difficulty
14. Use transformations to construct additional squares congruent to the smaller square, to form a 5-square cross that is similar to a "plus sign" or the symbol on the flag of Switzerland.		Moderate
15. Using additional graph paper onto which you trace the original square ABCD and any transformations, prove visually that all of the triangles created by transformations are congruent both to one another and to the small triangles within the large square ABCD.	Cut out pairs of triangles and lay one on top of another to demonstrate that each component of the top triangle has the same measure as (is congruent to) the corresponding component of the bottom triangle. This can also be done by folding the paper instead of cutting out the shapes.	Moderate
16. Using additional graph paper as needed, prove visually that all of the smaller squares are congruent.	Cut out the 5-square cross-shaped polygon. Crease the paper along each edge of the center square. Fold up the four "arms" of the cross so they lie flat on the center square. The squares are all the same size (corresponding parts are all congruent) because they cover each other without overlapping or having gaps.	Moderate

Investigation Questions	Suitable Response	Difficulty
17. The segment length calculated in Question 12 forms the hypotenuse of a right triangle. What is the number in degrees in the acute angles of this triangle? How can you determine the angle without measuring the angle directly?	 Use the trigonometric relationships sine and cosine, and the known lengths of the sides of the right triangle (from the previous question) to solve for the missing angles: $\sin a = \dfrac{opposite}{hypotenuse}$ $\sin a = \cos b$ $\sin a = \dfrac{5}{11.2}$ $\sin a = 0.446628$ $\sin^{-1} a = 26.5°$ $m\angle a = 26.5°$ $\sin a = 0.446429$ $\cos b = 0.446429$ $\cos^{-1} b = 63.5°$ $m\angle b = 63.5°$ Since angle c is a right angle (definition of a square), its measure is 90°. The sum of the internal angles of any triangle is 180°: $$m\angle a + m\angle b + m\angle c = 180°$$ $$26.5° + 63.5° + 90° = 180°$$ This serves as a further check on the method and calculations.	Difficult

Investigation Questions	Suitable Response	Difficulty
18. What theorem can you apply to prove that two triangles are similar? Apply this theorem to prove that any one of the larger triangles in square ABCD is similar to any of the smallest triangles you constructed within square ABCD.	 Use the Angle-Angle Theorem: If two pairs of corresponding angles in a pair of triangles are congruent, then the triangles are similar. We know this because if two angle pairs are the same, then the third pair must also be equal. When the three angle pairs are all equal, the three pairs of sides must also be in proportion. Prove that $\triangle abc$ $\sim \triangle a'b'c' \sim \triangle ade$ Proof Given: The outer square and the inner square are defined to be squares. 1. $\angle dea \cong \angle b'c'a'$ by alternate exterior angles ($\overline{ba'} \parallel \overline{a'g}$). 2. $\angle c'a'b' \cong \angle aed$ by alternate exterior angles ($\overline{ca'} \parallel \overline{a'h}$). 3. $\triangle ade \cong \triangle a'b'c'$ by the sum of the interior angles of a triangle is 180°. 4. $\triangle ade \sim \triangle a'b'c'$ by congruent triangles are also similar. 5. $\angle ead \cong \angle bac$ by reflexive property. 6. $m\angle aed = 90°$ by vertical angles with $\angle gef$ (given in definition of square). 7. $m\angle acb = 90°$ by definition of square. 8. $\triangle ade \cong \angle a'b'c'$ by the sum of the interior angles of a triangle is 180°. $\triangle abc \sim \triangle a'b'c' \sim \triangle ade$ by Angle-Angle Theorem	Difficult

Investigation Questions	Suitable Response	Difficulty
19. Show two different ways to find the area of the smaller square. Verify your results by shading in the grid squares to sum the total area.	Students may choose a variety of techniques to find the area of the small square; here are examples of two methods that are commonly used. *Method 1:* Use previous values for lengths of sides of $\triangle abc$ and the fact that it is similar to $\triangle a'b'c'$ to solve for unknown sides of the smaller triangle, using proportions. Dimensions of the smaller triangle: Base = 2.232 units; Height = 4.464 units The height of the smaller triangle $\triangle a'b'c'$ is equal to the length of the square's side, so the area of the square is 4.464^2 units^2 or 19.93 units^2. *Method 2:* Use previous values for lengths of sides of $\triangle abc$ and the fact that it is similar to $\triangle ade$ to solve for unknown sides of the smaller triangle. Since the area of the small square is equal to the sum of the areas of the trapezoid and a small triangle, subtract the area of $\triangle ade$ from the area of $\triangle abc$: 25 units^2 − 4.982 units^2 = 20.02 units^2. If rounded, the two values obtained from the different methods agree. (If dynamic geometry software is used, students may measure the area directly, and it will be found to be 20.00 units^2.) assuming the sides are 10.00 units in length.	Difficult

Synthesis Questions

Below are sample responses to the questions in the Synthesis Questions section in the student handout.

1. **How does the definition of congruent polygons allow you to prove congruence visually? What are some possible shortcomings of this kind of proof?**
   Polygons whose corresponding parts are congruent are congruent. To be congruent means to be the same or equal to. This allows two polygons to be superimposed, one on top of the other, so we can see that one exactly covers the other. This could only happen if all the parts of both shapes were equal. Using this visual method has the drawback that we must work very carefully to cut out two shapes perfectly, so they do "fit" each other. Any human imperfection in cutting or folding might make it difficult to see if the polygons were perfectly matched.

2. **If a classmate unfamiliar with your work on this project saw the diagram below and stated that one of the angles formed by the segments appeared to be obtuse (for example ∠BGA'), how could you verify without using a protractor to measure that the apparent obtuse angle contains more than 90°?**
   There are isosceles (2 sides congruent), scalene (no sides congruent), right (contains 1 right angle), acute (all acute angles), and obtuse isosceles (contains one obtuse angle) triangles in the original square.

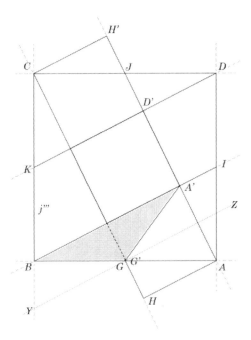

For the obtuse angle of the obtuse isosceles triangle ΔBGA', one method is to construct a line parallel to the base of the obtuse triangle (segment BI ∥ YZ) that passes through the vertex of the obtuse angle, then alternate or vertical angles and their complements to show that the sum of the angles must be greater than 90 degrees (see diagram).

3. **Integers that satisfy the Pythagorean equation for right triangles are called "Pythagorean triples." There are infinitely many such sets of integers, but the 3-4-5 right triangle is the smallest Pythagorean triple. The triangles you drew and used in first part of this project were multiples of the 3-4-5 right triangle. How can you confirm this?**

We constructed triangles with perpendicular sides of 15 and 20 units, which gave a hypotenuse of 25 units, confirmed by the Pythagorean equation and also visually on graph paper. The 15-20-25 right triangle can be obtained by multiplying the lengths of the 3-4-5 right triangle by 5:

$$3 \times 5 = 15$$
$$4 \times 5 = 20$$
$$5 \times 5 = 25$$

4. **How can you prove algebraically that pairs of adjacent segments that form the smaller square are, in fact, perpendicular and that opposite pairs of segments are, in fact, parallel? Use additional graph paper as needed.**

Two non-vertical lines are parallel if and only if they have the same slope. Two non-vertical lines are perpendicular if and only if they have slopes whose product is −1. This can be proven by plotting the lines that form the squares on a coordinate plane to determine their slopes by $m = \dfrac{\Delta y}{\Delta x} = \dfrac{y_2 - y_1}{x_2 - x_1}$ (see diagram).

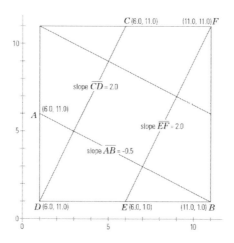

Extension and Real Life Application

Below are sample responses to the questions in the Extension and Real Life Application section in the student handout.

1. **Discuss at least one real life application (and extension) of concepts relevant to this entire project.**
   Designers of quilts or tile work can use transformations to produce a tessellation that forms a pattern based on only a few design elements. For example, some kinds of Islamic art are based on the orderly, repeating patterns of polygons. They can be simple shapes or complicated ones, and can cover large plane surfaces such as walls, floors, and ceilings. Space can be filled with color or left blank so that the absence of color creates what artists call "negative space." Quilt makers rely on shapes as well as colors of fabric pieces to create an overall interesting design. In both cases, transformations include reflections of shapes, translations, rotations, or even dilations.

   Zooming in and out of images, where the aspect ratio remains the same but size changes, is another application. For example, if an x-ray is taken of one's hand the doctor might need to zoom in on one small area to examine it for a break in a tiny bone. Zooming enlarges the bone in question without changing its aspect ratio. Digital imagery and software technology make this possible; in the past the doctor might have to take additional x-ray images with the lens closer to the body part, ion order to obtain a closer image. Digital technology allows for zooming to be done with less radiation administered to the patient.

2. **Create a set of four congruent right triangles that satisfy the Pythagorean triple of 5-12-13, and use these triangles to construct a small, inner square as you did in investigation Question 4. What is the area, in square units, of the inner square?**
   The area of the inner square is 41.75 units^2.

3. **Suppose a right triangle has its shortest side 8 units in length. If the dimensions of the perpendicular side and the hypotenuse complete a Pythagorean triple, what would be the area, in square units, of an inner square constructed as in the previous question?**
   The triangle would have sides of 8 and 15 units respectively, and hypotenuse of 17 units, according to the Pythagorean equation.

   The area of the inner square is 38.1 units^2.

4. **If you constructed the square from the right triangles in the previous question, what percent of the area of the largest possible square is the area of the smallest possible square you can make using the methods followed in this project?**

The largest possible area is formed by the twisted inner square of a 23 × 23 square (the sum of the 8 + 15 units of the triangles' sides). The area of this inner twisted square is the square of the hypotenuse, $17^2 = 289$ units^2.

The smallest possible area is formed by the square made of overlapped triangles, from the previous question, 38.1 units^2. That is about 13% of the area of the largest twisted square.

5. **The ancient Egyptians used ropes knotted at regular intervals to measure right angles. Three ropes were connected and each rope had a different number of knots tied at regular intervals. When pulled taut, a right triangle was formed which could be used to ensure that a stone block had each face perpendicular to the faces adjoining it. How many knots would have been tied in each rope? Explain your thinking.**
The Egyptians would have knotted ropes of 3 equally spaced intervals, 4 equally spaced intervals, and 5 equally spaced intervals. They would hold the ropes taut in a triangle, and align the 3-knot and 4-knot ropes with the stone block faces. This would verify the right angles at the corners.

6. **Suppose you have eight congruent right, scalene triangles with sides of length a, b, and c. Show how you can use four of the triangles to create two congruent rectangles of length a and width b, and another four of the triangles to create a square with sides length c. How can these figures be used to demonstrate the Pythagorean Theorem?**
Place the two congruent rectangles perpendicular and touching at one vertex. Arrange two right triangles so one long side and one short side, respectively, are placed together to form one side of a larger square. Place a short side next to each long side until four sides of a larger square are formed, leaving a twisted, open square in the middle (see reference to "negative space" in previous question).

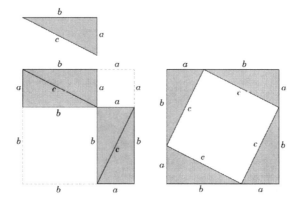

The larger square has an area that is the square of the sum of the two sides $(a + b)$ of the triangle, while the smaller, twisted inner square has an area that is the square of the hypotenuse of the triangle. The sum of the areas of the square that is a x a and the square that is $b \times b$ is equal to the area of the larger square that is c x c. Substituting values for a, b, and c (such as 3, 4, and 5 units respectively) yields a result that numerically agrees with the diagram shown.

7. **Suppose you can construct a point anywhere on the side of the larger unit square and connect that point to the opposite vertex. This point divides the side into segments of length a and $(1 - a)$. Create the smaller, inner square in this manner by constructing congruent points and segments on each side of the larger square. What must be the ratio of the lengths a and $(1 - a)$ such that the area of the smaller square is one-half that of the larger square?**

Construct a segment through the vertex of the smaller square (the smaller square is shown here parallel to the edge of the page) that is parallel to the side of the larger square, as shown. The length of the segment connecting the vertex to the opposite side of the small square is $1 - a$. The length of the corresponding segment in the larger square is $\sqrt{1 + a^2}$.

The ratio of similarity then becomes $\dfrac{1-a}{\sqrt{1+a^2}}$.

The ratio of the areas of the two (similar) squares is the square of the similarity ratio: $\dfrac{(1-a)^2}{\left(\sqrt{1+a^2}\right)^2} = \dfrac{1-2a+a^2}{1+a^2}$

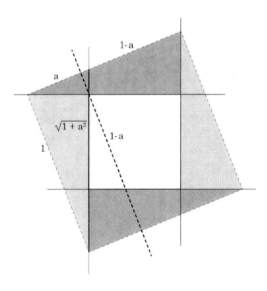

Setting the ratio of the areas equal to ½ and solving for the required length of *a*:

$$\frac{1}{2} = \frac{1 - 2a + a^2}{1 + a^2}$$

$$1 + a^2 = 2\left(1 - 2a + a^2\right)$$

$$1 + a^2 = 2 - 4a + 2a^2$$

$$a^2 - 4a + 1 = 0$$

$$a = 0.269$$

The other root of the quadratic equation, $a = 3.725$, can be disregarded because it exceeds the length of the side of the unit square.

8. **An artist wants to create a sculpture based on multiple rotations of a square tile, stacked one on top of the other. She plans to make a series of squares that are successively smaller, and rotate them by some fixed amount as she stacks each new layer. She has seen a 2-dimensional design on a Cartesian coordinate system with the vertices of a square at points (0, 0), (100, 0), (100, 100), and (0, 100) respectively. She observes that a rotated inner square was formed by plotting the vertex of an inscribed square at points (0, *a*), which is some distance above the origin. Another vertex of this inscribed square has been plotted at (*a*, 100). This defines a right triangle whose short leg has length *a*, whose long leg has length *b*, and whose hypotenuse is one side of the inscribed square. What must be the ratio of *a* to *b* so that each new square can be rotated by a fixed amount when she stacks it on top of the one below it? What is the ratio of similarity for the squares?**

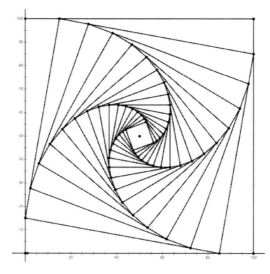

The number of degrees of rotation is arbitrary. For a rotation of 10° clockwise, for example, the ratio of side a to side b is equal to the tangent of 10°.

$$\tan 10° = 0.1763 = \frac{a}{b}$$
$$a + b = 100$$
$$a = 100 - b$$
$$0.1763 = \frac{(100 - b)}{b}$$
$$0.1763b = 100 - b$$
$$0.1763b + b = 100$$
$$1.1763b = 100$$
$$b = 85.01$$

This means that the second set of vertices can be plotted at (0, 14.99), (14.99, 100), (100, 85.01), and (85.01, 100).

The sides of the second square are formed by the hypotenuses of the four triangular regions. Each triangle has sides a = 14.99 units and side b = 85.01 units. The length of each triangle's hypotenuse is 86.32 units:

$$a^2 + b^2 = c^2$$
$$14.99^2 + 85.01^2 = c^2$$
$$\sqrt{7451.4} = c$$
$$c = 86.32$$

Since the hypotenuse of the triangular portion forms the side of the rotated square, the scale factor may be determined by the ratio of the hypotenuse to the side of the original square:

$$\frac{\text{hypotenuse}}{\text{original side}} = \frac{86.32}{100}$$
$$0.8632$$

Therefore the artist should make each square 86.32% the size of the one before it, and stack the squares on top of each other rotated by 10° in order to build up the sculpture.

2.C. MATHEMATICS-TWISTED SQUARE-*LEVEL I RUBRIC*

Mathematics Investigation Report – Assessment Rubric
Level I

Name:
Math Class:

Component	To receive highest marks the student:	4 Expert	3 Practitioner	2 Apprentice	1 Novice	0 No Attempt
1. Preparation and Research	Collaborated with group members on relevant research Brought and prepared all items necessary for their presentation Prepared supporting material for their presentation Prepared a thorough presentation for their classmates					
2. Demonstrations, Models, or Experiments	Obtained all necessary materials and used them to explore the guiding questions of the investigation Completed and documented results, data, and observations for guiding questions of the investigation Performed experiments or demonstrations proficiently for others, or explained clearly a model and the concepts the student investigated with the model					
3. Content	Presented written and spoken explanations that were mathematically accurate and paraphrased in the student's own words Answered all questions posed by their teacher or classmates correctly and thoughtfully Answered project synthesis and real-world application questions correctly and thoroughly Communicates clearly an understanding of the connection between their model or experiments and the driving question and theory behind the over-arching concept					
4. Real World Application and Extension	Identifies in written and spoken explanations the application of the topic to the real world, including specific examples Thoroughly discusses relevance of the topic to real life					
5. Collaboration and Contribution	Group members equitably shared responsibility for: Research of guiding questions Presentation and discussion of results					
6. Presentation	Delivered their content clearly and thoroughly, in an organized, logical manner with • Eye contact and poise • Appropriate voice level and clarity • Addressing the class/audience					

Total Points for Investigation (Maximum of 24 Points)

Guidelines for Marks:
4 = **Expert:** Distinguished command of the topic; students show insightful and sophisticated communication of their understanding
3 = **Practitioner:** Strong command of the topic; students show reasonable and purposeful communication of their understanding
2 = **Apprentice:** Moderate command of the topic; students show adequate but basic communication of their understanding
1 = **Novice:** Partial command of the topic; students show limited and insufficient communication of their understanding
0 = **No Attempt**

3.A. MAKING BEEHIVES-STUDENT HANDOUT-LEVEL II

Making Beehives

Driving Question

Which 3-dimensional shapes do bees use to make their beehives?

Background

Bees instinctively understand the need for efficiency when building their hives. They want to construct their nests so that they achieve a maximum amount of enclosed volume with a minimum of material and effort needed to build them. Bees could be considered to be one of nature's logistical engineers.

Logistics engineers apply mathematical and scientific principles of engineering to the distribution of services and goods that people need on a daily basis. They do this to optimize the infrastructure that provides us with the things we need. Logistics engineers work with the systems and processes related to distributing goods and services, often called the supply chain. They are interested in making the distribution of goods and services as efficient as possible because this helps to improve profits.

If you have ever had the chance to observe a container ship loaded with shipping containers, you have seen the results of a logistics engineer's work. The container ship is perfectly designed to carry the maximum load safely and as rapidly as possible from one port (a point of distribution) to another. You can imagine how the cost of goods would be impacted if those goods were transported across an ocean scattered across the deck of a sailing ship that depended on the wind for power. Logistics engineers, like bees building their hives, employ knowledge of math and science to produce the most efficient structures or processes possible with the materials available.

Project Objectives

In this project you will work with the members of your group to:

Mandatory

- Understand which polygons can be used to tessellate a plane, and extend this reasoning from two dimensions to three dimensions.
- Set areas of a square, circle, equilateral triangle, and hexagon equal to each other for comparison of the ratio of perimeter to area.
- Determine the polygon that would most economically hold the greatest volume of liquid based on comparison of base area. Compute the theoretical volume.
- Using available materials construct a set prisms and a cylinder of whose bases are of equal area, and whose heights are equal.
- Determine experimentally the volume of each prism and cylinder using liquid, and compare these results to the theoretical values previously computed.

- Relate bees' food energy needs to their optimization of resources used to build honeycombs.

Optional

- Derive the formula for the area of a regular hexagon from the formula for the area of an equilateral triangle.
- Compute and compare the area of a circle to the area of a hexagon inscribed in it, and relate these areas to the volume of the cylinder and hexagonal prism.
- Compute and compare the area of the annulus formed by circles inscribed in and circumscribed about a hexagon, to the area of the hexagon.
- Describe and explain which transformations (rotation, translation, reflection, dilation) can be applied to produce a hexagonal tessellation.

Materials and Equipment

Mandatory Equipment

- ☐ Water-resistant material for making shapes (such as plastic-coated card stock)
- ☐ Scissors
- ☐ Tape
- ☐ Water
- ☐ Ruler or straightedge
- ☐ Compass
- ☐ Drawing paper, several sheets

Optional Equipment

- ☐ Graduated cylinder

- ☐ Food coloring
- ☐ Pattern Blocks
- ☐ Dynamic geometry software

Key Concepts for Background Research

Research your project topic based on the driving question above. Use any resources available to research background information that will help you to complete your project.

Below is a list of key concepts that may be helpful when doing your background research.

- ☐ Regular polygon
- ☐ Polyhedron (plural - polyhedra)
- ☐ Non-polyhedron
- ☐ Geometric solids
- ☐ Volume of solids
- ☐ Surface area of polyhedra

- ☐ Tessellation
- ☐ Prism
- ☐ Cylinder
- ☐ Platonic solids
- ☐ Area of polygons
- ☐ Perimeter

263

Safety and Maintenance

Add this important safety precaution to your normal classroom procedures:

- A construction project involves the use of sharp objects. Handle all sharp objects carefully, including drawing compasses, scissors or craft/hobby knives.

Investigation

Use these guiding questions to help answer the driving question:

PART 1:
1. Which regular polygons can be used to tessellate, or tile, a plane, without overlapping or leaving gaps between them?
2. What three-dimensional solids can be formed from these polygons? How is a cylinder different from these three-dimensional solids?
3. Consider several types of three-dimensional solids, including hexagonal prisms, and cylinders. How can you compare the volume of one solid to another, both theoretically and experimentally?
4. Suppose you want to construct several two-dimensional figures that all have the same area, say 10 cm^2 for example. How can you use the area formulas for a quadrilateral, an equilateral triangle, and a circle to determine the length of each side (or circumference) of the figures?
5. What are the lengths of each side of a square and an equilateral triangle whose areas are both 10 cm^2? What is the length of the diameter of a circle whose area is 10 cm^2?
6. What is the length of each side of a regular hexagon whose area is 10 cm^2?
7. Of all the two-dimensional figures whose areas and lengths of sides you computed, which figures, if any, have shorter perimeters? Is there a "shortest perimeter" figure that can also tessellate a plane?
8. Imagine you need to construct a set of hollow geometric solids, using the least amount of material possible while still holding the largest volume of liquid possible. This is the same task that bees undertake when they construct their honeycombs from beeswax. Mathematically, which geometric solids are best suited for this task?
9. Biologists have shown that a honeybee needs to eat between six and eight grams of honey in order to produce one gram of beeswax. In terms of bees' food energy requirements, discuss why it is important for bees to use beeswax as efficiently as possible. Why do bees build their honeycombs using the shapes they do?

264

PART 2:   How can the formula for the area of a regular hexagon be derived
(optional) from the formula for the area of an equilateral triangle?

Suppose a certain species of honeybee made its honeycomb with circular cells packed as closely together as possible (hexagonal packing). What volume of beeswax would be necessary to fill in all the gaps between the one cell and the other six cells surrounding it? Since you don't know the size of this species of bee (and therefore the size of its honeycomb cells), express this volume in terms of the ratio of the area of a circle to the area of a hexagon inscribed in that circle.

PART 3:   Consider a hexagon that has a circle inscribed in it and a second
(optional) circle circumscribed about it. The annulus formed by the two concentric circles has an area A, while the hexagon has an area A'. What percent of A' is A?

Of the transformations mathematically possible, which could be applied to the hexagonal honeycomb pattern of beehives?

Synthesis Questions

The answers to the following questions will guide you to further critical thinking about your project topic and will build knowledge to help answer questions your classmates may ask when you make your presentation.

1. **Why do only certain kinds of polygons tessellate?**
2. **What are some other examples of how hexagons are used in nature?**
3. **How are hexagons used by people in daily life? Why are hexagons chosen as the shape in these examples?**

Extension and Real Life Application

The answers to the following questions will help you make connections between the concepts relevant to your project topic and their applications to real world problems, and will further add to your knowledge to help answer questions that your classmates may ask when you present.

1. **Discuss at least one real life application (and extension) of concepts relevant to this entire project, in addition to what you have discussed in the previous question(s).**
2. **Scientists estimate that one-third of food consumed by humans is dependent on insect pollination. Bees carry out the majority of this pollination. Discuss the implications for the world food supply if bees suffer some kind of crisis. Is there any such crisis currently affecting bees?**
3. **What is "closest packing" and how does it relate to the chemical structures of various crystalline substances?**

3.B. MATHEMATICS-MAKING BEEHIVES-TEACHER GUIDE-LEVEL II

Making Beehives

Student Objectives

Students answer their driving question and investigation questions through independent research, and then deliver this research to their classmates in a concise presentation form that includes a presentation website with video content. The student will:

Mandatory (Level I Projects)

- Understand which polygons can be used to tessellate a plane, and extend this reasoning from two dimensions to three dimensions.
- Set areas of a square, circle, equilateral triangle, and hexagon equal to each other for comparison of the ratio of perimeter to area.
- Determine the polygon that would most economically hold the greatest volume of liquid based on comparison of base area. Compute the theoretical volume.
- Using available materials construct a set prisms and a cylinder of whose bases are of equal area, and whose heights are equal.
- Determine experimentally the volume of each prism and cylinder using liquid, and compare these results to the theoretical values previously computed.
- Relate bees' food energy needs to their optimization of resources used to build honeycombs.

Optional (Level II, III Projects Only)

- Derive the formula for the area of a regular hexagon from the formula for the area of an equilateral triangle.
- Compute and compare the area of a circle to the area of a hexagon inscribed in it, and relate these areas to the volume of the cylinder and hexagonal prism.
- Compute and compare the area of the annulus formed by circles inscribed in and circumscribed about a hexagon, to the area of the hexagon.
- Describe and explain which transformations (rotation, translation, reflection, dilation) can be applied to produce a hexagonal tessellation.

TEKS Objectives

This lab correlates to the following TEKS objectives:

(c)1   The student uses mathematical processes to acquire and demonstrate mathematical understanding. The student is expected to:

   B.   use a problem-solving model that incorporates analyzing given information, formulating a plan or strategy, determining a solution, justifying the solution, and evaluating the problem-solving process and reasonableness of the solution;

   C.   select tools, including real objects, manipulatives, paper and pencil, and technology as appropriate, and techniques, including mental math, estimation, and number sense as appropriate, to solve problems;

   D.   communicate mathematical ideas, reasoning, and their implications using multiple representations, including symbols, diagrams, graphs, and language as appropriate;

(c)11   Two-dimensional and three-dimensional figures. The student uses the process skills in the application of formulas to determine measures of two- and three-dimensional figures. The student is expected to:

   B.   determine the area of composite two-dimensional figures comprised of a combination of triangles, parallelograms, trapezoids, kites, regular polygons, or sectors of circles to solve problems using appropriate units of measure;

   C.   apply the formulas for the total and lateral surface area of three-dimensional figures, including prisms, pyramids, cones, cylinders, spheres, and composite figures, to solve problems using appropriate units of measure; and

   D.   apply the formulas for the volume of three-dimensional figures, including prisms, pyramids, cones, cylinders, spheres, and composite figures, to solve problems using appropriate units of measure.

This lab correlates to the following Common Core State Standards:

HSG.GMD.A   Explain volume formulas and use them to solve problems:

   1   Give an informal argument for the formulas for the circumference of a circle, area of a circle, volume of a cylinder, pyramid, and cone.

   3   Use volume formulas for cylinders, pyramids, cones, and spheres to solve problems.

HSG.GMD.B   Visualize relationships between two-dimensional and three-dimensional objects:

4   Identify the shapes of two-dimensional cross-sections of three-dimensional objects, and identify three-dimensional objects generated by rotations of two-dimensional objects.

HSG.MG.A   Apply geometric concepts in modeling situations:

1   Use geometric shapes, their measures, and their properties to describe objects (e.g., modeling a tree trunk or a human torso as a cylinder).

2   Apply concepts of density based on area and volume in modeling situations (e.g., persons per square mile, BTUs per cubic foot).

3   Apply geometric methods to solve design problems (e.g., designing an object or structure to satisfy physical constraints or minimize cost; working with typographic grid systems based on ratios).

Project Background

People have observed for millennia that bees construct the cells of their honeycombs in the shape of hexagons. Anywhere in the world one looks inside a beehive, the same structure is found: regular, repeating patterns of hexagons. Bees seem to know instinctively to use this shape to build their honeycombs. Hexagons are one of three regular polygons that can tessellate, or tile, a flat region or plane. The angles formed by the sides of such polygons are a factor of 360, the number of degrees in one complete rotation.

Equilateral triangles and squares, whose sides form angles of 60 degrees and 90 degrees respectively, also tessellate a plane. Regular pentagons, on the other hand, do not tessellate because their sides form angles of 108 degrees, which is not a factor of 360. Three pentagons placed side to side so their vertices meet at one point complete 324 degrees of rotation, and adding another pentagon completes 432 degrees of rotation, with the consequence that a physical set of such pentagons could not lie flat on a surface.

The ability to tessellate is what enables hexagons to form a repeating pattern. The hexagon also encloses a maximum area for the length of its perimeter compared to squares or equilateral triangles. Circles maximize area for circumference, but do not tessellate (they leave gaps between successive circles even when closely packed). For bees building honeycombs, the hexagon strikes the best balance of volume enclosed by each cell for expenditure of resources to construct them.

In this project students will design, measure, and construct geometric solids that can hold liquid. They will use these containers to compare the volume of several shapes, holding base area and height of the containers constant.

Students will be able to use the formulas for the area of a square, a triangle, and a circle to complete the project. However, they will find the area formula for an equilateral triangle useful:

$$A_{\text{equi. triangle}} = \frac{s^2 \sqrt{3}}{4}$$ Eq. 1

Students should discover that a regular hexagon is composed of six equilateral triangles, so Equation 1 can be modified as follows:

$$A_{\text{hexagon}} = \frac{3\sqrt{3}s^2}{2}$$ Eq. 2

Materials and Special Preparation

Mandatory Equipment	*Optional Equipment*
☐ Water-resistant material for making shapes (such as plastic-coated card stock)	☐ Graduated cylinder
☐ Scissors	☐ Food coloring
☐ Tape	☐ Pattern blocks
☐ Water	☐ Dynamic geometry software
☐ Ruler or straightedge	
☐ Compass	
☐ Drawing paper, several sheets	

The student handout for this activity lists the mandatory and optional equipment shown above that can be used as part of the student's project. Please review these items and the preparation notes for each prior to providing them to the student.

Safety and Maintenance

Be certain that students add this important safety precaution to their normal classroom procedures:

• A construction project involves the use of sharp objects. Handle all sharp objects carefully, including a drawing compass, scissors or craft/hobby knives.

Presentation Guidelines

Use the following guidelines to assess the student's preparation, content knowledge, and presentation delivery.

Investigation Guidelines

Follow these guidelines to assess each of the investigation questions from three parts of the student project handout. The Part 1 investigation is mandatory, while Parts 2 and 3 are optional. The third column indicates the difficulty level of the concept addressed in the investigation question.

PART 1 Investigation Questions (Mandatory)	*Suitable Response*	*Difficulty*
20. Which regular polygons can be used to tessellate, or tile, a plane, without overlapping or leaving gaps between them?	A square, an equilateral triangle, and a regular hexagon can each be used to tessellate a plane.	Easy
21. What three-dimensional solids can be formed from these polygons? How is a cylinder different from these three-dimensional solids?	A square forms a cube or rectangular prism if its height is greater then the length of a side. An equilateral triangle forms a triangular prism or a tetrahedron. A regular hexagon forms a hexagonal prism. A cylinder has as its base a circle, which is not a polygon. The other solids are composed only of polygons.	Moderate
22. Consider several types of three-dimensional solids, including hexagonal prisms, and cylinders. How can you compare the volume of one solid to another, both theoretically and experimentally?	Theoretically, the area formula for the base polygon can be used to compare the area of each solid. The height of each solid should be held constant. Then, the general volume formula for the solids, $$volume = area_{base} \times height$$ can be applied. Experimentally, the solids' dimensions should be calculated and used to build hollow models into which liquid can be poured. The volume accepted by each model is compared by direct measurement.	Difficult

PART 1 Investigation Questions (Mandatory)	Suitable Response	Difficulty
23. Suppose you want to construct several two-dimensional figures that all have the same area, say 10 cm² for example. How can you use the area formula for a quadrilateral, an equilateral triangle, and a circle to determine the length of each side (or circumference) of the figures?	Solve each area formula for the dimension required, the diameter of the circle and one side of each of the regular polygons: Then use 10 cm² for each area and compute the required dimension. $$diameter = 2\sqrt{\dfrac{a}{\pi}}$$ $$side_{square} = \sqrt{a}$$ $$side_{eq.\ triangle} = \sqrt{\dfrac{4a}{\sqrt{3}}}$$ $$side_{hexagon} = \dfrac{3\sqrt{3}\left(s^2\right)}{2}$$	Moderate
24. What are the lengths of each side of a square and an equilateral triangle whose areas are both 10 cm²? What is the length of the diameter of a circle whose area is 10 cm²?	The dimensions are as follows: $side_{square}$ = 3.162 cm $side_{eq.\ triangle}$ = 4.806 cm $diameter$ = 3.568 cm	Easy
25. What is the length of each side of a regular hexagon whose area is 10 cm²	For the hexagon, the length is: $side_{hexagon}$ = 1.962 cm	Moderate
26. Of all the two-dimensional figures whose areas and lengths of sides you computed, which figures, if any, have shorter perimeters? Is there a "shortest perimeter" figure that can also tessellate a plane?	The perimeters are: Circumference of circle: 11.209 cm Perimeter of square: 12.648 cm Equilateral triangle: 14.417 cm Perimeter of hexagon: 11.771 cm The two shortest perimeters are the circle and the hexagon. Of these, only the hexagon can tessellate the plane.	Moderate

PART 1 Investigation Questions (Mandatory)	Suitable Response	Difficulty
27. How can you construct a set of hollow geometric solids, each of the same height and base area, using the least amount of material possible while still holding the largest volume of liquid possible? This is the same task that bees undertake when they construct their honeycombs from beeswax. Mathematically, which geometric solids are best suited for this task?	I used thin plastic recycled from a package, and packing tape, to build 3-D shapes. I chose a square prism, an equilateral triangular prism, and a hexagonal prism because they are the shapes that can tile a plane, or tessellate. I chose a cylinder because it has the largest volume even though it can't tessellate a plane. I made each shape so the base area was 10 cm^2 and the height of each shape was 10 cm. 	Difficult
28. Biologists have shown that a honeybee needs to eat between six and eight grams of honey in order to produce one gram of beeswax. In terms of bees' food energy requirements, discuss why it is important for bees to use beeswax as efficiently as possible. Why do bees build their honeycombs using the shapes they do?	Bees build their honeycomb cells this way because the more wax they need to use, the more they need to eat to have the energy to produce that amount of wax. By using hexagons to build the cells they minimize materials used to build, while maximizing the volume of honey each cell can hold.	Easy

PART 2 Investigation Questions (Optional)	Suitable Response	Difficulty
How can the formula for the area of a regular hexagon be derived from the formula for the area of an equilateral triangle?	Formula for area of an equilateral triangle: $$A = \frac{s^2 \sqrt{3}}{4}$$ A regular hexagon is composed of 6 equilateral triangles. Multiply by 6 the formula for the equilateral triangle: $$A_{\text{hex}} = 6A_{\text{eq. tri.}} = 6\frac{s^2 \sqrt{3}}{4}$$ $$A_{\text{hex}} = \frac{3\sqrt{3}\left(s^2\right)}{2}$$	Moderate
Suppose a certain species of honeybee made its honeycomb with circular cells packed as closely together as possible (hexagonal packing). What volume of beeswax would be necessary to fill in all the gaps between the one cell and the other six cells surrounding it? Since you don't know the size of this species of bee (and therefore the size of its honeycomb cells), express this volume in terms of the ratio of the area of a circle to the area of a hexagon inscribed in that circle?	If the hexagon is inscribed in a circle, then each vertex of the hexagon lies on the circumference of the circle. Therefore, the radius of the circle is also the length of the side of one of the equilateral triangles that composes the hexagon. The area of the circle is: $$A = \pi r^2$$ The area of the inscribed hexagon is expressed in terms of the circle's radius: $$A = \frac{3\sqrt{3}\left(r^2\right)}{2}$$ The ratio of the area of the circle to the area of the hexagon is: $$\frac{\pi r^2}{\frac{3\sqrt{3}\left(r^2\right)}{2}}$$ $$= \frac{\pi r^2}{1} \cdot \frac{2}{3\sqrt{3}\left(r^2\right)}$$ $$= \frac{2\pi}{3\sqrt{3}}$$ $$\sim 1.209$$	Difficult

273

PART 3 Investigation Questions (optional)	Suitable Response	Difficulty
Consider a hexagon that has a circle inscribed in it and a second circle circumscribed about it. The annulus formed by the two concentric circles has an area A, while the hexagon has an area A'. What percent of A' is A?	The area of the annulus is given by: $$A_{annulus} = \pi(R^2 - r^2)$$ Where R is the radius of the larger circle and r is the radius of the smaller circle, and $$r = \frac{R\sqrt{3}}{2}$$ Therefore $$A_{annulus} = \pi\left(R^2 - \left(\frac{R\sqrt{3}}{2}\right)^2\right)$$ $$A_{annulus} = \pi\left(R^2 - \left(\frac{3R^2}{4}\right)\right)$$ $$A_{annulus} = \pi R^2\left(1 - \frac{3}{4}\right)$$ $$A_{annulus} = \frac{\pi R^2}{4}$$ Hence $$\frac{A}{A'} = \frac{\frac{\pi R^2}{4}}{\frac{3\sqrt{3}R^2}{2}}$$ $$\frac{A}{A'} = \frac{\pi R^2}{4} \cdot \frac{2}{3\sqrt{3}R^2}$$ $$\frac{A}{A'} = \frac{\pi}{6\sqrt{3}}$$ $$\frac{A}{A'} = \frac{\pi\sqrt{3}}{18}$$ $$\frac{A}{A'} \approx 0.3025$$ $$\frac{A}{A'} \approx 30\%$$ The annulus has an area about 30% that of the hexagon with inscribed and circumscribed circles.	Difficult

PART 3 Investigation Questions (optional)	Suitable Response	Difficulty
Of the transformations mathematically possible, which could be applied to the hexagonal honeycomb pattern of beehives?	The transformations that could be applied to hexagonal honeycomb patterns are rotation, translation, and reflection. One cell can be rotated 120° and it is still congruent to all other cells. A cell can be translated by a distance equal to its dimensions and is still congruent to all other cells. A cell can be reflected about any of its segments and is still congruent to all other cells. A cell cannot be transformed by dilation because although it would still be similar, it would no longer be congruent to the other cells.	Moderate

Presentation Delivery Guidelines

Follow these guidelines to assess the student's preparation and presentation delivery to the class. To receive excellent marks, students have:

Preparation:	– clearly invested at least 3–4 hours doing topical research – brought and assembled all equipment necessary for their presentation – prepared a supporting handout for their presentation – prepared a thorough presentation discussion for their classmates
Delivery:	– delivered their presentation content clearly and thoroughly, not speaking so quickly that the student audience cannot follow – integrated their research and experimental setup into the presentation as visual support – answered all question posed by their classmates to the best of their ability – answered all question posed by their classmates correctly and thoughtfully
Website:	– prepared a website explaining their project and the driving question associated with it – included a thorough, well-written, explanation of the answer to their driving question and the theory behind the over-arching concept – included supporting pictures, videos, and research references (including web-links)
Video:	– recorded a supporting video for their website – edited the supporting video in an attempt to produce a good–excellent quality video – included a thorough, well-spoken, explanation of the answer to their driving question and the theory behind the over-arching concept – included footage of their experimental setup with an explanation

Handout:	– prepared a supporting handout for their presentation – included a brief, but well-written, explanation of the answer to their driving question, the theory behind the over-arching concept, and its application to real life – included pictures of their experimental setup with explanation – included references to all web-links and to the presentation website URL (or QR code)

Synthesis Questions

Below are sample responses to the questions in the Synthesis Questions section in the student handout.

1. Why do only certain kinds of polygons tessellate?

Polygons tessellate only if they have angles that are a factor of 360. For example, a square tessellates because its angles are each 90°, so that 4 successive rotations of a square complete 360°. An equilateral triangle must complete 6 successive rotations because its angles are each 60°. The rotations can be seen in a tessellation where the vertices of the polygons all meet at one point. A regular pentagon will not tessellate because its angles are each 108°, which is not a factor of 360 (360/108 = 3.33). The pentagons would leave a gap where their vertices meet, or adding another pentagon would result in an overlap.

2. What are some other examples of how hexagons are used in nature?

The Giants' Causeway in Northern Ireland has hexagonal formations of igneous rock. Snowflakes form in hexagonal patterns. Atoms of many kinds, including carbon, link together in hexagonal structures to form molecules. Certain types of crystals form hexagonal structures.

3. How are hexagons used by people in daily life? Why are hexagons chosen as the shape in these examples?

Hexagons are used by people in everything from quilt and knitting patterns to the structure of super-strong composite materials used to manufacture lightweight structures, such as airplanes. Soccer balls are made partially of hexagons (and also pentagons). They aren't the only shape used, because they lie flat (tile a plane) and a ball needs to be spherical. Hexagons are used because they form patterns that can be beautiful in the artistic sense, such as the tessellations that decorate buildings and outdoor spaces. Hexagons are efficient at optimizing volume for surface area or perimeter. Hexagons used in structures also do not shear as easily as a network of triangles or squares, because they do not have any straight lines running through the network.

Extension and Real Life Application

Below are sample responses to the questions in the Extension and Real Life Application section in the student handout.

1. **Discuss at least one real life application (and extension) of concepts relevant to this entire project, in addition to what you have discussed in the previous question(s).**
   Holding the greatest volume for the least material to make the container is important in any situation where economy or efficiency is a goal. This is also true in two dimensions as well, for example when trying to cut as many flat pieces of something from one sheet of material. Computer software and laser cutting are often used to be more efficient at cutting metal parts, clothing fabric, or upholstery material from the main sheet of metal, cloth, or leather. Cooks also use a technique of optimizing to get the most raviolis, pot-stickers, biscuits, or cookies cut out of a piece of dough or pasta.

2. **Scientists estimate that one-third of food consumed by humans is dependent on insect pollination. Bees carry out the majority of this pollination. Discuss the implications for the world food supply if bees suffer some kind of crisis. Is there any such crisis currently affecting bees?**
   Our food supply would suffer from scarcities of many items, which would drive up the cost beyond the reach of many people, especially in developing countries. Since food is a necessity, like water and shelter, people might go to war against one another to protect what they have.
   Bees around the world currently are suffering from colony collapse disorder, in which the bees abandon their hives for reasons that are not clear to scientists. There is a shortage of pollinator bees as a result, both in the United States and other countries around the world.

3. **What is "closest packing" and how does it relate to the chemical structures of various crystalline substances?**
   Closest packing in crystalline structures means that the atoms, ions, or molecules are arranged in the way that makes the most use of the space. The atoms or molecules can be modeled as spheres, which are closest packed in a hexagonal arrangement or a cubic arrangement. In chemistry the structure is described with the particles on the lattice points, or intersections of imaginary lines that connect the particles' centers. Chemists use these models to explain and predict the bonding and structural behavior or properties of different crystalline materials.

Mathematics Investigation Report – Assessment Rubric
Level 1

Name:
Math Class:

Component	To receive highest marks the student:	4 Expert	3 Practitioner	2 Apprentice	1 Novice	0 No Attempt
Preparation and Research	– Collaborated with group members on relevant research – Brought and prepared all items necessary for their presentation – Prepared supporting material for their presentation – Prepared a thorough presentation for their classmates					
Demonstrations, Models, or Experiments	– Obtained all necessary materials and used them to explore the guiding questions of the investigation – Completed and documented results, data, and observations for guiding questions of the investigation – Performed experiments or demonstrations proficiently for others, or explained clearly a model and the concepts the student investigated with the model					
Content	– Presented written and spoken explanations that were mathematically accurate and paraphrased in the student's own words – Answered all questions posed by their teacher or classmates correctly and thoughtfully					

	– Answered project synthesis and real-world application questions correctly and thoroughly – Communicates clearly an understanding of the connection between their model or experiments and the driving question and theory behind the over-arching concept				
Real-World Application and Extension	– Identifies in written and spoken explanations the application of the topic to the real world, including specific examples – Thoroughly discusses relevance of the topic to real life				
Collaboration and Contribution	– Group members equitably shared responsibility for: – Research of guiding questions – Presentation and discussion of results				
Presentation	– Delivered their content clearly and thoroughly, in an organized, logical manner with – Eye contact and poise – Appropriate voice level and clarity – Addressing the class/audience				
Total Points for Investigation (Maximum of 24 Points)					

Guidelines for Marks:

4 = **Expert:** *Distinguished command of the topic; students show insightful and sophisticated communication of their understanding*

3 = **Practitioner:** *Strong command of the topic; students show reasonable and purposeful communication of their understanding*

2 = **Apprentice:** *Moderate command of the topic; students show adequate but basic communication of their understanding*

1 = **Novice:** *Partial command of the topic; students show limited and insufficient communication of their understanding*

0 = **No Attempt**

4. A. PHYSICS-BALANCING DEMONSTRATIONS
STUDENT HANDOUT-*LEVEL II*

Balancing Demonstrations

Driving Question

How does an object balance, what is required to balance an object, and how can this be demonstrated?

Project Objectives

Students answer their driving question and investigation questions through independent research, and then deliver this research to their classmates in a concise presentation form that includes a presentation website with video content. The student will:

Mandatory

- Know the meaning of the terms "center of mass" and "center of gravity".
- Present five demonstrations showing how to balance a complex system, object, or shape. Each is to be built from one of the five sets of equipment selected from the Investigation section of the Student Handout.
- Demonstrate that an object in static equilibrium (balanced) has its center of mass (or center of gravity) above its base of support, or directly below its pivot point (point of contact).
- Demonstrate that an object whose center of mass (center of gravity) is not above its base of support, or directly below its pivot point, or point of suspension, will experience torque that will cause the object to rotate out of balance.
- Understand that a balanced object in static equilibrium experiences zero net torque.
- Show an obvious understanding of each demonstration and explain the requirements for balancing each system, and why those requirements are necessary.

Key Concepts for Background Research

Research your project topic based on the driving question above. Use any resources available to research background information that will help you to complete your project.
Below is a list of key words that may be helpful when doing your background research.

- ☐ Balance
- ☐ Center of mass
- ☐ Point of contact
- ☐ Lever arm

- ☐ Static equilibrium
- ☐ Center of gravity
- ☐ Torque
- ☐ Net torque

☐ Moment arm   ☐ Weight shift

☐ Rotational equilibrium   ☐ Linear equilibrium

Safety and Maintenance

Pay attention to the following maintenance recommendations, and add these important safety precautions to your normal laboratory procedures:

- All balancing objects may fall. Use caution to ensure that none of the objects you are balancing are in danger of breaking or causing injury if they fall.
- If you choose to use any tools to help construct a demonstration system, please use extreme caution and observe all safety recommendations from the tool's manufacturer.

Below is a list of ten sets of demonstration equipment. Choose five sets of equipment and determine how each chosen set can be used to demonstrate how a complex system, constructed from the equipment in the set, can be balanced about a singular point. For each demonstration you must be prepared to show the complex system created from the equipment in the set and explain what requirements are necessary to balance the system, and why those requirements are necessary?

SET #	Equipment	
1	☐ Balancing bear, or similar toy	☐ Thread
2	☐ Balancing bird ☐ Salt shaker	☐ Toothpick
3	☐ Fork (2), or 1 fork and 1 spoon ☐ Salt shaker	☐ Toothpick (2)
4	☐ Soda can	☐ Water
5	☐ Long-necked bottle, empty or full	☐ Wooden board, 1"× 4" × 18"
6	☐ Jenga® blocks	
7	☐ Inflatable, self-righting, punching toy (bop bag)	
8	☐ Hammer ☐ Ruler	☐ String
9	☐ PASCO Stability model	☐ Small flat wooden board, 20" x 10"
10	☐ Board with one 9" nail driven, vertically, into the center of the board	☐ 9" nails (10)

Synthesis Questions

The answers to the following questions will guide you to further critical thinking about your project topic and will build knowledge to help answer questions your classmates may ask when you make your presentation.

1. **What do the terms "center of gravity" and "center of mass" mean, and how are they different?**

2. **If an object is not moving (static equilibrium) what is the net force acting on it? What is the net torque? How do you know?**

3. **The Tower of Pisa is a famous cathedral bell tower in Italy. It may be most famous for its unique tilt as a result of the ground under one side of the tower being too soft to support it. To the right is an image of the Tower of Pisa. Although the tower appears as if it is about to topple over, it does not. Explain why this is so.**

4. **Observe the crane to the right. Assume the vertical tower is fixed and the horizontal arm can rotate freely (vertically and horizontally) a top the vertical tower. If the horizontal arm is in static equilibrium, where is its center of mass located? How do you know?**

5. Without moving its position, imagine the crane lifted a piece of metal whose mass was greater than that of the entire horizontal arm. How would the center of mass of the horizontal arm change once the metal was lifted? How would that change its equilibrium?

6. Assuming the horizontal arm on the crane rotates freely, what is one thing you could do to the crane to keep the horizontal arm in equilibrium when the metal from the previous question is lifted?

   =producing torque? If yes, how do you know?

7. Why does a person carrying a heavy package while walking lean back slightly? What would happen if the person didn't lean backward while carrying the package? Why?

8. Below is an image of a solid metal ring with an inside diameter equal to 2d. If the ring has uniform density throughout, where is its center of mass? How can you balance the ring on a single point? Explain your answer. Would you need any additional materials to balance the ring? If yes, what would those materials be and how would you use them?

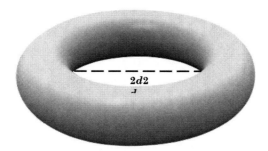

$2d2$

Extension and Real Life Application

The answers to the following questions will help you make connections between the concepts relevant to your project topic and their applications to real world problems, and will further add to your knowledge to help answer questions that your classmates may ask when you present.

1. Discuss at least one real life application (and extension) of concepts relevant to this entire project, in addition to what you have discussed in the previous question(s).

2. Why should engineers have to consider center of mass of the structure while constructing the buildings?

3. Scientists found that Human's center of mass changes, as they get fatter.

What kind of health problems will they have as their center of mass changes?

Figure 2. Sample Level II project that shows balancing demonstrations (Task 12).
(Please use your QR reader to scan the QR codes to watch the video and/or see the
e-portfolio website).

Figure 3. Sample brochure showing balancing demonstrations (Task 11).

4.B. PHYSICS-BALANCING DEMONSTRATIONS
TEACHER GUIDE-*LEVEL II*

Balancing Demonstrations

Project Objectives

Students answer their driving question and investigation questions through independent research, and then deliver this research to their classmates in a concise presentation form that includes a presentation website with video content. The student will:

Mandatory

- Know the meaning of the terms "center of mass" and "center of gravity".
- Present five demonstrations showing how to balance a complex system, object, or shape. Each is to be built from one of the five sets of equipment selected from the Investigation section of the Student Handout.
- Demonstrate that an object in static equilibrium (balanced) has its center of mass (or center of gravity) above its base of support, or directly below its pivot point (point of contact).
- Demonstrate that an object whose center of mass (center of gravity) is not above its base of support, or directly below its pivot point, or point of suspension, will experience torque that will cause the object to rotate out of balance.
- Understand that a balanced object in static equilibrium experiences zero net torque.
- Show an obvious understanding of each demonstration and explain the requirements for balancing each system, and why those requirements are necessary.

TEKS Objectives

This lab correlates to the following TEKS objectives:

P.3   The student uses critical thinking, scientific reasoning, and problem solving to make informed decisions within and outside the classroom. The student is expected to:

      B. communicate and apply scientific information extracted from various sources such as current events, news reports, published journal articles, and marketing materials.

Project Background

The center of mass of an object (sometimes called center of gravity) is the point about which the total mass of the object is distributed equally, both in magnitude and distance: the point at which an object would be perfectly balanced if suspended from.

For example: a sphere constructed from a material with uniform density (the same mass per unit volume throughout) would have its center of mass (CM) exactly at its center (Figure 1). There are equal amounts of mass distributed in distance and magnitude about that point. If the sphere didn't have a uniform density, its center of mass would not be at it center, but rather, in a location near the area of highest density (Figure 2). Also, the location of an object's center of mass may not be within the boundaries of object at all, similar to the semi-circular rod in Figure 3.

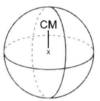

Figure 1. Uniform density sphere

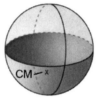

Figure 2. Non-uniform density sphere

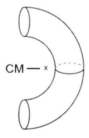

Figure 3. CM outside shape

Perfectly balanced objects are said to be in "static equilibrium:" a state in which an object is at rest and the total net force experienced by the object is zero. Balanced objects include things standing as well as things that are hanging, but in both cases there is a similar thread that helps these objects to stay balanced: static equilibrium can only occur when an object's center of mass is above its base of support for standing objects, or directly below its point of suspension (point of contact) for hanging objects.

If the center of mass of a standing object were to exist in an area not above its base of support, or not below its suspension point for a hanging object, the object would experience an unbalanced force from Earth's gravity that would cause the object to rotate, fall, or topple over (Figure 4). This force can be assumed to act on the object's center of mass, and the rotation produced is about the object's base of support for standing objects, or the point of suspension for hanging objects. This rotation, brought on by a force, is described by the *torque* experienced by the object:

$$\tau = \mathbf{r} \times \mathbf{F}$$

$$\tau = rF \sin\theta$$

Eq.1

Where torque τ is equal to the cross product of the unbalanced force vector $\mathbf{F}$ and the displacement vector $\mathbf{r}$ (the vector connecting the rotational axis to the applied force vector).

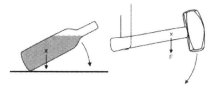

Figure 4. Objects experiencing torque due to their CM being not above the point of contact/suspension

To summarize, perfectly balanced objects in static equilibrium experience zero net force, and consequently, zero net torque. Non-zero net torque, as a result of gravitational force, will exist if the center of mass of a standing object is not directly over its base of support, or the center of mass of a hanging object is not directly under its point of suspension.

In this project, the student will choose five sets of equipment, each set associated with a specific balancing demonstration, from a list of ten equipment sets found in the Investigation section of the student handout. It will be the responsibility of the student to determine how each chosen set can be used to demonstrate how a complex system can be balanced about a singular point. In each demonstration, the student must show a complex system created from the equipment in the set, what requirements are necessary to balance the system, and why those requirements are necessary.

For a short description of the demonstration generally associated with each set of equipment listed in the Investigation section of the student handout, please see the table in the Presentation Guidelines section below.

Materials and Special Preparation

The student handout for this activity lists ten sets of equipment that the student will choose from. Of that equipment, the items listed in the table below require special preparation. Please review these items and the preparation notes for each prior to providing the items to the student:

Equipment	*Preparation Notes*
☐ Soda can	The soda can must be empty.
☐ Board with 9" nail	Hammer one 9" nail vertically into the very center of a small piece (2" × 4" × 10") of wood. Only hammer the nail in approximately 0.5" to 1" deep.

Safety and Maintenance

Be certain that student pay attention to the following maintenance recommendations, and add these important safety precautions to their normal laboratory procedures:

- All balancing objects may fall. Have students use caution to ensure that none of the objects being balancing are in danger of breaking or causing injury if they fall.
- Students may choose to cut the bottom of, and drill a bottle-neck-sized hole into, the piece of wood that is part of Set #5. Have students use extreme caution when using power tools or other tools and always follow the safety guidelines published by the tool's manufacturer.

Presentation Guidelines

Use the following guidelines to assess the student's preparation, content knowledge, and presentation delivery.

Investigation Guidelines

Although the student has the freedom to determine how each set of equipment listed in the Investigation section of the student handout can be used to create a balancing demonstration, each set of equipment listed has a specific demonstration associated with it. These demonstrations are specified in the table below as "Suggested Demonstrations" for each equipment set. A short description of each demonstration is also included, as well as an indication of difficulty level associated with each to provide information that can help assess student knowledge.

SET #	Equipment	Suggested Demonstration	Difficulty
1	• Balancing bear, or similar toy • Thread	Tie the thread between two elevated points (one point slightly higher than the other). Set the wheel on the balancing bear on the suspended thread at the elevated end. Allow the bear to balance on the string and roll down the string. The balancing bear does not tip over or fall off the thread because the system's center of mass (bear and all) is directly below the thread (the point at which the system is suspended), between the counterweights. Because the center of mass is directly below the point at which the bear is suspended, it experiences zero net torque.	Easy
2	• Balancing bird • Toothpick • Salt shaker	Place a toothpick into one of the holes on the salt shaker so the toothpick stands vertically out of the salt shaker. Set the beak of the balancing bird on the tip of the vertical toothpick. The bird will balance on the tip of the toothpick. The bird does not tip over or fall off the toothpick because the bird's center of mass is directly below the tip of its beak (the point at which the system is suspended). A majority of the mass of the bird is in the tips of its wings which are below its beak. This causes the center of mass to be lower than the bird's beak and directly below the tip of the toothpick. Because the center of mass is directly below the point at which the bird is suspended, it experiences zero net torque.	Easy

SET #	Equipment	Suggested Demonstration	Difficulty
3	• Fork (2), or 1 fork and 1 spoon • Toothpick (2) • Salt shaker	Press the tines of the two forks together (or the spoon into the tines of the fork) so the two form a "V" shape. Slide a toothpick firmly between the tines so the toothpick extends inward between the forks, and just slightly above the plane formed by the two forks. Place a toothpick into one of the holes on the salt shaker so it stands vertically from the salt shaker. Balance the forks and toothpick system on the toothpick extending vertically out of the salt shaker by resting the toothpick extending from the forks on the tip of the other toothpick. The forks and toothpick system does not tip over or fall off the toothpick because the system's center of mass is directly below the tip of the vertical toothpick (the point at which the system is suspended). A majority of the mass of the system is in the handles of the forks. This causes the center of mass to be lower than the tip of the toothpick. Because the center of mass is directly below the point at which the system is suspended, it experiences zero net torque.	Moderate

SET #	Equipment	Suggested Demonstration	Difficulty
4	Soda can Water	Fill the empty soda can approximately 1/3 full with water. Place the can onto a table and lean the can with water at a 45° angle so the groove around the bottom of the can rests on the table. The can will balance at a 45° angle on its own, but only with water in the can. Without water, or with additional water in the can, the can will not balance at that angle. When the can is empty, or completely full of water, the center of mass of the can is approximately in the center of the can. When the can is leaned at a 45° angle, the center of mass is not directly above its support base and the can experiences a non-zero torque that causes it to tip over. When the can is only 1/3 full and leans at a 45° angle, its center of mass is directly over its support base, causing the net torque to be zero, and the can balances.	Moderate

SET #	Equipment	Suggested Demonstration	Difficulty
5	• Long-necked bottle, empty or full • Wooden board, 1" × 4" × 18"	Drill a hole slightly larger in diameter than the neck of the bottle into one end of the board, approximately 1.5 inches away from the end of the board. Cut the opposite end of the board flat at a 45° angle. 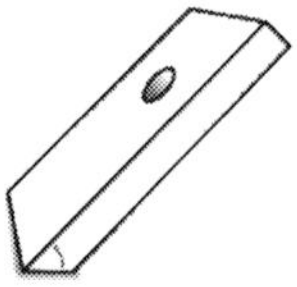 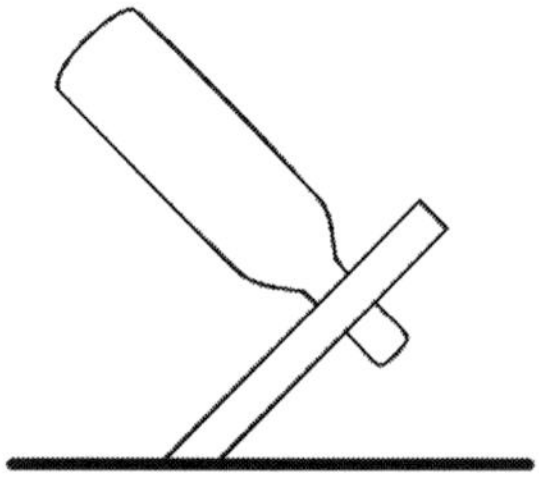 Place the bottle neck into the hole and rest the bottle and board on the table. If the system doesn't balance, adjust the position of the bottle by sliding it further into the hole. If the system still doesn't balance, cut an additional 1" of length off the angled end of the board, maintaining a 45° angle at the end. Check for balance, and keep removing length from the board 1" at a time. The system will eventually balance, similar to Figure 11. This system balances because the center of mass of the system is just under the bottle, but directly above the support base of the board, which causes the net torque on the system to be zero.	Difficult

SET #	Equipment	Suggested Demonstration	Difficulty
6	• Jenga® blocks	Assemble the Jenga blocks similar to the pattern shown in the figure. Add more Jenga blocks to the top of the structure in a horizontal block–vertical block pattern until the structure has at least five horizontal pieces and five vertical pieces. Slowly remove the left support piece from beneath the structure and the structure will balance on its own. 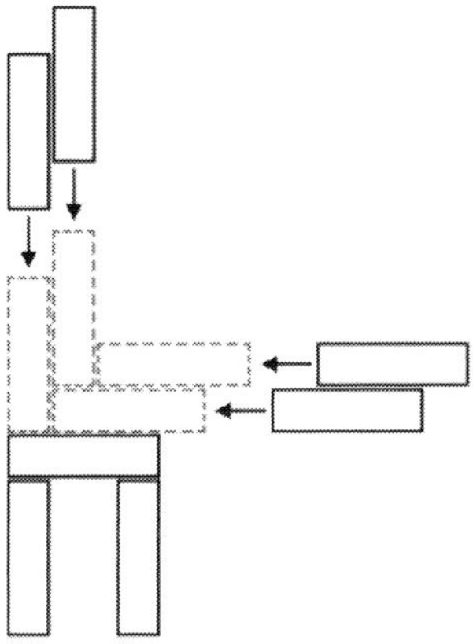 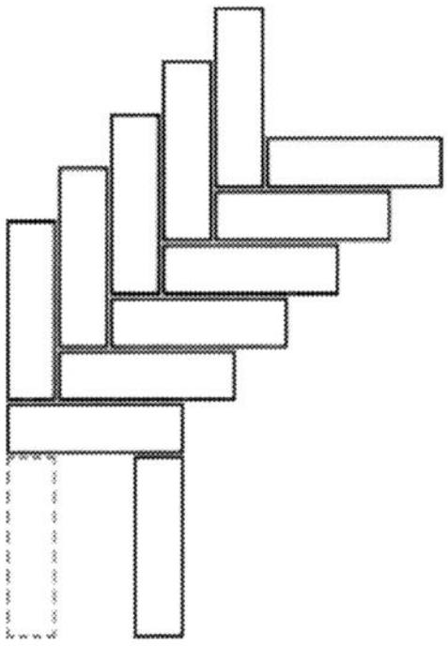 This system balances because the center of mass of the total system is directly above the lowest vertical piece, which is directly above the support base of the entire system. Because of this the net torque on the system is zero and it maintains static equilibrium.	Difficult

SET #	Equipment	Suggested Demonstration	Difficulty
7	• Inflatable, self-righting, punching toy (bop bag)	When the toy is inflated and placed upright it maintains static equilibrium because the majority of the mass in the toy is at its base, over the point of contact between it and the floor. When the toy is punched or pushed, it experiences a torque that causes it to rotate, but then it rotates right back to equilibrium because the center of mas is no longer directly over the point of contact between itself and the floor. Gravity causes a torque that rotates the toy when the center of mass is no longer over its support base. This torque causes the toy to right itself until the center of mass is over the point of contact again.	Easy
8	Hammer String Ruler	Tie a loop of string approximately 2–3" in diameter. Hold the hammer under the ruler length-wise and place the loop of string around both, similar to the figure. Slide the string and the hammer down the length of the ruler until approximately 2–3" of the hammerhead extends beyond the end of the ruler. Place the end of the ruler onto the edge of a table with the hammerhead hanging under the table. The ruler will extend horizontally in equilibrium with just a small piece of the ruler being supported by the table. The system maintains static equilibrium because its center of mass is directly under the point of contact between the ruler and the table. The result is a zero net torque on the system. The reason the system's center of mass is in a strange location is because most of the mass within the system is in the hammerhead, which extends under the table.	Moderate

SET #	Equipment	Suggested Demonstration	Difficulty
9	• PASCO Stability model • Small flat wooden board, 20" × 10" ×	Place the stability model vertically on the board with the longer base touching the board. The hanging arrow indicates the center of mass of the model and where it aligns vertically with its base. When the model is standing on its longer base, the center of mass is above its base of support, implying that the net torque on the model is zero and it will maintain static equilibrium. Flip the model over so the shorter base is touching the board. In this position the center of mass is not over its base of support, so when it is released it will experience a torque that causes it to rotate and topple over. Place the stability model vertically on the board with the longer base touching the board. Place your finger on the board at the front edge of the model and begin to lift the other end of the board. Slowly continue to tip the board until the arrow indicating the center of mass is pointing at your finger, at which time the model will topple over due to the center of mass no longer being over is base of support.	Moderate

SET #	Equipment	Suggested Demonstration	Difficulty
10	• Board with one 9" nail driven, vertically, into the center of the board • 9" nails (10)	Place one nail on its side on the table. Lay 8 nails atop the first nail with their heads touching the first nail in an alternating pattern.  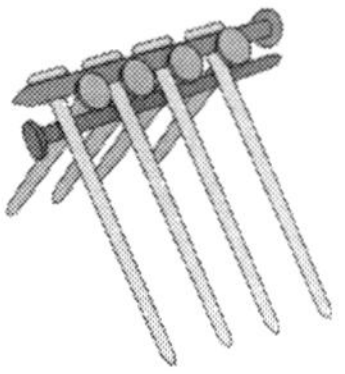 Lay the last nail atop the 8 alternating nails just above the first nail with its head opposite that of the first, as in the figure above. While carefully squeezing the first and last nails together (this will capture the 8 alternating nails), lift the entire system and balance it atop the vertical nail in the board. The system will remain in static equilibrium because its center of mass is directly under the point of contact between the vertical nail and the horizontal nail. The center of mass of the system is lower than the point of contact due to the majority of the system's mass being in the ends of the 8 hanging nails.	Difficult

Presentation Delivery Guidelines

Follow these guidelines to assess the student's preparation and presentation delivery to the class. To receive excellent marks, students have:

Preparation:	• clearly invested at least 3–4 hours doing topical research • brought and assembled all equipment necessary for their presentation • prepared a supporting handout for their presentation • prepared a thorough presentation discussion for their classmates
Delivery:	• delivered their presentation content clearly and thoroughly, not speaking so quickly that the student audience cannot follow • integrated their research and experimental setup into the presentation as visual support • answered all question posed by their classmates to the best of their ability • answered all question posed by their classmates correctly and thoughtfully
Website:	• prepared a website explaining their project and the driving question associated with it • included a thorough, well-written, explanation of the answer to their driving question and the theory behind the over-arching concept • included supporting pictures, videos, and research references (including web-links)
Video:	• recorded a supporting video for their website • edited the supporting video in an attempt to produce a good–excellent quality video • included a thorough, well-spoken, explanation of the answer to their driving question and the theory behind the over-arching concept • included footage of their experimental setup with an explanation
Handout:	• prepared a supporting handout for their presentation • included a brief, but well-written, explanation of the answer to their driving question and the theory behind the over-arching concept • included pictures of their experimental setup with explanation • included references to all web-links and to the presentation website URL (or QR code)

Synthesis Questions

Below are sample responses to the questions in the Extension and Synthesis Questions section in the student handout.

1. **What do the terms "center of gravity" and "center of mass" mean, and how are they different?**
   "Center of mass" is a term used to describe the point about which the total mass of an object is distributed equally, both in magnitude and distance; the point at which an object would be perfectly balanced if suspended from. "Center of gravity" describes the point at which the weight of a system is distributed equally, both in magnitude and distance. Without the presence of gravity, "center of gravity" does not exist, but "center of mass does.

2. **If an object is not moving (static equilibrium) what is the net force acting on it? What is the net torque? How do you know?**

   If an object is in static equilibrium, the net force acting on it is zero, and so is the net torque. We know this because the system is not rotating and because torque is the cross product of the net force vector and the distance from the rotational axis of the object. Because force is zero, so is torque.

3. **The Tower of Pisa is a famous cathedral bell tower in Italy. It may be most famous for its unique tilt as a result of the ground under one side of the tower being too soft to support it. To the right is an image of the Tower of Pisa. Although the tower appears as if it is about to topple over, it does not. Explain why this is so.**

   The tower is leaning but doesn't fall because the center of mass of the tower is still over itᵉ base of support, despite its leaning angle.

4. **Observe the crane to the right. Assume the vertical tower is fixed and the horizontal arm can rotate freely (vertically and horizontally) atop the vertical tower. If the horizontal arm is in static equilibrium, where is its center of mass located? How do you know?**

   If the arm is in static equilibrium its center of mass is either directly above or directly below the point at which attaches to the vertical tower. For an object to be in static equilibrium it must be at rest and experience zero net force and zero torque. This will only happen if an object's center of mass is directly over or directly below its point of support.

5. **Without moving its position, imagine the crane lifted a piece of metal whose mass was greater than that of the entire horizontal arm. How would the center of mass of the horizontal arm change once the metal was lifted? How would that change its equilibrium?**

By lifting a heavy piece of metal, the center of mass of the system (arm plus metal) would shift toward the area of the highest mass density. This would be near the metal being lifted, considering that it is nearly the same weight as the entire arm. If the center of mass of the arm system was shifted away from the point of contact between it and the vertical tower, the crane would then experience a non-zero net torque that would cause the arm to rotate.

6. **Assuming the horizontal arm on the crane rotates freely, what is one thing you could do to the crane to keep the horizontal arm in equilibrium when the metal from the previous question is lifted?**
    A counter-weight could be added to the other side of the crane, farther from the rotational axis. This would help to keep the center of mass over the point of contact between the arm and the vertical tower.

7. **When a person opens a door is the person producing torque? If yes, how do you know?**
    Yes. When the person opens the door it begins to rotate (a change in rotational motion). An object that experiences a change in rotational motion must be experiencing a non-zero net torque.

8. **Why does a person carrying a heavy package while walking lean back slightly? What would happen if the person didn't lean backward while carrying the package? Why?**
    When a person carries a package, the added mass of the package changes the location of that person's center of mass. To keep from experiencing a torque that would cause one to fall over, a person leans to keep their center of mass over their base of support.

9. **Below is an image of a solid metal ring with an inside diameter equal to 2d. If the ring has uniform density throughout, where is its center of mass? How could you balance the ring on a single point? Explain your answer. Would you need to any additional materials to balance the ring? If yes, what would those materials be and how would you use them?**

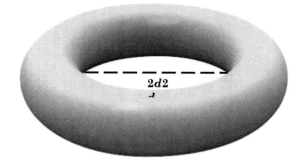

$$2d2$$

Because the metal ring is uniform in size and density, its center of mass would be directly in the center of the ring's opening. To balance the ring you would need to have some way to make the point of contact directly above the center of the ring's opening. One could use string or rope tied across the opening of the ring so the ring hangs just below the point of contact.

4.C. SUMMATIVE ASSESSMENT

Balancing Demonstrations

Multiple Choice Questions

Select the best answer to each of the questions below. Record your answer on the answer sheet using upper case letters.

The diagram below shows a handle to open a propane gas valve. The pivot on the right side of the handle is a distance **r** from the point where force **F** is applied to turn the handle. The angle θ is the angle between vectors **F** and **r**. Use the diagram below to answer questions 1 through 3:

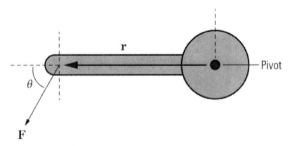

1. **What is the equation that expresses the magnitude of the force that produces rotation about the pivot?**

   A. $F \cos \theta$ B. $F \sin \theta$ C. $F \cos \theta + F \sin \theta$ D. None of these

2. **As a result of the force F, the torque on the handle is _____.**

   A. at a maximum because it is being applied perpendicularly

   B. at a minimum because it is being applied perpendicularly

   C. at some value between the minimum and maximum because it is being applied at an angle with respect to the position vector **r**

   D. zero because the handle is not in motion

3. **In which direction does the torque vector point?**

   A. Out of the page

   B. To the right

   C. To the left

   D. In the direction of rotation

4. **Someone has over-tightened the cap on a bottle of barbecue sauce. A bottle lid opener is to be used to open the lid. How much force is necessary to apply 50.0 N m of torque to the cap if the lid has a diameter if 4.00 cm and the bottle opener has a handle 20.0 cm? Assume the force is applied perpendicularly to the handle.**

   A. 227 N   B. 250 N   C. 208 N   D. 288 N

5. **A hexagonal bolt is tightened by applying a force to a wrench, as shown at right. What is the magnitude of the torque about the center of the bolt? What is the direction of the torque vector?**

   A. 7.2 N m, into the page

   B. 7.2 N m, out of the page

   C. 5.4 N m, into the page

   D. 5.4 N m, out of the page

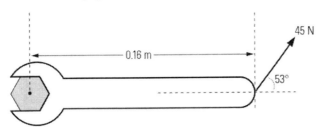

45 N

0.16 m

53°

6. **Which of the following statements are true regarding center of mass and center of gravity:**

   I. Center of mass and center of gravity are the same thing; the terms can be used interchangeably.

   II. Center of gravity is the location of an object's weight and coincides with its center of mass.

   III. On earth, center of mass and center of gravity are located at the same point for an object.

   IV. The center of mass of an object may not be located within the object.

   A. I and II
   B. II and IV
   C. Only III
   D. II, III, and IV

7. **How does stable static equilibrium differ from unstable static equilibrium?**

   A. Objects in stable static equilibrium may be able to slide but must not be able to roll.

   B. Objects in stable static equilibrium return to equilibrium after being displaced by a force.

   C. Objects in stable static equilibrium have more kinetic energy than those in unstable static equilibrium.

   D. The vector sum of all the external forces acting on objects in stable static equilibrium must be zero.

8. **Two children ride a seesaw at the playground. One of the children is seated at one end of the toy, while the other child is seated much closer to the fulcrum, or pivot point of the seesaw. The seesaw remains motionless and horizontal because _____.**

   A. the seesaw experiences no component of force from the children's weight perpendicular to the lever arm

   B. the torques produced by each child's weight act in the same direction but are counteracted by the fulcrum

   C. the seesaw is a special example of a first class lever

   D. the torques produced by each child's weight must sum to zero

9. **Consider a tablet sitting motionless on a table, the blades of an airplane's rotating propeller, a truck's tire as it travels in a straight line at constant speed, and a hockey puck sliding across a frictionless surface with constant velocity. Which of these objects is in equilibrium? Which of these objects is in static equilibrium?**

   A. Equilibrium: truck's tire, hockey puck; Static equilibrium: propeller blades

   B. Equilibrium: truck's tire, hockey puck; Static equilibrium: tablet

   C. Equilibrium: all the objects; Static equilibrium: hockey puck

   D. Equilibrium: all the objects; Static equilibrium: tablet

Many sailboats have keels, as shown in the diagram. Although this increases a boat's mass and therefore density, it helps to stabilize the boat in the water by prevent it from tipping over.

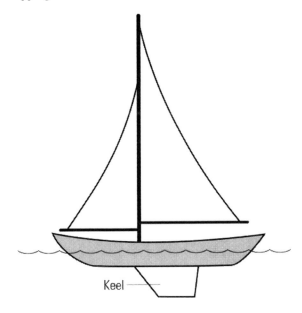

10. This type of sailboat design provides stability because _____.

A. the keel helps counteract the torque created by the wind's horizontal force on the sails

B. the keel helps the boat to move forward through the water, instead of sideways

C. the change in mass affects the buoyant force on the sailboat, which is associated with stability

D. the change in mass and density alter the sailboat's position in the water, such that the hull displaces more water

11. A mountain bike rider pushes against the pedal of his bike with a 110-N force, as shown in the image at right. The pedal shaft is 20.0 cm in length. Find the magnitude of the torque about point P.

A. 18 N m

B. 19 N m

C. 3.8 N m

D. 6.2 N m

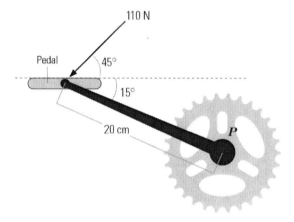

Kendama is a game of skill in which the player tries to catch a ball, connected by a string to the handle, in one of three small cups or the spike on the handle of the toy, as shown.

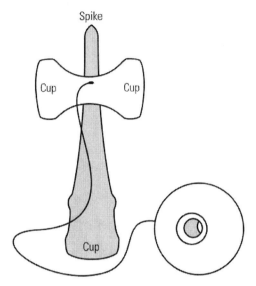

12. In terms of equilibrium, why is the central point, or spike, of the handle considered the most difficult place to catch the ball?

A. The spike acts as a pivot about which all the torques and forces on the ball must balance.

B. The ball has its maximum potential energy, relative to the handle, just as it begins to rest on the spike.

C. The spike represents an unstable equilibrium point until the ball's hole becomes aligned with the spike.

D. All of these statements are true.

13. **Consider three items of laboratory glassware: a graduated cylinder, an Erlenmeyer flask, and a beaker, as shown, but not to scale. Each vessel has the same mass, and each contains the same volume of water (density 1.0 g/mL). Rank the containers in order from greatest to least stability.**

   A. beaker, flask, cylinder

   B. cylinder, beaker, flask

   C. flask, cylinder, beaker

   D. flask, beaker, cylinder

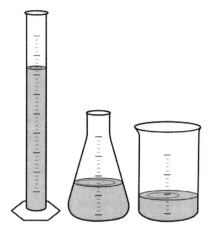

Hero of Alexandria is credited with building an aeolipile, a type of action-reaction steam engine, as seen here. Historians and engineers disagree as to whether his engine could have done useful work. Replicas of this engine are often built by science and engineering students.

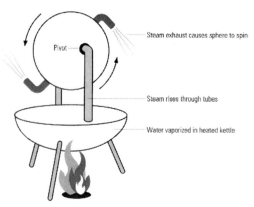

14. **Rank the following aeolipile designs in order from largest to smallest torques:**

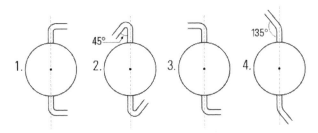

A. 1, 2 and 4 tie, 3   B. 2, 3 and 1 tie, 4   C. 3, 2 and 4 tie, 1   D. 4, 2, 3, 1

15. **A log weighing 500.0 N is laid across cinder block supports on each bank of a stream to form a bridge, as shown in the diagram. What is the magnitude of the normal force from the block on the right? Assume the log has uniform density.**

A. 333 N

B. 167 N

C. 228 N

D. 375 N

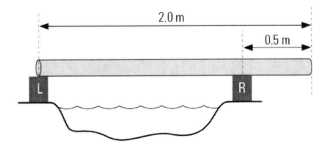

FOR MORE STEM SOS STUDENT SAMPLES AND ACTIVITIES;

Like Harmony STEM on Facebook:
www.facebook.com/HarmonySTEM

Follow Harmony STEM on Twitter:
twitter.com/STEMCONNECT

Harmony Public Schools Center of STEM Education website:
stem.harmonytx.org

CPSIA information can be obtained
at www.ICGtesting.com
Printed in the USA
FSOW02n1056100315
5558FS

9 789463 000178